Blood on the Altar

Tobias Jones is the author of two travel books, *The Dark Heart of Italy* and *Utopian Dreams*, and two novels, *The Salati Case* and *White Death*. He has been a columnist for the *Observer* and *Internazionale*, and has written and presented documentaries for the BBC and RAI. He currently runs a woodland shelter in Somerset with his wife.

by the same author

NON-FICTION
The Dark Heart of Italy
Utopian Dreams: In Search of a Good Life

FICTION
The Salati Case
White Death

BLOOD ON THE ALTAR
In Search of a Serial Killer

TOBIAS JONES

faber and faber

First published in 2012
by Faber and Faber Ltd
Bloomsbury House
74–77 Great Russell Street
London WC1B 3DA

Typeset by Ian Bahrami
Printed and bound by CPI Group (UK) Ltd, Croydon, CR0 4YY

A CIP record for this book
is available from the British Library

ISBN 978–0–571–27494–9

2 4 6 8 10 9 7 5 3 1

This book is dedicated to the memory of Elisa Claps

Plates

Elisa Claps (© Bournemouth News/Rex Features).

Elisa's mother, Filomena, with her daughter's diary and a lock of her hair (© Bournemouth News/Rex Features).

The Via Pretoria entrance of the Chiesa della Santissima Trinità (© Getty Images).

Potenza (© Alinari Archives/Getty Images).

A view of the Tyrrhenian Sea from Monte San Biagio, Maratea (© Tobias Jones).

Heather Barnett (© Bournemouth News/Rex Features).

Danilo Restivo (© Bournemouth News/Rex Features).

Police outside Heather Barnett's flat (© Bournemouth News/Rex Features).

Gildo Claps putting up posters in memory of both his sister and Heather Barnett (© Bournemouth News/Rex Features).

Gildo Claps talking to reporters outside Winchester Crown Court (© Press Association Images).

Professor Francesco Introna oversees the removal of Elisa's remains from the church (© Press Association Images).

Elisa's funeral, 2 July 2011 (© Getty Images).

Elisa's white coffin (© Getty Images).

Author's Note

The geographical terms Basilicata and Lucania are synonymous, and I've used both interchangeably; the adjective 'Lucano', and its variant suffixes, refers to a person from Lucania/Basilicata. The Chiesa della Santissima Trinità is often called simply La Chiesa della Trinità (or just La Trinità), and I have followed that usage.

The entirety of this book is factual and the vast majority of the conversations reported here are taken from primary sources, eye-witness accounts and legal documents. I have occasionally, however, imagined conversations and the protagonists' inner thoughts where faithful reconstruction was, for whatever reason, impossible. It should also be noted that various interviews I've conducted and travels I've undertaken don't necessarily appear in the book in chronological order, but have been placed in the narrative where it was thought to be most appropriate.

Map of Basilicata

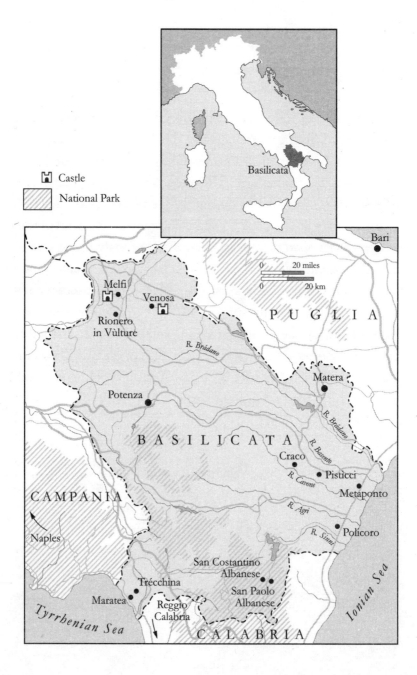

Castle

National Park

Basilicata

Bari

0   20 miles

0   20 km

Melfi

Venosa

Rionero
in Vùlture

P U G L I A

R. Bràdano

Potenza

Matera

B A S I L I C A T A

R. Bràdano

R. Basento

Craco

R. Cavone

Pisticci

CAMPANIA

Metaponto

R. Agri

Naples

R. Sinni

Policoro

San Costantino
Albanese

Trécchina

San Paolo
Albanese

Maratea

Reggio
Calabria

Ionian Sea

Tyrrhenian Sea

C A L A B R I A

Preface

'In Southern Italy life is reversed; the simplest thing
becomes the most complex.'
    Ann Cornelisen, *Torregreca*

As you journey south of Naples towards the remote region of
Basilicata you'll see its monumental, majestic mountains rising
ahead of you. They're rocky, barren peaks, sometimes capped with
snow, a church or a crucifix. The mountains turn an ever fainter
blue until, in the distance, they blanch and blend into the wide sky.

Basilicata is the forgotten land of Italy. My dog-eared, twenty-
year-old guide book to the peninsula has only six pages, out of
over eight hundred, on the region. When I stop in a service station
to buy a map of the area, the man behind the counter looks at me
with surprise.

'Basilicata?' he asks gruffly, frowning as if I've made a mistake.
He spins the map stand and pulls out alternatives. 'We've got
Campania. There's Calabria, or Sicily.' There are dozens of guides
to other regions but not one for Basilicata. It's not somewhere that
tourists travel to.

Even most Italians would be hard pushed to say exactly where
Basilicata is: it straddles the instep and the metatarsal of the Italian
boot, dipping into both the Ionian and Tyrrhenian seas. It's the
second most sparsely populated region in Italy after the Valle
d'Aosta, its 10,000 square kilometres containing under 600,000
souls. Ninety two per cent of the region is classified as either
mountainous or hilly.

Many people don't even use the name Basilicata. The Romans
called the area Lucania, a name revived under Mussolini, and
today people still refer to the place as Lucania and to themselves

as being Lucani. There's much debate as to the origin of the word. It derives, possibly, from one of the tribes that settled here, either the Lyki or the Lucani. Others say that it comes from the Greek for 'brightness', *leukos*, or from the Latin for 'forest', *lucus*, or possibly from the Greek *lykos*, meaning 'wolf'. When you've spent enough time in Lucania, all of these origins seem plausible. It has a remarkable combination of light and dark, of settled history and sudden danger, of dense forests and open spaces.

'It's wetted by two seas,' wrote Francesco Saverio Nitti of his homeland in his famous book *Heroes and Brigands* in 1899, 'and both one and the other have very melancholy coastlines.' It doesn't, he admitted, 'have blossoming cities or industries. Its countryside is sad and its inhabitants are poor.' The title of his book referred to the brigands who had led a ferocious insurgency against the imposition of the Piedmont monarchy in the years immediately after unification. Such was Lucania's distance from the centres of power – Rome, Milan, Turin – that men like Carmine Crocco became folk heroes for their resistance to the 'northerners' and the 'Piemontesi'. More than a century after that era of *brigantaggio*, Lucania was still sufficiently remote that it was the perfect place to hide the kidnapped John Paul Getty III in the 1970s.

That remoteness was also the reason for Mussolini sending political opponents of his regime to Lucania (he called it, after all, 'the most forgotten land'). Intellectuals like Carlo Levi or *mafiosi* like Calogero Vizzini ended up exiled here in the 1930s, the former writing the most famous book ever published on the region, *Christ Stopped at Eboli*. It was during his exile that Levi met the dogged, endearing peasants living in a land 'hedged in by custom and sorrow, cut off from history and the State, eternally patient . . . a land without comfort or solace, where the peasant lives out his motionless civilization on barren ground in remote poverty, and in the presence of death'.

'This shadowy land', he noted, was 'almost exiled from time'; the cemetery was 'perhaps the least melancholy' spot in the village. Levi wrote about the 'gloomy resignation' and 'primitive solemnity', noticing the 'tragic beauty' of the place and the mountaintop houses that 'appeared to teeter over the abyss'. Long after he left, there were still people in Lucania living, literally, in caves, in the famous *sassi* of Matera. There's something primitive and timeless about this backdrop. It's not surprising that this lonely land, with its rocky, rugged mountains, was where Mel Gibson chose to film *The Passion of the Christ*.

Even today it's a place that often appears untouched by modernity. You'll see old women bent double in the fields, scarves protecting their heads from the insistent sun as they slowly hoe the dusty soil. Some of the mountain villages are so isolated that the inhabitants still speak Albanian. There are almost no railways. The signs you see most often as you're driving are '*strada con buche*', 'road with holes', or else '*strada dissestata*', meaning 'uneven road'. It's a part of the world that feels primitive and elemental. It's a region of such hardship that between 1875 and 2006 almost a quarter of a million people emigrated. Set against that barren backdrop, human life seems somehow surprising and unexpected, almost incidental. The most common thing people say to you is '*Qui nun g'è niend*': 'There's nothing here'.

That's not quite true, of course. There are, in every village and town, fascinating glimpses into the history of the peninsula. The food and, especially, the wine are wonderful. There are many sites of astonishing natural beauty: wild places that, for once, seem untamed and untouched by human greed. And, in many ways, the region is actually thoroughly modern. There are wind turbines on some of those majestic mountains. Oil has been discovered in the region, meaning that huge pipelines run parallel to some of the dual carriageways. People talk optimistically of Lucania as the

Texas of Italy. There are large industrial plants, trunk roads, occasional riches. This is where Italy's largest telescope is to be found. Many of the sofas in Europe are made in Matera.

But none of that explains why it is that I've become so attached to Lucania. I don't even know how it happened, but this, of all the places in Italy, feels like my spiritual home. There's something here that, a long time ago, just got under my skin. It's more a question of the people than the place. Perhaps because it's an area almost entirely untouched by tourism, the Lucani are extraordinarily hospitable and generous. If you ask directions of someone, they'll invariably walk you there themselves, stopping on the way in their cousin's bar to offer you a coffee. '*Offro io*' – 'I'll pay' – is one of the most common phrases you hear. They often seem both astonished and delighted that a foreigner should come to this forgotten land, and are always eager to share the treasures of their region.

And, I discovered, there are many treasures, most of all the Lucani themselves. When I first moved to Italy in the late 1990s, I lived with three young men from Matera. It was, to say the least, a baptism of fire. They would have ferocious arguments and then, seemingly without reason, they would be laughing and joking together as if nothing had happened. They spoke a dialect that was incomprehensible to me. Lunch was rarely before three and dinner was always well after dark, normally at nine or ten. There was something about their impetuousness, about their pride in the land they had left behind, something about their passion and humour that intrigued me.

I remember being told by one of them that Lucania produced the best bread in the world. I sat there for over an hour, gently trying to suggest that Genoa, or France, or Germany, or – God forbid – even Britain produced some pretty decent loaves, but he was having none of it and got increasingly irate as he realised I wouldn't be persuaded that, in the whole world, only Lucania produced the perfect loaf.

Years later, I had a similar experience of Lucania's culinary pride. I was supposed to be giving a lecture at a literary festival in Potenza and, given the unconventional approach to punctuality, my hosts took me to dinner half an hour after my event was supposed to have started. When we arrived in the lecture hall much later, my event still couldn't start as there was a heated discussion going on about which town in Lucania produced the best peppers. Two men were standing up in the auditorium, shouting at each other about who produced the finest specimens, while two dozen people laughed and clapped at their rhetoric and passion and sophisticated palates. I had no desire to interrupt them to start my own lecture, and neither, clearly, did anyone else. This is a region that loves its food. They say that people get what's called *vozza*, an uncontrollable appetite that leads you to binge on the wonderful grub to the point of acute intestinal pain. People here eat more pasta per capita than in any other region of Italy.

The poet Leonardo Sinisgalli, himself Lucano, once wrote rather beautifully about his people: 'There are many Lucani in the world,' he said, 'but nobody sees them. They're not exhibitionists. The Lucani, more than every other people, live well in the shadows . . . No one knows how they got so much patience, so much endurance . . . This', he wrote intriguingly, 'is a people that wisdom has brought to the very edge of insanity.'

That patience and endurance is something that writers have noted down the ages. There's a weary acceptance of hardship that borders on the fatalistic. Some people have suggested that such fatalism is fairly Hispanic, and indeed the whole region was, for centuries, under Spanish rule (in dialect, the word for 'yesterday' is *ayer*). But although the Lucani are famed for their patience, when they lose it they really lose it. Their history is full of iconic dates on which the people rose up against some perceived injustice: 1485, 1647, 1728, 1820, 1943. The cause of the revolt might appear minor (the imposition of duty on flour, for example, in 1728), but after decades or centuries of injustice, the people would suddenly rise up and say, '*Mo' basta*' – 'That's enough.' Lucania is a land of rebels. Not the superficial sort who constantly gripe against authority, but the instinctive sort who have a deep sense of natural justice, the sort who have been constantly ignored by history and rulers and who patiently put up with so much until, unable to take any more, they revolt in unforgettable ways. It's no surprise that this is where *brigantaggio* was born, or that Matera was the first city in the whole of southern Italy to rebel against the Nazi occupation after 8 September 1943. For all their instinctive patience, when a Lucano says, '*Mo' basta*,' it's best to listen.

And that, in some ways, is what this book is about. It's about an event so terrible and tragic that the Lucani's instinctive sense of justice was profoundly offended. It's about one iconic crime that resonated with a whole region and led it to search its side streets and its conscience for almost two decades. The disappearance of a sixteen-year-old girl, Elisa Claps, from the centre of Potenza in September 1993 was unlike all the other *cronaca nera*, black chronicles, I had reported on over the years. Ever since I had moved to Italy in the late 1990s, I had been fascinated by a series of mysteries: the Piazza Fontana massacre; the Monster of Florence atrocities; the disappearance of Emanuela Orlandi, a teenage citizen of Vatican City; the murders of Marta Russo and little Samuele; the Ustica tragedy; the Montesi scandal . . . The country seemed to have no end of gruesome but gripping enigmas, murders or missing-person cases that remained unresolved for years and decades. Each one would usually evolve and mutate, maybe overlap with other crime stories. Each would become more confused and complicated, allowing ample space for magistrates, journalists and barflies to indulge in conspiracy theories and offer their own elaborate and incredible explanations.

The fascination lay in the fact that each mystery offered a cast of carnival characters that sometimes seemed plucked from a Fellini film. Each mystery granted a unique insight into Italian life: it took you into strange suburbs and back alleys; it would introduce you to extremists and loners, to petty criminals and heroic, mourning families. Those mysteries seemed to ricochet through Italian society, and if you followed them closely they could lead you towards hidden corners of this wonderful, bizarre and bewildering country. All countries, of course, have their mysteries, but there was something unique about Italy's iconic crimes. It often appeared, as Pirandello wrote almost a century ago, as if the search for truth in Italy really was futile, and that sanity could only be maintained if you gave up the search altogether and just enjoyed the fantastic make-believe. Such was the illusionism of Italian life that anyone searching for the truth would risk going deranged.

I had researched and written about many of the Italian mysteries, and had wearily forgotten the details about most of them. But there was something about the Elisa Claps case that stuck with me. It haunted me somehow. I had never known Elisa, but I found myself spending many melancholy hours gazing at her carefree face, at the photograph that was always used on posters pleading for information: pitch-black eyes, long dark hair falling onto a white jumper, a hint of a smile on her lips. Everything I heard about her made her disappearance all the more tragic. Here was a girl who was sixteen, just on the cusp of adulthood. She was the youngest daughter of an extraordinarily strong and loving family. She was honest and idealistic. She wanted to work for Médecins Sans Frontières. She wore jumpers knitted by her mother. That carefree face kept me up at night, and over the years I went through a kind of – I hope it's not presumptuous to say this of someone you never knew – bereavement. I felt I was mourning her, and not just because of what might have, or must have, happened to her, but because she had become, for me and many others in Italy, a symbol of the disappearance of truth, a constant reminder of injustice and a summons to do something about it. And, of all the iconic Italian crimes, it was a mystery in the purest, simplest sense: it seemed to defy logic that a girl could vanish without trace from a city centre on a busy Sunday morning.

I started travelling to Potenza whenever I got the opportunity. It wasn't easy: Potenza is a remote, isolated city, far from the country's main road and rail links. It's over five hundred miles south of Parma, where my wife's family is from, and is not the kind of place you just happen to be passing. When you do eventually get there, it is, as my usually complimentary guide book says, 'unlovely'. The city's been razed to the ground so many times that, almost uniquely in Italy, there's precious little that seems old or picturesque. It was razed in 1268, when Carlo I took revenge on the local nobles for daring to revolt. An earthquake struck five years later, then again in 1694 and in 1857, when over nine thousand lives were lost. The most recent struck in 1980, once again collapsing buildings and stealing lives. Blighted by those earthquakes and illegal building, the city spreads out from the central summit like a lumpy concrete skirt.

For years I had seen Gildo and Filomena, Elisa's brother and mother respectively, on television. Their sad, stony faces made it very clear that they were determined underdogs who would fight, with dignity and devotion, until their very last breath for justice. I had admired them from a distance and had longed to help them, if I could, in that fight. I tentatively made contact with them, and over the years we became good friends. I listened to their suspicions and fears and slowly became acquainted with an extraordinary cast of characters: there was a dysfunctional, dangerous man with a hair fetish; his powerful Sicilian father; a dodgy priest and a heroic one; an enigmatic Calabrian doctor; a forgetful Albanian; and a devout, good-looking private detective. There were many lies and fantasies and false leads, and, seemingly, a classic cocktail of conspiracy and cock-up. It was a story in which the villains appeared pretty pitch-black, but there were also some notable heroes: Elisa's mother, a diminutive, combative woman for whom my admiration grew every time I met her; the private detective who worked for the family, pro bono, for years; and the other priest, a brave, good man who refused to be cowed in his search for the truth.

I knew, sadly, that I wouldn't solve the mystery, but I wanted at least to try and solve a different one, something that had always intrigued me: why does Italy have such a strange relationship to the truth? Why is it that Italian crimes are always like this, confusing, misleading and, above all, inconclusive? Why is nothing ever really resolved? In Britain there are occasional mysteries – Lord Lucan, Jack the Ripper, and so on – but here there are hundreds of complex, cold cases. I wanted if not to solve the Elisa Claps case, then at least to understand the society that made it possible; to understand the anthropological backdrop to the tragedy and to peer deeper into the soul of a region, Lucania, that I loved.

And what emerged, over the years, wasn't just the fact that one girl's innocence and life had been brutally stolen; with that came the suspicion that certain sections of society in this land of the eternal underdog might have somehow cut a deal with the powerful, allowing that innocence to be slain with impunity. Lucania had always imagined itself as an *isola felice*, a 'happy island' unique in southern Italy for having been able to hold the tentacles of organised crime at bay. The disappearance of Elisa Claps led many to realise that those tentacles were much closer than had previously been thought. It also led many to believe that there was, sometimes, a wafer-thin line between organised crime and organised religion. Like much of southern Italy, Lucania is steeped in the rites and rituals of the Catholic Church. The disappearance of Elisa revealed the dark side of that Church and showed how, in this case, it prized its reputation far more than it valued the truth.

It's been an incredible, melancholic and, sometimes, uplifting journey. You never know where a book will lead you, and this one truly took me by surprise: I thought I was writing about an iconic crime in a remote corner of a foreign country when, suddenly, the story took an unexpected turn and led me back to my own roots in the south-west of England. I realised that the book had been a quest, and, like all quests, this one had brought me home after a long adventure. But when I got there, I wasn't the same any more and home looked different somehow. Everything had changed. I had, in the past, rather relished the idea of Italy being a land of smoke and mirrors, of cloaks and daggers. I lapped up the noir, the intrigue and the convoluted conspiracy theories. I enjoyed the conjecture and the vertiginous paranoia, the whispers about hidden powers and sinister puppeteers. But now, now that it's all over and we know what really happened, I've finally understood that, as with great mathematical equations, the truth is revealed not in complexity, but in simplicity. The truth, we realised too late, was staring us in the face all along.

One

'. . . strada facendo vedrai
che non sei più da solo
strada facendo troverai
anche tu un gancio in mezzo al cielo
e sentirai la strada far battere il tuo cuore
vedrai più amore vedrai
e una canzone neanche questa potrà mai
  cambiar la vita
ma che cos'è che ci fa andare avanti e dire
  che non è finita
cos'è che ci spezza il cuore tra canzoni e amore
che ci fa cantare e amare sempre più
perché domani sia migliore, perché domani tu
strada facendo vedrai.'
  Claudio Baglioni

On the morning of Sunday 12 September 1993, Antonio and Filomena Claps were preparing for a family lunch in the countryside. They had driven the short, ten-minute drive to their house in Tito with Luciano, their middle child, a few hours earlier. It was an easy journey, a brief jump on the dual carriageway that took them away from the crowded, bustling city of Potenza. It was a warm, sunny day: the sky was dark blue and, after the torrential downpours of the day before, the air felt fresh.

Antonio was a short man. He was barrel-chested, gruff and kind. He had a glint in his eye and liked to make people laugh. He ran a tobacconist's in the centre of the city and was well known, and well liked, by everyone. His unusual, un-Italian-sounding surname – Claps – was common around here. There were a few hundred Clapses in Lucania but hardly any others in Italy. Filomena was a diminutive but strong woman: she worked every morning as

[1]

a public official in the Ufficio del Catasto, the local land registry office, before going home to cook lunch for everyone and then spending the afternoon working at the tobacconist's. She was a woman who loved children. Whenever young kids used to come into the tobacconist's with their parents, she would instantly be drawn to them, making them smile or laugh. But she would also correct or discipline them, telling them to wrap up or study hard. She was a devout Catholic and had strong opinions about right and wrong. She knew how to prepare all the old-fashioned delicacies of the region. She was a typical *mamma*, a woman who had, with Antonio, created a family home full of warmth and laughter and good food.

That Sunday morning, Antonio and Filomena chatted about their children, about the food they were going to eat, about what needed doing in the weeks ahead. They longed to retire out here in the country, where there was more space and quiet. A few more years in the city and they would move here for good.

The couple had three children. The eldest, Gildo, had been a regional swimming champion. In many ways he was a typical man: he loved motorbikes, cars, Roma football club and Tex, the popular comic hero created by Gian Luigi Bonelli. But he was also a serious student. He had almost finished his law studies, and his parents would proudly tell their friends that he only had to pass two more exams and he could finally graduate. Luciano, their middle child, was about to go off to do his military service. He wanted, eventually, to join the police. Their youngest was a girl, an adored daughter called Elisa. Everyone loved Elisa, the baby of the family. Even now, at sixteen and on the cusp of womanhood, they still thought of her as the *cucciolo*, the special puppy or pet. Her father, particularly, was besotted by her. There was something about Elisa that was naïve and innocent, and she still had all the idealism of a teenager: her ambition was to become a doctor in Africa. Her friends sometimes became impatient with her exceptional tenderness. On one occasion she had spent hours trying to help a butterfly take off again after it had somehow damaged its wings. She had been ecstatic when it had finally fluttered away. She had had a setback that year when she had failed some exams, but she had studied for much of the summer and had easily passed her retakes. She was attractive in a simple, natural way: thick, black hair, a disarming smile, a slightly round face.

With their three children becoming adults, Antonio and Filomena felt as if life was easier now than it had been in the past. It had often been tough, not least in 1980, when a powerful earthquake destroyed large parts of Potenza and its suburbs and the whole family had been forced to live first in a caravan and then in a converted shipping container. Many families round here had suffered a similar fate during the early 1980s as buildings either collapsed or were designated unsafe. Antonio and Filomena had suffered not only the difficulty of losing their house; they were also, briefly, separated from their children, who were sent to live with an aunt in Scanzano Jonico, on the Ionic coast. It was during that time that Antonio and Filomena decided to save money to build a house in the countryside. Their place in Tito, although it didn't have a phone line and was still a bit rudimentary, was the realisation of a long-cherished dream.

As Filomena began preparing lunch, Antonio read the newspaper. For once there was good news. On the front page a photograph showed Yitzhak Rabin and Yasser Arafat. Bill Clinton stood between and behind them, his arms raised as the two shook hands having just signed the Oslo Accords. It was a shot that seemed to represent the optimism of the so-called New World Order: finally it looked like there was to be peace between the people of Israel and Palestine. It was an optimism that was misplaced. So too was the apparent calm in the Clapses' country house. Later, Filomena

[3]

would say that she felt a sense of foreboding that morning, a vague notion that something was terribly wrong.

*

Back in Potenza, in Via Mazzini 69, Gildo was awake long before Elisa. He had stayed in the city to study and was up early with his books. His plan, if he managed to graduate the following summer, was to enter the legal profession. Elisa had decided to stay with him for a lie-in: she would have struggled to be up at eight, when her parents and Luciano had left the house. And anyway, she wanted to see her friends and go to Mass before heading to the country.

Shortly after ten, Gildo woke his sister. She rolled over and groaned, but soon afterwards he heard, from his room, the running water of the shower and Claudio Baglioni's song '*Strada facendo*'. It was Elisa's favourite, and he could hear her singing along. Gildo smiled to himself at his younger sister's taste: the evening before she had watched, for the umpteenth time, the film *Ghost*. He saw her come out of the bathroom ready to go out. She was wearing blue trousers and a white jumper knitted by their mother.

Shortly after eleven, the doorbell sounded. Gildo went to the intercom in the hall to open the front gate. It was Eliana, a friend of Elisa's. They were going to go to Mass together before both heading to the country with Gildo. Gildo heard the lift rising up through the building and opened the front door to find the red-haired Eliana holding a tray of sweet pastries. Eliana left the pastries in the flat before heading out with Elisa, the two teenagers waving at him as the lift doors closed. It was the last time Gildo would ever see his sister.

It was a sunny morning. Elisa and Eliana walked up the steps towards the city centre. Via Pretoria was the central street where everyone went. It was one long, pedestrianised area where couples would walk arm in arm; where groups of friends chatted while sat on their mopeds; where cafes and bars were full of customers reading the papers and shouting their orders. There was a genteel bustle to the place on this late summer morning. Some people were buying their pastries for their Sunday lunch; others were buying polystyrene boxes of ice cream. By comparison with the bright sunlight outside, the Chiesa della Santissima Trinità was dark and cool. There was a background hiss of whispering as worshippers spoke quietly to each other during the rituals of the Mass.

An hour later, Gildo was hungry. He was keen to get going, to drive over to join his parents and enjoy a large lunch. As soon as his sister got back, they could leave. He didn't even know why she went to Mass. He found the whole thing daft. Elisa and his mother were always going to church. Elisa even sang in the cathedral choir. But Gildo thought the Catholic Church was full of superstition and hypocrites. It was, he reckoned, a throwback to the Dark Ages. He had to be careful how he said such things to his mother. She had a strong faith and was forthright about the virtues of the Church.

Eventually the doorbell went. That, he thought, would be Elisa at last.

'I'm coming down,' he said, slightly impatiently as he picked up the intercom.

'Is Elisa there with you?' It was Eliana's voice.

'No, she's not,' Gildo said. 'What's happened, why aren't you together?'

'Don't worry, nothing's happened. We lost sight of each other coming out of the church, and I thought she must have come here to wait for me.'

'No, she's not here.' Gildo's impatience grew now. How was it possible to lose sight of someone you were with? He was hungry and just wanted to get going.

'I'll go back and look for her,' Eliana said. 'You wait here. I'll find her and we'll come back.'

Even then Gildo had what he would call, years later, a 'subtle worry'. He switched on the TV but didn't really watch it. Elisa could be a bit dizzy sometimes but she was always reliable. She knew they were all due to go to lunch in the countryside. It wasn't like her to keep everyone waiting. He waited in the flat for almost half an hour, getting increasingly frustrated. By one o'clock he was properly worried. He decided to go out and walked down the six flights of stairs to the street. For half an hour he waited on Via Mazzini, looking left and right in the hope that he would see Elisa. Friends walked by and said hello, but he barely replied. Every time someone came into view, he would scrutinise them from afar, hoping that the distant figure would turn into his sister. It never did. Eventually one of his oldest friends, Cesare, came by, and together they walked up the thin steps of Via IV Novembre and, reaching the top, split up, walking along parallel streets.

Gildo wandered towards the Chiesa della Santissima Trinità, but it was locked. Over the next quarter of an hour the central street and its side alleys began to empty as people slowly made their way home for lunch. For the first time Gildo's apprehension gave way to a mild terror. Everything seemed so normal, but he knew something wasn't right. It was so unlike Elisa to mess them around. The relaxed Sunday morning crowds were almost all gone now, and Elisa wasn't with them.

By then it was gone two o'clock, and Gildo walked back home, desperately hoping that Elisa was there. Just beyond the entrance to the Clapses' block of flats he saw Eliana, Elisa's friend, by a phone box. By now Gildo was acutely concerned and was quite aggressive in demanding from the evasive Eliana the truth. She reiterated what she had already told him, that the two of them had lost sight of each other on leaving the church. Gildo was unconvinced but told her to go and wait upstairs in the flat in case Elisa returned. Meanwhile, many of his closest friends were gathering to help organise a search party.

*

Back at the country house in Tito, Antonio, Filomena and Luciano are getting irritated. It's well past two o'clock, and Gildo and Elisa haven't shown up. A phone hasn't yet been installed in the house and so they can't even call to ask why there's such a delay. Everyone is hungry and feeling peeved. The table is laid, the jugs are full. Everything is ready. It was ready over an hour ago. The food's overdone now, it's going dry. Eventually they decide there's only one thing for it: to abandon the table and the food and head home, back to the city.

'I'm sure everything's fine,' they say to each other. 'Gildo probably lost the car keys.' But despite the reassurances they give each other, they sense something's not right. Gildo and Elisa are, if not always punctual, certainly responsible. They wouldn't just not show up for a family meal. Antonio drives fast, feeling fear but trying to disguise it for the sake of his wife. The three in the car start thinking silently about all the possible reasons for the delay, their minds moving as fast as the car, careering from one unpleasant thought to another. Perhaps one of them had fallen and broken something. Maybe they had been involved in a crash. Nothing they imagined, though, nothing they thought, could ever have been as terrible as the reality they were about to go through. And not only the reality, but the lack of reality, the absence of answers. Little did they know, as they drove back to Potenza, that thinking and fearing the worst was to become

[7]

habitual, a state of mind, a way to try and guess what might have happened to young Elisa.

*

There was something shifty or evasive about Eliana that Gildo didn't trust. She wasn't, he felt sure, telling him the whole story. He went back upstairs, now in a fury, and as soon as Eliana opened the door he forcefully asked her to tell the truth.

'Where's Elisa?' he almost shouted.

The young girl began to stutter.

Gildo pushed home the advantage. 'Tell me the truth: where is she? What happened?'

Eliana didn't look at him but at her shoes. She confessed quietly that they had never gone to Mass together, but that Elisa had an appointment with Danilo Restivo that morning at the Chiesa della Santissima Trinità. He had, she said, wanted to give Elisa a present for passing her retakes.

'We were supposed to meet up after a quarter of an hour in the *piazza*,' she said, her voice quivering now. 'I went to the *piazza* but she never turned up. So I went to the church and she wasn't there either. That's why I thought she was here, with you.'

Gildo continued to shout questions at her, but she was on the brink of tears and kept repeating the same thing – 'I went to the *piazza* but she never turned up.'

He stared at her with disdain. She should have said all this over an hour ago. His apprehension was now on the cusp of panic. He knew the name Danilo Restivo. He was a vague friend of Luciano's, one of those people you often saw in and around Via Pretoria. Now that he thought about it, Gildo had heard his sister talking to him on the phone the previous evening, presumably making plans for this morning's appointment. There was something not right about

Restivo, something decidedly strange. He was the butt of jokes and had to try hard to be accepted. He had a soft, almost feminine voice and the kind of manner that suggested he was always gentle and solicitous. He had bushy dark hair, thick lips and rather bulbous eyes behind his glasses. There was something unnerving about him, especially since he had been insistently courting Elisa for a while. He had even bumped into them, Gildo and Elisa, on holiday a few months ago, in Montegiordano. Elisa had hung on tightly to her brother back then, apparently fed up that a man who was pestering her in Potenza had even followed her to Calabria. Gildo had wanted to get rid of him, but Elisa had felt sorry for him, saying he was just a hanger-on who did no harm. She asked Gildo to let it go.

Gildo was very worried now. He began to ask question after question, angry that his little sister's friend had lied about what they were doing. Hunger and fear were getting the better of him as he aggressively tried to get all the information he could out of this worried teenager.

'I just walked her to the church,' she said, beginning to cry. 'I just walked her there, that was all.'

Gildo went to find the phone book and flicked furiously through the pages until he got to the surname Restivo. He picked up the phone and, when it was answered, asked for Danilo. Shortly afterwards, he recognised Danilo's sing-song voice.

'Where's Elisa, what's happened to her?' Gildo asked immediately.

Restivo stuttered. 'We met in front of the Trinità,' he said. 'We went in and sat behind the altar and chatted. We were there for little more than a quarter of an hour and then we said goodbye and Elisa got up to leave. I stayed for a while to pray.'

Gildo kept asking questions, and Restivo confessed that Elisa seemed troubled. She had said that a man had harassed her that morning.

'What do you mean "harassed"?'

Gildo heard a voice on the other end of the line, someone demanding to have the phone: 'Give it to me.' Then there was silence for a few seconds until a deeper, sterner voice came on. 'We're having lunch and my son has already told you everything he knows.' The line went dead. The father had hung up.

Years later, Gildo would write that it was at that exact moment that he knew something had happened to Elisa. 'I felt', he wrote, reflecting on that instant in his own memoir, 'a strong pain in my stomach, and then a sense of emptiness, of absence . . . a sombre malaise.'

At around three o'clock, another of Elisa's friends arrived. Angelica was one of Elisa's closest friends. Their mothers were colleagues at the land registry office. Angelica tried to reassure Gildo, and together they decided to call all Elisa's friends. They put her diaries and notebooks on the living-room table and called them one by one. Angelica called Luca, an ex-boyfriend of Elisa's, a young man from Sicily who had been doing military service in Potenza. Luca had returned to Capaci at the conclusion of his posting and the relationship had finished, but the two had remained close friends. He hadn't, he said, seen or heard from Elisa. Slowly Gildo and Angelica went through the names and numbers one by one, methodically phoning and getting the same questions and concern from those who answered. Angelica also phoned Danilo Restivo. He had had a brief chat with Elisa, he said. He had wanted to ask her advice about what to do about a girl he liked but who didn't reciprocate his affections. He wasn't sure whether to pursue it or let it lie. Having told him to let it go so he and the girl could stay friends, Elisa had gone off, he said, and he had remained there to pray.

As soon as Antonio and Filomena walked through the door they knew something was seriously wrong. They saw Elisa's things all over the table, and one look at Gildo's stony face was enough.

'Elisa's missing,' was all he said.

[10]

The questions came thick and fast, and he answered them as quickly as possible. He told them everything about the last few hours, relieved to be able to share things with them but horrified by the devastating effect on his parents. His father was frowning, staring at the carpet as if he hadn't understood. His mother was repeating prayers and imprecations and her beloved daughter's name.

'I'm going round to Restivo's house,' Luciano said. He looked at everyone to see if they approved, and they nodded, knowing it was the logical thing to do. Luciano picked up his keys and headed out.

*

That Sunday is the saint's day of Danilo Restivo's mother. The family have organised a large lunch to mark the occasion, but Danilo is very late. No one knows where he is. His sister, Anna, goes downstairs to look for him and then doesn't come back. Eventually they both turn up, very late for the lunch, with Anna's boyfriend, Giovanni. They explain that they've been to hospital for a little cut on Danilo's hand. He has a single stitch in the wound.

They finally sit down for lunch shortly after two o'clock, but it's not a peaceful meal. The phone keeps ringing. First Gildo calls, demanding to speak to Danilo. Some friends of a young girl called Elisa keep calling, wanting to speak to Danilo too. Then a man rings the buzzer and asks to see Danilo. His father realises something is wrong and knows, though he barely admits it consciously, that his son is in trouble.

When his son comes back to the flat, his father stands up from the table. Maurizio Restivo is a large man with a jowly, heavy face. He's the director of the Potenza branch of the National Library, a slightly austere, cerebral and intimidating man.

'Come here,' he says sternly.

Danilo follows his father into his study. Maurizio knows his odd son. He knows he lies and fantasises, that he does odd things for which there's no rational explanation. But he knows his weak spots. He probes and coaxes and questions, sometimes raising his voice or, something Danilo finds even more worrying, whispering quietly. Nobody other than father and son will ever know what was said in that room in those frantic few hours after Elisa's disappearance. But from it Danilo emerges calmer. He seems more at ease. The next time Luciano rings the buzzer, wanting more information and clarity about the morning's events, he finds Danilo almost normal: no longer sweating and shaking, but once again himself, his soft voice and spooky smile the same as ever.

*

When Luciano returned to the Claps home half an hour later he only increased the concern.

'He's lying,' Luciano said. 'They saw each other, but Restivo's telling a load of bullshit. He must have done something to her, I'm sure of it.'

Luciano said that Danilo had been highly agitated, sweating heavily. He had replied to all of Luciano's questions with uncertainty and hesitation. He had had a large plaster on the back of his hand. When Luciano had asked what had happened, Danilo had stuttered, embarrassed. He had said that after seeing Elisa, he had gone to a building site where they were building escalators to help pedestrians up to the city centre. He had slipped and got a cut on his hand, so he had gone to hospital. It all sounded, to say the least, suspicious.

The four family members looked at each other and then stared vacantly at the floor. They didn't trust Restivo at all. They knew about his reputation, and the wound on his hand only made them more suspicious. If he had been wounded, they wondered what Elisa might have suffered. Desperation was beginning to sink in. The brothers felt impotent. Restivo was the son of a powerful Sicilian, a man who was part of the Potenza *bene*, the great and good of the city. They were just the children of a humble tobacconist. The Restivo family seemed to realise the gulf in social standing between them and was treating their despair with contempt.

Antonio was pacing up and down. There must be a rational explanation, he hoped. Teenage girls could be unpredictable. She must have gone off somewhere. She would reappear any minute, and they would all be surprised and amused by their unnecessary terror. There wasn't anything to worry about, he told himself and his wife. But he was worried. Elisa wasn't unpredictable. She was thoughtful and reliable. She would never have gone off without saying anything.

The atmosphere was horribly surreal. The Claps family was surrounded by normality, but nothing felt normal any more. There was an emptiness, an absence at the heart of the home, as if their most precious possession, their daughter and sister, had been stolen. As the hours went by, the reassurances they offered each other were beginning to sound hollow. They all knew something was terribly wrong. Gildo and Luciano phoned as many friends as possible, persuading them to scour the city centre, to ask questions of everyone they met. Filomena was almost catatonic, rocking backwards and forwards in her chair repeating one sentence: '*Mia figlia non torna più*' – 'My daughter's not coming home.'

In the early evening that same day, Gildo and Luciano decide to go and see Restivo again. They ring the intercom at the bottom of his block of flats, but his parents inform them that Danilo has already left the city. He had to go to Naples to take an entrance exam for a dentistry course. There's a click over the intercom as once again the line is closed. It was as if doors were already being slammed in their faces.

Gildo and his father went to the police station to report Elisa as missing. At the reception there was a bored official. It was a sleepy Sunday evening, and in this small, provincial city nothing ever happened. Father and son were ushered into another room and eventually another official came in and took down a few details. A typewriter rattled away as the bare facts of Elisa's appearance and date of birth were recorded. The official tore out the piece of paper and asked them to sign it. That was the extent of the investigative procedure. It wasn't the calm objectivity of the professional, they felt, but the begrudging going-through-the-motions of a snooty bureaucrat who resented the disturbance. There was no sense of urgency, no notion that the situation called for decisive action.

On leaving the police station Gildo could see that his father was broken-hearted. Years later, he would write that his father 'was coming round to the knowledge that a tragedy had taken place, and that knowledge would in the course of the years fold and smash his spirit to the point that he would refuse the memory itself of what had happened that day'. All the family were bewildered, but Antonio, more than any of them, was already beginning to lose not only his daughter, but also a part of himself and his own sanity.

Gildo escorted his father home and then decided to go, with his friend Cesare, to the Chiesa della Santissima Trinità. When they got there they were told that the priest in charge of the church, Don Mimì, had also left the city that afternoon. He had gone for a retreat to the spa town of Fiuggi. He wouldn't be back for a few days. The two friends wandered around the empty church, looking for any sign of Elisa. It was cool and quiet in there, the empty pews and echoing footsteps only increasing the emptiness Gildo felt. He tried to open a small door, but it was locked. He was told that in Don Mimì's absence, the upper storeys of the church were inaccessible.

As he was approaching his home, Gildo saw groups of people standing outside the front door. A young girl walked up to him, looking determined.

'I'm Danilo's sister,' she said aggressively. 'People are saying strange things about my brother. He hasn't done anything.'

'He hasn't told the truth,' Gildo said coolly. 'He saw my sister this morning, and she hasn't been seen since.'

The young girl tried to interrupt him, but Gildo demanded Danilo's number in Naples.

'There isn't a phone line there,' she said, 'and anyway he needs to study. He's got an exam tomorrow.'

'I want to know what's happened to my sister,' Gildo said, allowing hours of tension to spill over as he grabbed the girl's wrist.

'My brother hasn't done anything,' she said, pulling her arm away and walking off.

Gildo watched her, amazed again at the way in which people seemed more concerned about their reputations than the truth. Within hours of Elisa's disappearance, it was as if her desperate family were being treated as a nuisance, as trouble-makers who were disturbing the peace of this sleepy province. Phones were put down; doors were slammed. Arrogant officials were nonplussed.

He decided to go back to the Questura, the police station. He was told to wait upstairs as the flying squad was now in charge. For almost three hours he was subjected to a cross-examination, having to answer questions about his family, his sister, her habits, her friends, her relationships, her secrets. Every minor detail of the family's life was probed. It was as if the entirety of the feeble investigation was centred on the Claps family, as if they were somehow responsible for the disappearance of Elisa. Gildo became increasingly angry, constantly trying to persuade the official that it was necessary to contact Danilo Restivo in Naples and cross-examine him. The official smiled patronisingly and continued his only line of enquiry, asking for more details about Elisa, about her parents and her brothers.

The coolness of the officer irritated Gildo. He asked impertinent questions calmly, repeatedly going over what Elisa was wearing, what she was like.

'Go and interrogate Restivo, Danilo Restivo,' Gildo urged frantically. 'He was with her. He's unstable. Everyone knows he's not right in the head. He's even got a cut on his hand. Go and talk to Restivo.'

The officer listened and took notes. His manner was calculated to exude authority and gravitas. The officer and his superiors would decide who to interrogate. They were never bounced into decisions by frantic relatives.

'You need to get hold of Restivo.' Gildo could barely contain himself. 'He saw her last.'

'No urgency,' the official said calmly. 'When the magistrate has been appointed, they'll consider the question of this Restivo.'

By the time Gildo emerged it was dark. He realised with horror that his sister wouldn't be coming home that night. He spent the whole night wandering around the city with Luciano and their friends. He felt like his strength had been sapped. It was cold now and the only people he saw were other friends in the search party, slowly driving around the city or else walking its side streets, looking in every corner and back alley. Each time they came across each other they pursed their lips, shaking their heads silently to say there was no news, no sighting. Occasionally one of them would say one word to the other: '*Niente*.' That was all. '*Niente*' – 'Nothing.'

'Nothing becomes even worse than terrible news,' Federica Sciarelli wrote years later. She's the host of *Chi l'ha visto?*, an Italian programme about missing persons. 'Because nothing accompanies you everywhere, day after day, month after month, year after year. You keep going, sure, but with a boulder that weighs on all the body, on the heart, on the head, even on the muscles. You keep going, but nothing is ever the same.'

The phone at the Clapses' home kept ringing, and every time it rang there was tension and a tiny slice of hope. 'Maybe that will be her calling now,' Filomena thought. 'Maybe they've discovered something terrible.' Usually it was just a friend asking if Elisa was back yet, if there was anything they could do. Journalists called for quotes and information. There was so much bustle and disturbance, but at the centre there was just a hole.

That night the family experienced something that would recur often over the following months. The telephone would ring and everyone would look at it, hoping that it would bring good news or, failing that, at least news. But all evening and throughout the night they would answer the phone, and at the other end there would simply be a long silence.

'*Pronto*,' Filomena would say. '*Pronto. Chi è?*'

Nothing. They hoped these silent calls might be a reason for hope, perhaps someone who had news but was too scared to share it. But over the following months, as those terrible, toying phone calls continued, that hope was replaced by frustration. Whoever was calling seemed to be relishing their pain and desperation.

None of the family wanted to go to bed that night. There was no point trying to relax or to sleep. It was impossible and pointless. Eventually the phone stopped ringing. The lights of the city were slowly going off. The first of many long, dark nights for the Claps family had begun. Nobody slept. There was a terrible feeling of impotence: the sense that there was nothing they could do to help Elisa. All four of them felt that it was possibly already too late. They didn't say so; they spoke to each other about not giving up hope, about doing everything possible to bring her home. But they knew now that she was in very serious trouble, if, indeed, she was even alive. And there was nothing they could do.

Filomena, in particular, feared the worst. She felt sure that something terrible had happened, that her beloved daughter had been done in. There was no other explanation. Everything about Restivo was suspicious and shifty. Everyone knew his reputation. He had that cut on his hand and had come out with the ridiculous explanation that he had fallen down an escalator. '*Quel fetente*,' she says to herself. 'That skunk.'

*

The following day, Monday, brought no good news. Luciano went to a friend who owned a printer's and together they ran off hundreds of posters with Elisa's face and, underneath, a plea for information. He and his friends began to put them up all over the city, at bus stops and at the railway station. Gildo, meanwhile, picked up Elisa's diaries and notebooks. He paused briefly, looking at them wistfully: he didn't want to rifle through her private possessions, but he didn't want, either, to miss any vital hint about what might have been going on in her life. He sat down and slowly started to turn the densely written pages. It was too much for him. The tension and lack of sleep suddenly overwhelmed him and he sobbed silently as he looked at the innocent, sentimental pages. There were two pages Elisa had written about splitting up with her Sicilian boyfriend Luca. Then, suddenly, Gildo saw something that caught his attention. It was a reference to Danilo.

'This evening,' the diary said, 'he stopped me again in Via Pretoria. I tried to avoid him but as always he stuck to me; the others had suggested I shouldn't get too close to him but at the end of the day I'm sorry, he's a bit strange and I always see him on his own. I walked around with him a couple of times and then left him with some excuse . . .' Gildo stared at the page, certain now that Danilo Restivo was the key to unlocking the whole case. He remembered that Danilo had called Elisa the evening before she went missing, on the Saturday. Eliana had said yesterday that Danilo wanted to give Elisa a present for passing her retakes. That was the reason Danilo had called and the reason he had wanted to meet up with Elisa.

But just as Gildo was thinking about Danilo Restivo, another strange personality entered the story. Angelica, Elisa's friend, said that she had something to tell him, something she had been thinking about because it seemed odd.

'Go on,' Gildo said, clutching at any straw he could.

Angelica said she'd been phoning everyone she had seen in the city centre yesterday, everyone she had glimpsed in and around the church where Elisa had met Danilo Restivo. She had remembered seeing a young man, an Albanian called Eris Gega. He was one of the people she and Elisa used to see around the place. They had originally met at a church summer camp. He was a bit older than them, twenty, she thought. Angelica remembered he had been wearing a short-sleeved, light-coloured shirt and greenish trousers.

By now Angelica had made dozens of hopeless phone calls, but she decided to make one more. When she eventually got hold of Eris, she told him why she was calling.

'You've heard about Elisa?' she asked. 'She's been missing since yesterday.'

'I know,' he said.

'I just wondered if you had heard from her or seen her.'

'Why would I?' he said defensively.

'I saw you in the *piazza* yesterday morning. I just wondered if you had seen anything.'

'I wasn't in the *piazza* yesterday.'

Angelica shut her eyes briefly, trying to recollect exactly what she saw. 'I thought you were there with Marco . . .'

'No, not yesterday.'

Angelica said goodbye and stared at the phone for a second. She was sure she had seen him. It was strange that he should immediately deny it. It wasn't as if he could have forgotten what he was doing only yesterday. She went and told Gildo, who immediately called the flying squad to inform them of the discrepancy.

That afternoon the whole Claps family was summoned back to the Questura. What they were told shocked them. The official in charge said that their haste in covering the city with posters and fliers, along with the appeals they had organised on a local TV channel, made them objects of suspicion. The family, they were told, were clearly trying to deflect attention away from themselves and must know more than they had so far let on. They were told to sign another statement and ushered out by a dismissive official.

At the same time, Danilo Restivo was returning from his entrance exam in Naples. He was on the bus that meandered through Campania and Basilicata and back home. At the penultimate stop, just before the bus arrived in Potenza city centre, he saw his father standing by his car with another man. They beckoned him to get off the bus. They were gesturing quickly, as if he should get off before the bus pulled away. Danilo grabbed his bag, walked to the front of the bus and down the stairs.

His father was looking like he meant business. Danilo was slightly scared of him. He didn't know what he and this man were doing here, waiting for him.

'Get in,' his father said gruffly, holding open the door to his car.

Danilo got into the car, putting his bag on the seat beside him. The other man got into the front seat beside his father and turned round to talk to Danilo in the back seat.

'Danilo,' he said, 'I'm a lawyer. The authorities are waiting at the end of the bus line to take you in for questioning. Your father and I thought it wise to take you there ourselves, to have a little chat about what happened yesterday.'

The young man nodded, not sure what to say.

'So, what happened?' the lawyer asked.

Restivo repeated the story he had told the previous day. That he had met Elisa at the church and that she had left after about ten minutes or a quarter of an hour. He had wanted to see her because he wanted to ask about a friend of hers, Paola, a girl that he liked but who wasn't keen on him. He didn't know what to do, whether to pursue it or let it drop. Elisa suggested he let it go, that he shouldn't ruin the friendship with Paola. He also said that he noticed that 'Elisa was worried, and I don't remember in what context she told me that she had been hassled by a man that morning.' He had stayed in there for ten minutes to pray, he said, and then went over to another church, San Michele, to look for friends. But he didn't see anyone and walked home towards his parents' flat in Viale Marconi, near the football stadium. He had taken a strange route, going via the escalators that were under construction between Via Dante and Piazza XVIII Agosto. He had fallen over and hurt his hand, his arm and his hip. He wrapped his injured hand in his jacket and went home. There his sister Anna and her boyfriend, Giovanni, saw him and he showed them the injury. The cut didn't seem too serious, but Anna suggested he go to hospital to get it cleaned up. The three of them got in Giovanni's Fiat Panda and went to the San Carlo hospital. They had to wait for half an hour and it was almost two before a doctor put a single stitch in his hand.

The lawyer nodded, looking briefly at Restivo's father for confirmation. They asked him question after question, trying to fix in his mind the details, probing for inaccuracies or inconsistencies. Eventually they drove him to the Questura, where Danilo was questioned by an inspector, Vito Eufemia.

Years later, Eufemia would recall that Restivo appeared 'prepared, cool, very cunning, precise in his answers'. Restivo was questioned again and again about his exact movements the previous day, and his story never changed. He repeated what he had told Luciano, and his father, and his father's lawyer. Every detail was the same, only each time that he told the story he added little facts, embellishments and clarifications. The inspector was sufficiently suspicious about the story to insist that Restivo accompany the officials to the escalators to demonstrate exactly where and how he had fallen. Restivo took them there and insisted that he had fallen the entire length of the staircase, falling head over heels until he came to rest head first on the level landing below. He had covered his teeth and stomach as he was falling, which was how, he said, a small piece of sheet metal became lodged in his left hand. His glasses were entirely undamaged, even though they were left halfway up the staircase. Asked why he had gone there at all, he said he was curious, that he considered the escalators a fascinating feat of engineering. In fact, he had been there just a few days before with a young woman, Paola (something she subsequently denied had ever happened).

In compiling his report, Eufemia would write that Restivo's version of events was 'extremely unlikely'; he wrote of its 'unreliability', adding that the whole reconstruction was 'unimaginable'. 'It clearly emerges that the witness isn't to be considered credible, which could hint at facts much more serious that would see him directly involved in the disappearance of Elisa Claps.'

Back at the Questura, Eufemia asked Maurizio Restivo, Danilo's father, if he would hand in the clothes – the jacket and jeans – that his son had been wearing the previous day. Restivo consented, saying that he would accompany Eufemia to his house to pick up the clothes. Restivo, his wife and Inspector Eufemia walked down to their respective cars. Eufemia overheard Restivo's wife telling her husband that their son's clothes had already been washed and were drying on the balcony.

Once at the Restivo household, Restivo's parents handed over various clothes.

'I'll also need', Eufemia said firmly, 'the clothes that are drying on the balcony.'

'Eh?'

'The clothes on the balcony . . . I'll require those as well.'

'Indeed,' said Maurizio Restivo, fixing the inspector with his dark eyes. 'One minute.'

Restivo walked inside and called his lawyer, Mario Marinelli. Eufemia, standing in the doorway with two colleagues, couldn't hear the words, only the sound of Maurizio's low, languid voice. The man came back towards them a couple of minutes later.

'You have a search warrant, of course?'

'I understood you had consented to hand over the clothes. There was no need.'

'There is now.' Restivo was firm, his jowly face looking at the impertinent inspector with contempt.

Eufemia was taken aback. Restivo had appeared happy to collaborate, but suddenly, when specific clothes were asked for, he had insisted on a search warrant. It was demanding behaviour for a man who apparently had nothing to hide.

'Very well, I'll make a call.' Eufemia walked down the steps and phoned his boss, the head of the flying squad, Luigi Grimaldi. Grimaldi told him to wait there, that he would get the necessary warrant signed by a magistrate. Eufemia waited, still wondering why Maurizio Restivo had appeared so co-operative only to become so obstructive. Twenty minutes later, Grimaldi called Eufemia and ordered him to return to the Questura. The two had a brief, heated discussion. Eufemia couldn't understand why Danilo's clothes, clothes that he admitted had blood on them from his small cut, weren't going to be sequestered. He went back upstairs to summon his two colleagues and returned to base empty-handed.

At 22.30 that evening, Eliana De Cillis made a statement about the events of the previous day. She reaffirmed everything she told Gildo about Elisa's meeting with Restivo. Pressed about the relationship between Elisa and Danilo, Eliana said: 'Elisa had known Danilo Restivo for a couple of years. He was courting her but she wasn't interested and so sometimes kept him at a distance. He was insistent, though, phoning her and asking her to go out.' Elisa, she added, 'had never confided to me any notion about leaving home or any other irrational gesture . . . she was tranquil and never showed any problems with her family'.

*

It was another surreal night for the Claps family, their second without Elisa. No one could sleep properly, if at all. It just seemed impossible, unbelievable that something like this was happening to them. They walked through the dark house in a daze, nibbling on any food they could find and making cups of coffee.

They veered between activity and paralysis, between trying to do something useful and feeling that everything was useless. There was nothing they could do. But they had to do something. Filomena prayed, raising her palms to the ceiling and slapping her hands on her forehead in anguish. As soon as daylight came, Gildo and Luciano tried to find the energy to make phone calls, to talk to people, to question them. They were walking the streets, putting up posters, fielding questions from journalists and investigators. Gildo went back to the Questura to hear about the previous evening's interrogation of Restivo, but was told little other than generic details.

Their father wanted to go after Danilo. That was the only useful thing to do, he insisted. Danilo had to pay for what he had done. They all knew by now that, almost certainly, Elisa wasn't coming home. At least not alive. And Danilo, they felt sure, knew why. Antonio had thought about little else for the last few hours. All he could think about was forcing the information out of that idiot or, failing that, exacting revenge. He wanted to go after Restivo as soon as possible. That was the only justice for his daughter. Restivo had to pay, to pay the highest price. Elisa had been his little girl. His precious, only daughter. She had always been a daddy's girl, going to him when she had fallen over or was hurt. They were inseparable. He was strict, it was true, but she had always melted his heart. In recent years she had become a young woman; she was beyond that age of sitting on his lap to be tickled. But the deep, deep bond was still there. And now he felt as if his insides had been ripped out. There was a terrible emptiness in the home, in him. And Restivo, he knew, was responsible.

'Where does he live, then, this bastard?' Antonio asked.

'Who?' The brothers stalled. They knew precisely who he meant.

Antonio just looked at them. He knew that they knew. 'Where is he?'

The conversation was interrupted by the telephone ringing. Everything stopped each time it rang. They all looked at it, then Gildo walked over and picked it up. It was the Tribunale dei Minori, requesting to see Elisa's parents as soon as possible. Filomena and Antonio put on shoes and tried to make themselves look presentable. When Filomena glanced briefly in the mirror, she saw that her face betrayed her terrible exhaustion.

When they came back shortly afterwards, however, they were almost clinging onto each other, visibly distraught. They slumped down on the sofa in the living room and quickly gave their sons an outline of what they had heard.

'He's got a record,' Antonio said, his stare lost in the far distance. 'Who? Restivo?'

The parents nodded. 'Back in May 1986, he blindfolded two children and tied their hands behind their backs. They were only twelve and fourteen. He said he had a surprise for them and took them to a hideout he had. There he put on surgical gloves and cut the younger boy's neck with a bread knife and then locked them both in the shack. The boy had to have a couple of stitches in hospital.'

'Was he arrested?'

Both parents shook their heads. 'The incident was reported, but the children and their families dropped all the charges. Apparently Restivo's father paid them a million lire to forget about it.'

'What's he going to offer us?' Gildo said bitterly under his breath.

The more facts the family gleaned, the more they became convinced that their initial suspicions were correct, and that Danilo Restivo was responsible for Elisa's disappearance. But each time they felt sure of it, there was always something that planted a seed of doubt, that made them consider the tiny possibility that, actually, something completely different had happened. That evening, as they were fretting about the track record of Restivo, the phone rang. As always, everyone stopped, hearing the rings and praying that it was good news. Gildo's aunt, Rosetta, answered.

'No,' she said with a solemn voice that made the family listen, 'no, I'm not the mother, I'm Elisa's aunt.'

Rosetta twisted the phone away from her ear so that everyone could hear the voice. 'I'm from Montalto Uffugo. Elisa is here with us. She's well and you don't need to worry.'

'Let me speak with her, put her on please.'

'That's not possible, *signora*. At the moment she's not very well and she can't come to the phone. We'll call tomorrow evening at the same time. We want to speak to her father.'

The line went dead. Nobody spoke for a long time. There was the faintest hope that Elisa was alive. Perhaps not well, perhaps not even free, but at least alive. One or two of the family dared to hope that it was true.

There were, after all, other reasons to hope. At 23.30 on the Monday after Elisa had gone missing, the police interviewed a young man who lived in the same block of flats as the Claps family. Giuseppe Carlone claims that he saw her at 13.40 on the Sunday in front of the cinema Ariston in Via IV Novembre, that thin staircase that leads up to the city centre from the Clapses' block of flats in Via Mazzini. Carlone is convinced that he saw Elisa. He describes her as wearing blue trousers and a white top. Carlone says he was walking towards his home and that he walked past Elisa, said hello, but got no reply. He got home at exactly 13.45, so he thinks he must have seen Elisa five minutes previously.

Gildo is unconvinced. He was on precisely that staircase between 13.30 and 13.50 and he saw neither Carlone nor Elisa. Carlone was adamant that it was that same Sunday, that he had even been to Mass in the Chiesa della Santissima Trinità, staying there until around 13.00, but that he hadn't seen either Elisa or Danilo there. But he had seen Elisa, he said, on Via IV Novembre. Another young man, Massimiliano Carlucci, thought he saw her in the central Via Pretoria at around 12.40.

Various other people came forward, convinced they had seen Elisa long after she must have left the church. Adelaide Masella, a friend of Elisa's, is sure she saw both Elisa and Eliana in Via Mazzini soon after 12.30. Adelaide had been in a car with her sister and mother when the traffic forced them to stop exactly outside number 69, the Clapses' block. Adelaide described in precise detail what both girls were wearing: Elisa, she says, 'was wearing a pair of dark trousers tending towards blue, a pink top tending towards white, with a wide collar and three-quarter sleeves. She had a light pink key ring with a slightly darker border that she was playing with.'

Eliana, she said, was sitting astride her Piaggio moped. 'It was electric blue or black, a dark colour.' The details Adelaide was able to provide seemed precise and credible: Eliana 'held the moped in balance with both feet resting on the ground, keeping her hands on the handlebars. On her right arm she had a white-coloured helmet held upside down.' The trouble was that if Adelaide was right, Eliana must have been lying: she was adamant that she hadn't seen Elisa since they had separated at 11.30.

Investigators didn't know what to believe, who to trust. Elisa's friends seem to have seen her everywhere: in Via Pretoria, in Via IV Novembre, in Via Mazzini. None of the times appear to coincide, to make any sense. And no one seems to have seen Elisa at the one place she was supposed to have been: in the church itself. Some of her friends might have made an innocent mistake, thinking they had seen her when it was just another young girl with dark hair. But others, the investigators felt, were obtuse or misleading. From those very first, vital few days the investigation was hampered by misinformation, by accidental and wilful lies. The investigation had no clarity, no direction, no certainties. And there was no explanation of why Eliana De Cillis had, as she confessed days later, Elisa's key. Elisa, she said, had given it to her, but it seemed highly improbable: Elisa always kept the single key in her pocket.

The night after the mysterious phone call claiming that Elisa was alive but unwell, the family gathered around the phone. They were all waiting for it to ring, for that same, unknown voice from Montalto Uffugo to call back.

The phone did ring a few times, but it was never that same voice. There was no call from any kidnappers or any demands for a ransom. The call they longed for simply didn't come. It almost felt as if some people were deliberately trying to add to the sense of mystery, as if some citizens enjoyed stoking the suspense and disorientation caused by a missing sixteen-year-old. Just a few days after Elisa disappeared, some spooky graffiti was written on a wall in the city's Montereale Park: 'I had a cat, she was called Alice, she sang too much so I killed her. Elisa I've buried with a stone on top. I have only my cat on my conscience. Where's Elisa?'

It sometimes seemed as if people were using the horror of a missing teenager to settle scores and incriminate enemies. Witnesses came forward to point fingers, sending investigators off on futile, false leads. Tip-offs arrived from all over Italy – from Seregno, Vaglio and Brindisi – but none of them proved reliable or fruitful. A young woman called Elisabetta Postiglione came forward three days after the disappearance claiming that she had seen two men abducting Elisa, forcing her to get into a red Renault 5. One assumption, recurrent throughout the ensuing years, was that Elisa had been abducted in order to be forced into prostitution. Elisabetta draws sketches of the two men in question, but a week later withdraws her statement in its entirety. No one understands the motivation for the initial declaration or the retraction. Four years later, Elisabetta is discovered in Puglia, a prostitute under the control of Albanian pimps.

Just as the Claps family were dealing not only with Elisa's absence, but also with the endless leads and false dawns, Luciano received his call-up for military service. He was going to be posted in Persano, about sixty miles from Potenza. Gildo was distraught: having apparently lost his sister, he now had to do without his younger brother, just when he needed him. Gildo drove Luciano to the barracks, and the two spoke at length about Elisa and their parents. They were both worried about their father. He was beginning to seem distracted, almost in denial. He had initially wanted to deal with Danilo Restivo himself, but having been stopped by his family, he had increasingly retreated into his shell. He seemed suddenly aged and weighed down, almost immobilised by the futility of all their efforts. Filomena, their mother, was by contrast suddenly feisty, full of fury and energy and determination. Gildo hugged Luciano outside the barracks and then got back in the car for the lonely journey home. From now on, Gildo and Filomena would front the fight for justice.

*

Part of the difficulty, for both the investigators and the Claps family, was the lack of reliable information. It was impossible to know who was telling the truth because there was so much contradictory information, if not deliberate lies. Eliana had mentioned to investigators the name of a young man that Elisa had been spending time with recently, an Albanian called Eris Gega. She claimed the two liked each other, and Eliana said that Eris had been in the Piazza della Prefettura at 13.30 that Sunday. Eris was originally from Durazzo, in Albania, and following the collapse of communism was one of many Albanians who came to Italy in the early 1990s looking for a better life. Eris had arrived in Potenza in June 1991 with his parents, being put up by the city council first in a hotel, the Miramonti, and then in a prefab in a suburb called Bucaletto. He had worked as an apprentice mechanic for a while before heading to Bologna briefly. On returning to Potenza in the spring of 1993, he had met Elisa in a parish camp. He had liked her and had wanted to go out with her, but she had told him she had a boyfriend, the Sicilian Luca.

Like so many other witnesses and suspects, Eris Gega consistently fails to give a convincing account of what he was doing on the Sunday Elisa went missing. He contradicts himself, changes his story and gets confused. When he's first questioned, on 22

September, he claims that he never left Bucaletto all day. He hung around a nearby church in his suburb until 12.30, went home and had lunch, and stayed in until around 18.00. While he was at home having lunch, he claims to have received a call from one of Elisa's friends, asking if he had seen her. He was questioned again on 11 October and 3 December, when he names the friends he was with that Sunday. He refers to a wedding that took place in the church in the suburbs.

But when the authorities check with the friends he names, all of them say he wasn't in Bucaletto, that they saw him in the centre of Potenza, near a telephone box at midday, 'as if he were waiting for someone'. Both Elisa's friend Angelica and her boyfriend, Vincenzo, claim to have seen him there, near the phone box, between 12.00 and 12.30. So too does Eliana De Cillis. Many others claim to have seen him at a vintage-car show in the centre that day, and it emerges that the wedding he claims to have attended in the suburbs happened the Saturday prior to Elisa's disappearance. The phone call from Elisa's friend Angelica wasn't, as Eris claimed, at lunchtime but towards the evening.

It's clear that Eris, too, had repeatedly changed his story regarding his whereabouts. Investigators are unsure why he would continually make up unreliable stories. A young, vulnerable immigrant, he may simply have been wary of being dragged into a case that was increasingly dominating the local news agenda. Or he may have been trying to obscure his own involvement.

Most importantly, however, Eris Gega had at his disposition a white Fiat Uno. It was a car that many, many witnesses claimed to have seen that morning with, they said, Elisa inside. In October, a cousin of Gildo, Angelo, told him that one man was sure he had seen Elisa between 13.30 and 13.40 on that Sunday. The man was called Ernesto Sonzogni. Gildo went to see him, hoping, not for the first time, that this was a lead that could help resolve the mystery. Sonzogni claimed to have seen Elisa get into a Fiat Uno with a Matera number plate at the bottom of the steps that lead from Via Ravenna to Via Mazzini. Gildo wasn't overly impressed with the new witness: he was a man who had problems with alcohol, and he occasionally seemed vague and confused about details. But it was a version of events that appeared to be confirmed by another man called Nolè. He too had seen a young woman being shoved into a white Fiat Uno. The authorities follow the lead and it emerges that Eris did, indeed, have a Fiat Uno, and he also had an Albanian friend who had lent him another Fiat Uno. Sonzogni was shown both a video and a photograph of Eris Gega; Sonzogni wasn't at all convinced that Gega was the man he had seen, from a distance, driving the Fiat Uno, but eventually, and reluctantly, he admitted that there might be a similarity. He signed a statement, and Eris Gega was arrested on 22 December 1993.

*

By mid-October, Eliana was under investigation too. She appears in the Tribunale dei Minori on 13 October. Eliana repeats everything she had declared in the past, but her original lies to Gildo about where she and Elisa had gone, and what they had done, come back to haunt her. She's thought to be unreliable. She strenuously denies that she was in Via Mazzini with Elisa soon after 12.30, as their friend Adelaide, the one in the car, had claimed. Adelaide says she saw Eliana on her moped that morning and describes the exact clothes she was wearing. Eliana says she left her moped at home that day.

Eliana is one of the leads in the case, and her situation becomes even more complicated in December. That month an anonymous phone call to the police suggests that Elisa had been seen in Rome getting horribly beaten up and then forced into a white Fiat Uno.

'Help her and help me,' the voice says weakly. A specialist laboratory in Forlì identifies the voice of the caller as that of Eliana De Cillis. Quite why she would deliberately mislead investigators and plead for help in such a way is unclear. The only explanation seems to be that she is deliberately trying to shift attention away from herself and back onto the mysterious Fiat Uno.

*

On 5 October, almost a month after her disappearance, *Chi l'ha visto?*, the hugely popular TV programme about missing persons, features the disappearance of Elisa Claps. As always, the production team receive many phone calls, but one, in particular, is intriguing. A woman called Caterina Urciuoli calls from Potenza.

She talks at length about a young man who, she says, is disturbed; a man who has the worrying habit of cutting young girls' hair on the back of buses. Many people in Potenza knew about it. It was something young girls warned each other about. But no one, until now, had known the name of the man. The person Caterina Urciuoli mentioned was well known to everyone involved with the investigation: Danilo Restivo.

It's another lead, but, again, the information doesn't seem entirely disinterested. It turns out that the woman with the tip-off is the mother of Eliana De Cillis's boyfriend. It's possible, Gildo thinks, that she's just doing her civic duty, informing investigators about Restivo's bizarre hair fetish; but it's equally possible that she's deliberately deflecting attention from her son and his girlfriend, both of whom are feeling the heat.

Attention duly turned back to Danilo Restivo and his account of the events of that Sunday morning. There was something in his version that failed to convince the authorities. Of all the people who had been to Mass in the Chiesa della Santissima Trinità that

Sunday, no one had seen either Elisa or Danilo. The mother of Angelica, Elisa's best friend, didn't see them. Nor did the priest. Danilo's account of falling in the building site seemed absurd: the rolling head over heels down a whole flight of steps seemed fanciful and the injuries sustained incompatible with such a fall. He had told investigators that he knew the building site because he had already been there with his friend Paola. When investigators talk to Paola, she denies that she's ever been there with him. She says that Danilo once boasted to her that 'when he got angry he was capable of doing any manner of evil to someone'. It might have been an idle boast, she says, and Danilo had always been courteous with her. But gossip about him was on the increase as the desperate search for Elisa went on. It was well known that he hung around churches, trying to make friends with priests and parishioners. He had once claimed to have the keys to the church of San Michele, saying that he knew 'all the secrets' of the place since he was the one who locked up. People begin to repeat things they've heard as a strange sort of Chinese whispering takes place around the city: someone alleges that Restivo had once locked a young girl in a room above the Chiesa della Santissima Trinità and that they had had to knock down the door to release her. Everyone talks about his mania for cutting girls' hair.

*

The investigation had been placed in the hands of a young female magistrate called Felicia Genovese. She was proceeding slowly and cautiously, and treated the Claps family with curt politeness. Gildo was frustrated by her lack of urgency, especially as far as Restivo was concerned, and he started taking any new information he had to a rival force, the *carabinieri*, and, particularly, to Marshal Vincenzo Anobile. As well as Anobile and Genovese, there were two police

[34]

inspectors working on the case, Vito Eufemia and Donato Pace, under the direction of the head of the flying squad, Luigi Grimaldi.

By Christmas 1993, however, little progress appeared to have been made. Gildo and Filomena requested an appointment with the *Questore*, Antonio Mastrocinque. When mother and son were ushered into his office, Filomena immediately started asking him questions, demanding to know why more wasn't being done to investigate and apprehend Danilo Restivo. The police chief was evasive and discourteous, clearly irritated by the insistence and impatience of the Claps family. Eventually he stood up and said: '*Signora*, what more do you want? When will you understand that your daughter has run away from home? What do you want us to do?'

Both Gildo and Filomena were stunned. For months they had had to put up with the arrogance and incompetence of the investigators. Now, worse, those idiots were saying that there was nothing to investigate in the first place, that Elisa – their beloved daughter and sister – had simply run away from home. Months of tension and anger rose up in Filomena and she bent down, took off a shoe and threw it at the man. He stood up and started shouting, saying that he would have them both arrested. Filomena stood her ground, continuing to make it very clear what she thought of him and his colleagues. For a few seconds the two gave full vent to their feelings, neither hearing the other as they shouted loudly. The man's subordinates rushed into the room, and Filomena and Gildo were brusquely ushered out and escorted back to the car park. Once sat in the car, Filomena sobbed uncontrollably as Gildo stared out of the windscreen. His mother's tears only made him more angry at the officials responsible for finding his sister.

'It's difficult to explain', he wrote years later,

> what one feels in a case such as this: the absence, the emptiness that devastates you, the waiting that slowly grinds you down,

the hopes that light up and then shatter in a perverse see-sawing of emotions. From one side logic and reason were bringing us ever closer to a deduction that none of us dared to disclose out loud, from the other side the heart and expectations induced us to consider the most fanciful hypotheses in the illusion that Elisa could be still alive who knows where and that soon everything would be over. In the meantime, days became weeks and then months, making the hope that Elisa could return to us ever more feeble.

Life went on, but it would never be the same. The family got through the day on auto-pilot, mechanically doing the usual tasks but doing them without their normal concentration or feelings. The only reason to continue living was to fight the battle for Elisa. Everything else was irrelevant. That terrible uncertainty was, in many ways, even worse than the dreaded possibility that Elisa would never come home. Elisa's family were almost certain that she was dead, but they also had to live with the merry-go-round of elaborate theories and exotic explanations; they had to explore each crackpot idea and deliberate *depistaggio* or sidetracking. They had no evidence, no proof of what they knew, of what they instinctively felt. And while some people seemed to be revelling in the hypnotic pleasure of speculating on the fate of Elisa, her family were unable even to bury their beloved daughter, let alone bring anyone to justice. Elisa's father longed to wreak his own revenge on his own terms, but his wife and sons forbade it; they wanted justice the legal way and began a long, lonely fight to find their daughter and her killer.

Time went by in a daze. Gildo would have bursts of energy, pursuing every possible lead and going over again and again the single frames of that terrible Sunday morning. He spoke to all of Elisa's friends, questioning them repeatedly in case he had missed anything. He would pursue the authorities, harrying them and pushing them, insisting that they needed to do more. But then he would collapse, exhausted and disillusioned, aware again of the futility of all his efforts. He would flop onto the sofa, watching the news on TV and realising that, if his family's life had radically changed, so too had the outside world.

The aftershocks of the end of the Cold War were still being felt. It was as if the plate tectonics of geopolitical power had shifted drastically, creating an unexpected peace in certain places and terrible conflicts in others. The tortuous peace process in Northern Ireland had begun, only to be repeatedly blasted off course by the sheer brutality of extremists on both sides. The autumn of 1993 was particularly bloody: an IRA bomb in a fish shop on Belfast's Shankill Road killed both the bomber, Thomas Begley, and nine Protestants, including four women and two children. There was further outrage when Gerry Adams, who had begun peace talks, was pictured carrying the bomber's coffin. A revenge Loyalist attack on the quiet village of Greysteel later cost the lives of eight people. In the space of one week, twenty-three people had died. Russia, meanwhile, teetered on the brink of civil war. Boris Yeltsin had dissolved the country's legislature because it was blocking his reforms. Parliament responded by beginning impeachment proceedings against him, claiming that his actions were unconstitutional. The crisis was eventually resolved by tanks firing on the parliament and fierce street fighting in which almost two hundred people lost their lives. Algeria was in the middle of a bloody civil war, as Islamic guerrillas splintered into ever more violent groups and army militias were drawn into the dirty war. In Egypt, too, there were frequent fundamentalist bomb attacks targeting tourists. Although the World Trade Center in New York had been bombed back in February, killing six and injuring over a thousand, it still appeared that Islamic fundamentalism was a remote problem, largely restricted to the Middle East.

Things were barely more peaceful in Italy. The country was in the throes of a surreal revolution as a handful of determined judges pursued corruption in the highest echelons of power. By the autumn of 1993, almost two hundred parliamentarians were under investigation by the so-called 'Clean Hands' investigators. Nearly a thousand businessmen and public officials were also being pursued. Every day brought new accusations and astonishing downfalls as former ministers and prime ministers, including Giulio Andreotti and Bettino Craxi, came under the microscope. As in Russia, there seemed to be a stand-off between parliament and the outside world, as the politicians repeatedly blocked efforts to lift parliamentary immunity. The case of Duilio Poggiolini, director for the previous twenty years of the pharmaceutical department of the Ministry of Health, was representative of the entire system of corruption: billions of lire were found in his, and his wife's, possession, some of it stuffed inside a lilac-coloured footstool.

The crisis was accentuated by economic factors. Just a year earlier the Italian lire had been devalued. In 1993, for the first time since the end of World War II, consumption fell, dropping by 2.5 per cent. GDP fell by 1.2 per cent. The country had an epic debt problem, and a succession of 'technical' governments attempted to force-feed the country the bitter medicine required to lift it out of recession. The cuts were so deeply felt that in Venice the superintendent of the port, Antonio Di Ciò, was knifed to death in his office by an embittered workers' representative.

Sensing that the nation was on the brink, and that political instability represented an opportunity, the Mafia launched a frontal assault on the symbolic arteries of the state. Throughout 1993, bombs exploded in Milan, Rome and Florence, costing lives and further reducing the credibility of the country's security forces. Throughout the autumn of that year, details began to emerge of the murky dealings of various security and military officials. As the old certainties of the First Republic collapsed, stories began to emerge of extraordinary collusion between state officials and the criminal underworld. Corrupt judges were arrested in Sicily, and the careers of secret agents like Francesco Delfino seemed to overlap with many of the mysteries of the previous thirty years. Even military officials appeared on the wrong side of legality: one colonel's wife, Donatella Di Rosa, revealed that the military were so concerned about instability that a *coup d'état* was being organised. No one seemed safe any more. In Palermo, a respected priest called Pino Puglisi was assassinated for his courageous stance against Cosa Nostra.

As iconic Italians of the post-war period died, it seemed like the passing of an era. Pietro Barilla, the Parma pasta magnate who had turned his grandfather's business into a global brand, died in September. So too did Edmondo Bernacca, the man who had, for decades, been the country's most charismatic weather forecaster. A day after his fiftieth wedding anniversary, and having fallen into a coma after a second stroke, Federico Fellini – one of the greatest film directors of the twentieth century – also died. Bruno Pontecorvo, an Italian atomic physicist who had been an assistant to Enrico Fermi and had subsequently defected to the Soviet Union in 1950, passed away in Dubna, on the outskirts of Moscow.

The consequences of the collapse of communism were felt acutely in Italy. Not only did the country's old Communist Party lose much credibility, so too did those parties whose main *raison d'être* was to be a bulwark against communism. In the early 1990s, both the Christian Democratic and Italian Communist Parties were on the brink of imploding, not least because the entire party political system of the First Republic seemed caught up in the corruption scandal. New political forces were emerging: in the north, particularly in Lombardy and the Veneto, a separatist movement called the Northern League was exploiting the widespread antipathy towards traditional Roman politics. The League's leader, Umberto Bossi, was a populist rabble-rouser, a man not averse to resorting to staggering gangster-like language. 'If a judge', he said in the month Elisa disappeared, 'involves us in Tangentopoli they should know that their life is only worth a bullet.' It was the first of many warnings that the cure for the ills of the First Republic might be worse than those ills themselves. In fact, a few days later a poll of public attitudes revealed that, given the incredible corruption of the political system, 26 per cent of Italians would be in favour of a tax strike. Once again, it was a warning of a dark future, a hint that a possible solution to the illegality of the First Republic would be simply a different kind of illegality in the Second. Tax evasion, it was felt, was suddenly an almost moral practice.

It was mid-October, a month after Elisa's disappearance, when a highly secret manifesto was revealed: it was an outline of political ideals that was calculated to appeal to the vast majority of the electorate. It had been created through focus groups, market research and opinion polls. The manifesto was put together like an advert, with carefully constructed slogans and buzzwords. It was about to be sold to the public by the most charismatic, and controversial, salesman on the peninsula: Silvio Berlusconi. A few weeks later, on 5 November 1993, a national association called Forza Italia came into being. It was a shrewd move: not only was there clearly a power vacuum at the heart of Italian politics, but Berlusconi's company, Fininvest, was saddled with colossal debts. The government of Carlo Azeglio Ciampi was also contemplating dismantling the near monopoly Berlusconi enjoyed in the arena of commercial television. It seemed like a propitious time to seize power, to rescue both the nation and his empire from the external threats. To many Berlusconi was the ideal riposte to the grey, dour and sometimes dirty world of the Christian Democratic Party. He was flash, entrepreneurial, magnetic and, above all, successful. Everything he did

– in construction, television and football – seemed to turn to gold. He appeared to be the answer to Italy's prayers.

It wasn't, in short, a time in which the provincial story of a missing teenager was likely to find space in any national newspapers. The Elisa Claps story was still just a family tragedy rather than – as it would become over subsequent years and decades – a national, even an international one. As the Claps family endured their first Christmas without Elisa, it seemed as if only they, and a handful of relatives and friends, really remembered her at all.

Two

'They have only one colour, the colour of their
sad, sorrowful eyes and their clothes, and it is not
a colour at all, but rather the darkness of earth and
death. Their pennants are black, like the face of the
Madonna. All other flags have the motley hues of
another civilisation which does not belong to them
as it moves along the main road of History, towards
progress and conquest.'
    Carlo Levi

Matera is the most memorable, and arresting, place in Italy. One
of the oldest human settlements in Europe, it looks timeless and
primitive and picturesque. For millennia, men and women have
lived here in the white caves, turning openings in the rocks into
homes by digging out the *tufa*, the soft, porous stone rich in
calcium carbonate. These are the famous *sassi*, meaning literally
'stones' but implying the rocky, rugged places that people called
home.

It's almost impossible to get your bearings in the two ravines
that make up the *sassi*, Barisano and Caveoso. There are narrow
staircases and winding paths, petite roads and sudden gullies.
Every path and building is roughly the same shade: an off-white,
beige or mild ochre. The bare beauty of the stones is stunning, and
when you reach a vantage point you see balconies and bell towers,
a fantasy of imagination and adaptation. Nothing is regular: the
houses and churches have to go along with what the rocks dictate,
so that rectangular blocks of stone melt into the random, rolling,
curving forms of nature. Straight lines give in to natural contours,
and flat *piazze* are interrupted by eruptions of stone. The whole
place looks kind of cubist and curvaceous at the same time.

And if humans have had to accommodate rocky interruptions, the glaring white stone, too, has been worn and weathered by humans. These caves have been inhabited since paleolithic times and the huge white slabs that make up the roads and paths have been polished by millennia of shoes and hooves and rubber. The wonderfully clean feel of white cascading caves is set off by green shutters, flowers and mossy roofs. Other roofs have become the neighbours' balconies or even paths. It all feels like a long-forgotten fantasy, somewhere that you can relax in the splendour and surprise of human ingenuity.

Matera is now a UNESCO world heritage site, but not so long ago the whole place was, according to critics, a national disgrace. Twenty thousand people used to live in these caves, all packed densely one on top of the other in only 3,300 'rooms'. Extended families and livestock – goats, pigs, sheep, donkeys – would cram into what were little more than crevices in the rocks, with no sanitation or health care. Malaria and trachoma, an infection of the eye, were rife. Matera was a teeming human anthill and, to many sophisticated observers, the place felt more animalistic than human. Carlo Levi's sister, journeying through Lucania to visit her exiled brother in the mid-1930s, painted a very different picture of Matera. The *sassi*, she said,

> were like a schoolboy's idea of Dante's Inferno. And, like Dante, I too began to go down from circle to circle, by a sort of mule path leading to the bottom. The narrow path wound its way down and around, passing over the roofs of the houses, if houses they could be called. They were caves, dug into the hardened clay walls of the gully, each with its own façade, some of which were quite handsome, with eighteenth-century ornamentation . . . The houses were open on account of the heat, and as I went by I could see into the caves, whose only light came in through the front doors . . . On the floor lay dogs, sheep, goats and pigs.

Most families have just one cave to live in and there they sleep all together; men, women, children and animals.

Appalled by the scene, she described children 'with the wizened faces of old men, their bodies reduced by starvation almost to skeletons, their heads crawling with lice and covered with scabs. Most of them had enormous, dilated stomachs, and faces yellow and worn with malaria.' People followed her about, begging for quinine. She noticed 'the thin women, with dirty, undernourished babies hanging at their flaccid breasts'. Levi's sister echoed what many visitors felt in the interwar years: that Matera was something of which Italy should be ashamed, that humans being essentially cave-dwellers in the twentieth century was a disgrace. Matera was something that people tried to hide or deny: in the great film *Anni ruggenti*, set in the 1930s, an outsider is told, in so many words, 'No, no, we don't have people living in caves here,' just as the heavies are trying to evacuate and demolish them before his visit to the *sassi*.

In fact, Matera has often been used by film directors precisely because it appears timeless. It was the setting for Pier Paolo Pasolini's *Il vangelo secondo Matteo*, for Mel Gibson's *The Passion of the Christ*, and for dozens of other films that required a biblical, or primitive, backdrop. Many of the great Italian directors, including Francesco Rosi and Roberto Rossellini, deployed Matera as a setting in order to contrast the modernising, sophisticated Italy with the earthy, historical one. In Rosi's *Tre fratelli*, the urbane prodigal sons return to the deep south and their Matera roots for a funeral, and their philosophies come up against the blunt realities of life and death. It was Rosi who adapted Levi's *Christ Stopped at Eboli* for the big screen and who used Matera as the backdrop for his fable *C'era una volta*, starring Sophia Loren and Omar Sharif. It seems de rigueur that almost any film about Italian history – Rossellini's *Viva l'Italia* and *Anno uno*, or Paolo and Vittorio

Taviani's *Allonsanfan* – must pass through Basilicata in general and Matera in particular. The fact that Francis Ford Coppola's Italian roots are in nearby Bernalda, where he's starting an academy for aspiring screenwriters, cements the link between this region and the film industry.

But while film-makers have, for decades, come to Matera looking for an earthy, rugged backdrop, Matera itself has changed. In the late 1950s and early 1960s, there was a concerted political effort, headed by a politician from Basilicata called Emilio Colombo, to evacuate the caves and provide modern housing for people. Thousands of families were moved to the suburbs of the town, into concrete apartment blocks with running water and central heating. Slowly the caves were emptied and abandoned. It was only in the 1980s and 1990s that – probably partly because of the glamour of filmic representation – people began to appreciate their beauty once more. The *sassi* were slowly modernised themselves and plumbing and electricity were introduced. Suddenly those caves that had so appalled Carlo Levi's sister were transformed into light, clean living spaces. They're now among the most expensive and desirable properties in southern Italy, and almost all have now become chichi apartments, boutiques, museums or restaurants. Rather than trying to hide the *sassi*, people are now proud of their earthy beauty.

And they're certainly right to be proud. Matera is a stunning, surreal place. Even now that many of the caves have become boutiques and bars, they still feel enjoyably rudimentary somehow. The white interiors are bare. When you sit in a swanky restaurant you know that you're really eating in a cave: its curved ceiling looks like a vault or railway tunnel and it feels blissfully cool after the insistent, glaring sun. Service, like everything around here, is very polite and very slow. There's time to read a chapter or two of your book before they bring you a glass of Aglianico, the rich red wine that's produced round here. Aglianico is a black grape that was introduced to Italy by the Greeks when Lucania was part of Magna Graecia. That's how it got its original name, Ellenico. Over the centuries the name simply warped into Aglianico. Later, tiny plates of local delicacies arrive: *ciambotta*, a rich vegetable broth; *soppressata*, a prized salami made solely with fillet of pork; pickled aubergines; and *peperoni cruschi*, red peppers dried by the sun. A lot of the food has generous amounts of chilli. It reminds me of a saying round here: '*Se non pizzica non stuzzica*,' which means, more or less, 'If it isn't hot it doesn't hit the spot.'

Matera, like everywhere in Italy, seems to have churches on every corner and in every *piazza*. But although some have the usual grand facades, many are just doorways into the rock. When you walk into a place like the Madonna dell'Idris, it's stunning for being unadorned. Instead of the usual baroque and gold of so many flamboyant churches, this is just another cave, a comforting sanctuary: it's cool, simple, *spoglia* – nude. It feels elementary, the kind of place in which one could really be contemplative.

That beautiful church is on a small mass of rocks called, rather grandiosely, Mount Errone, and from here, looking back at the beautiful disorder of the *sassi*, you can see why the place has often been used in films to represent Jerusalem. It looks, at a stretch, a bit like Jerusalem does from the Mount of Olives: a teeming, stony, historical settlement. Or perhaps, at even more of a stretch, like Cappadocia in Turkey, another place where human ingenuity has turned the volcanic landscape into something extraordinary and unexpectedly hospitable.

If you turn away from the city, there's a deep gorge, almost a mini-canyon that descends to the River Gravina. And beyond that, slightly higher on the other side, is yellow scrubland dotted with occasional trees and, set in the rocks, black holes like eyes that seem too aligned or symmetrical to be natural. These are the famous *chiese rupestri*, the 'rocky churches' that were, like the *sassi* themselves, little more than cavernous holes carved out of the rocks.

Because of that deep ravine, it takes a long time to get from the old city to the archaeological park where those *chiese rupestri* are: you go back through the beautiful, timeless *sassi*, through the suburbs and the large factories where they produce literally millions of sofas. The road also takes you past the modern quarries of this ochre stone that look like enormous swimming pools with no water. Once you've reached the other side of the ravine, there's a fresh breeze and you can see Matera in the distance, its glorious chaos below you. Up here it feels a rugged, barren landscape. But when you look closer it's full of colour: there are tall agaves, their yellow flowers dotting the landscape. There are small, durmast oak trees and wild orchids and a rich smell of thyme. The whole landscape is carpeted with the herb.

In this archaeological park there are thought to be about 160 of these cave-churches. Many became places of worship over a thousand years ago as monks fled the Islamic expansion in the Middle East, northern Africa and even southern Italy. The nearby city of Bari, in neighbouring Puglia, was a Saracen emirate from 847 to 871. These churches were refuges for monks from all over the Mediterranean, becoming hermitages, mini-monasteries and chapels. They are, perhaps deliberately, not always easy to find. You often have to walk dangerously close to the precipice of the ravine to find the black openings. It's moving to see these caves, to wander into their dark interiors with flaking paintings and plain stone and think that this is where monks had to flee to escape persecution. It's hard to imagine a more rugged Christianity.

But then so much of the history of Lucania is about people fleeing from persecution. The reason so many settlements are way up in the mountains or in hidden caves is precisely because the inhabitants were fugitives, trying to escape the wrath of one colonial power or another. The very name Basilicata comes from *basilikos*, the Greek for 'imperial'. After the Greeks came the Romans (who took reprisals in Basilicata since the people had unwisely allied themselves with Hannibal), the Visigoths, the Ostrogoths, the Saracens, the Lombards, the Byzantines, the Normans, the Swabians, the Angevins, the Aragonese, the Hapsburgs, the Bourbons and the Bonapartes and the Bourbons again. Even the Savoy and the 'Piemontesi' from the north were, in the 1860s, considered not patriotic unifiers but rather just more invaders intent on taxation and suppressing revolt. Lucania's history is one of centuries of occupation but also of occasional, violent revolt against that occupation. Round here people still talk about one infamous Count of Matera, a certain Giovanni Carlo Tramontano. The King of Naples, Ferdinand II of Aragon, had appointed Tramontano Count of Matera in 1494. For two decades he was a much loathed figure in Matera, a man who ran up debts and expected the people to pay for them. When on 28 December 1514 he demanded 24,000 ducats from the citizens, a plan was hatched to rid the city of him. The next evening he went to church, unarmed as custom dictated. He was set upon when he emerged, stripped naked and beaten to death with halberds. The bells of the city's churches rang to announce his death, and the people flooded into the streets to celebrate. Even now, the little side street near the cathedral where he was murdered is called Via Riscatto, 'Liberation Way'. And, just in case anyone was uncertain about the pride of these people, the motto on the crest of Matera is '*Bos Lassus Firmius Figit Pedem*' – 'The tired ox puts down his foot harder' – implying that the people will only endure so much until they, too, put their foot down. Lucania might be a region that has seen centuries of invasions, but arrogant invaders should never take their acquiescence for granted. That occasional ferocity is now ritualised once a year at the city's famous festival for the Madonna della Bruna, when, at the end of the procession and once the Madonna has been safely removed, the crowds descend on the wagon that had carried the statue and literally rip it to shreds. It's known as the 'assault on the wagon'.

*

I get back in the car and head towards Metaponto. The road, for once, isn't hairpinning madly but is levelling out as I approach the region's only plain. It's on the south-east edge of Lucania, the part that dips into the Ionian Sea. There are five major rivers that slowly meander towards that sea: the Brádano, the Basento, the Cavone, the Agri and the Sinni. They look fairly dry at this time of year. It's late April, but it's clear, from the vast amount of polytunnels by the side of the road, that this is the most fertile area of the region. This is where they grow all the famous vegetables – the peppers and chillies and aubergines and tomatoes. That fertility is one of the reasons the Greeks settled here in the eighth century BC. As you drive around, you can feel the echoes of that ancient presence in the place names: Policoro, Nova Siri, Salandra, Pomarico, and so on.

Even back then, this was a land of rebels. The people of Metaponto allied themselves with Pyrrhus (he of the famous Pyrrhic victory) against Rome, and it was in nearby Policoro that the historic battle between the two took place. In 207 BC, the area allied itself with Hannibal and was duly sacked by Roman forces, who set up a *castrum*, a fortress of soldiers permanently garrisoned in the town. When in 72–73 BC Spartacus came this way, however, the people once again showed themselves to be instinctive rebels and many allied themselves to his cause. As Plutarch later wrote, 'Many herdsmen and shepherds of the region, young and robust, united with them.'

As you approach on the quiet dual carriageway that links Bari to Reggio Calabria, large columns come into view. This is the majestic temple of Hera, nicknamed the *Tavole Palatine*, the Paladin Tables, as this was where knights or paladins were thought to have assembled before heading off to the crusades. As you approach along a gravel path between two hedges, you can see fifteen huge Doric columns still standing, giving a sense of the size and splendour of the place. There are five monumental columns on one side and ten on the other. Even though it's a ruin of sorts, it feels strangely solid, almost permanent. Because it's open to the deep-blue sky and you can see the view through the columns, it feels like an integral part of the landscape, like something that has always been here. George Gissing wrote about these Paladin Tables in *By the Ionian Sea* in 1901, talking of being 'possessed by the pathos of immemorial desolation; amid a silence which the voice has no power to break, nature's eternal vitality triumphs over the greatness of forgotten men'. This was where Pythagoras established his 'school' in the sixth century BC and, despite the sound of traffic a stone's throw away, it's just possible to imagine what this place must have been like that long ago. The land all around is flat; you can smell the sea a mile or two away. This was one of the most important trading posts in Magna Graecia, a town where grain and wine were constantly being bought and sold.

Apart from the grand temple, though, this place feels like its glory years are far in the past. Camped outside the temple are various families who have been housed in the visitors' reception ever since severe floods last month, on 1 March, forced them to leave their homes. Their animals – horses and cows – have turned a small courtyard into a stable. They've put bed sheets up, their slogans complaining to the passing traffic on the dual carriageway that they've been forgotten by the authorities. Their fate isn't dissimilar to that of Metaponto itself, which over the centuries became a marshy swamp and was slowly abandoned. Only a small, seaside settlement called Torre di Mare remained. Standing here in the relentless sun looking at those august columns, it seems as if civilisation came and went a long time ago.

I drive on a couple of miles and look for the large archaeological park, with its well-preserved temples and theatres. I follow the small signs and end up driving along a narrow track, feeling, instinctively, that this isn't a well-trodden, or driven, road. I get to the large gates, but they're closed, padlocked with a fat chain. I check the opening hours and it's supposed to be open, but it's definitely closed. I ring the intercom but see loose wires coming out of the side of the box. It hasn't been connected.

Through the wire enclosure I can see the ancient stones. There are the remains of 'temple D', thought to be the temple of Artemis. There are a few squat Ionic columns sitting on mushroom-like lined plinths. Balancing precariously on two of those columns is the only remaining bit of the temple's architrave. It's thought to date from 470 BC. There are the remains of other temples, the beautifully clean white stone glistening in the hot sun. There's a theatre, its perfect semi-circle and gentle slope towards the stage still preserved after almost twenty-five centuries.

It's frustrating not to be able to go in. I drive into the tiny town and look, at least, for the archaeological museum. Even that's not easy. There are no signposts. I lean out of the window and ask a man for directions. He starts telling me not just where the museum is, but about everything inside it and what I mustn't miss. He's talking so long that it seems rude to be sat in the car, so I get out. We stand there for quarter of an hour, chatting idly about old artefacts they've found about the place. As usual, I get the sense that there's no rush here, no urgency to do anything; it's more important to be civil and generous, to share life rather than race after it somehow.

Eventually I get to the place, a rather grandiose building whose car park has sticks and branches woven over a metal frame for shade.

'Any idea', I say to the man on the front desk, 'why the archaeological park is closed?'

'Eh?'

'The park . . . it said on the board outside it was open at this time of morning.'

'It's closed.' He smiles at me, happy to help any tourist.

'Why's that? I thought it was open in the mornings.'

'Giuse',' he shouts over his shoulder to a colleague, 'why's the archaeological park closed?'

A debate ensues and it slowly emerges that they've decided to close it in the mornings for a while since no one ever goes there anyway. It saves time and money. That seems to be a recurrent theme in Lucania. They don't have any tourists, so they shut things early or don't even open them, and so the precious few travellers who do come this way decide it might not be worth the effort to hang around. It was the same over a hundred years ago: George Gissing discovered that the museum he was looking for had been transferred to Naples. 'Metaponto', he concluded, 'is a railway station, that and nothing more.'

'Do you want to come in here?' the man asks, readying himself to peel off a paper ticket from his block.

'Sure.'

The museum is full of coins and clasps and urns and so on. All the coins have an ear of barley, the symbol of Metaponto's fertility. The sophistication of ancient civilisation is apparent. It's strange to think that this place, now so sleepy, was once the centre of a bustling culture, that this was a busy trade route and vibrant town. Although the museum is full of fantastic objects and information and leaflets and boards and books, there are many more employees than visitors. I feel mildly self-conscious as two or three attendants watch me while I lean in to look at this or that. It's as if this place was dreamt up by optimistic tourism departments and local politicians long before the demand was there.

I drive towards the lido, to the long stretch of sand that runs all along this coast. It feels like many similar seaside towns in Italy: the perpendicular streets near the beach have sandy pavements and low, tidy houses. There are a few kiosks and stalls and, dotted at intervals along the beach, wooden bars, beach huts and boats. Unlike the beaches in the north, it all feels uncrowded and open. Standing on the sandy beach, you can see for miles to the north and south, and there are only a few dozen other people around. Gentle, clear waves lap at the fine sand; the sky is a deep blue and there's just enough breeze to take the edge off the heat. It's a great beach and I sit down at one of the bars and order a drink. It's an unpretentious place and I wonder whether, despite all the grand brochures and conferences about promoting tourism, they're actually happy that they're not overrun with tourists.

There's a rather overweight boy on the beach playing football with some friends, and, just as he begins to peel off his white vest, a woman beside me shouts over to him.

'Luca. Luca! Don't take your vest off.'

'But', he says, disgruntled, 'it's so hot.'

'You'll catch a cold. You know what your chest is like.'

'It's thirty-five degrees,' he protests. He's sweating profusely, but his mother is insistent and his vest stays on. His mother and I watch him playing as he gets redder in the face and his vest gets wetter with sweat. She begins to explain to me the various ailments he has, or she thinks he might have, or will have if he takes his vest off. There's something touching about her hypochondria. Every mother I've ever met round here is an expert on common ailments, especially the digestive system.

As we're talking a man sitting near us, a large man with shaved grey hair, asks where I'm from.

'Is my accent that obvious?'

He smiles, too polite to say yes. When he hears I'm from England, he draws up a chair and he starts telling me of all the wonderful places I should visit while I'm here. He's particularly keen that I should go to an abandoned village called Craco.

'It's a very suggestive place, very . . .' he rubs his fingers and thumbs together looking for the right word, 'evocative. It's unreal, almost other-worldly. Go and see it. It's something else.' He grabs hold of my forearm and tells me that he'll make a call on my behalf. With his other hand he pulls out a phone, and I hear him asking to talk to 'the mayor'.

'I have here a dear friend from England . . .' I hear him say, giving no hint that we only met a couple of minutes ago. He gets off the phone and assures me that he has opened every door possible.

On the way to Craco, I stop in another of those remote, high towns. The road, as always, doubles back on itself again and again as you climb the mountainside. It's dangerous to look too long, but behind you it's possible to see the dry, arid, beautiful landscape, the combination of grey rocks and green shrubs. Pisticci is a town of two halves. Like so many of the mountain-top towns and villages in Lucania, it was built on the very peak of a hill, the houses huddling as close as possible to each other. They say round here that all the towns are balanced on the *cocuzzolo*, which is the word for the crown of a hat or a summit. Pisticci couldn't defy gravity, however, and on 9 February 1688 almost half the town collapsed in a landslide. Around four hundred people lost their lives.

After the landslide there was a move to transfer the people into the valley, where it would have been safer, and cheaper, to construct new houses. But the townsfolk opposed leaving their ancestral home on the summit, and so Dirupo, a new district, was born. This is where they built the so-called *casedde*, terraced, whitewashed houses. From the top of the town, those *casedde* look unusually geometric, almost ordered, compared to the usual labyrinthine streets of mountain towns. Even many of the roofs have new, rust-coloured tiles. It feels tidier, somehow, than the chaotic, wonderfully improvised settlements on most mountain peaks.

As you walk through the centre, most of the buildings are whitewashed, so that the sun glares off them. Occasionally there are buildings made from rich, beige bricks, usually the older churches like the Chiesa Madre, the 'mother church', with its beautiful, bare brickwork and natural, sandy render that makes it feel plain and clean. That church, and the arched, brick ramparts of the old castle are in the part of the town that survived the landslide, the so-called Terravecchia, the 'old land'. Here the streets are more as I've come to expect round here: narrow, steep, surprising. It always feels, as you pass the open doors and nod hellos to old women on small chairs, that you're walking through someone's front room. Since all the windows are flung wide open, neighbours shout greetings and questions to each other from one house to the next. When you come out to the edge of the 'old land', the view from up here is magnificent. The sky is still deep blue and there's a constant soft breeze. There are no major roads and no other settlements in sight; only mountains and rocks and woods. Standing there, leaning on the railings overlooking the valley of the River Cavone, I wonder why all villages in Basilicata seem to seek this isolation; why, against all the advantages of a simple life in the valleys and plains, Lucani tend to huddle together on the most precarious peaks. There are, I guess, defensive benefits to being so high; and it's certainly cooler in summer, although that seems a small advantage when the winters, at this altitude, can be so bitter. The fact that there are recycling skips here for ash give an idea of how much wood must be burnt through the cold months. There must just be something deep in the psyche of Lucani that makes these beautiful, lonely summits so appealing.

I get back in the car and head towards the abandoned town of Craco. The road weaves down one mountain, along the valley floor and then starts climbing round another peak. Craco, too, suffered a landslide, only this time the vast majority did move into the valley, meaning that what remains is an eerie ghost town. It's a weird sight: the small mass of houses seem to be clinging onto the very summit of the mountain and, both being grey interspersed with green vegetation, they seem almost camouflaged against it, as if over the years they've become almost indistinguishable. Only the black openings – the empty windows and arches – and the geometrical shapes of the houses suggest that this was once a village. There's a large, rectangular tower at the very summit and a bell tower with small arches, but otherwise the village is an accumulation of cubic houses that are slowly cracking and collapsing back into the rocks from which they came. You can hear wooden shutters slamming and squeaking open in the mountain wind and, as you get closer, it's increasingly clear that this is a place that has been uninhabited for almost fifty years: there are fig trees and thistles and poppies growing in the cracking brickwork and tufts of grass appearing in the spaces between tiles. There are overgrown cacti on balconies and steps that lead nowhere. Diagonal cracks on the walls show that subsidence and earthquakes have clearly taken their toll as much as neglect. It's a spooky place, but unexpectedly absorbing. You kind of want to hang around, to walk through the narrow lanes and steep staircases and just feel the melancholia of absent humanity.

It's a kind of melancholia that Lucania has long been used to. Craco is far from being the only abandoned settlement. There are places like Campomaggiore Vecchio, an even more extraordinary, and august, ghost town that also emptied after a landslide in 1885. It had a baronial manor and a large church, the church of Santa Maria del Carmelo. It too looks both beautiful and bereft, an Ozymandias-like warning to the pretensions of humanity. It's become, as much as anything in this forgotten region ever does, something of a tourist attraction: it's floodlit at night and called, rather bizarrely, the 'city of Utopia'.

Many of these places are abandoned because of earthquakes and landslides, but most are empty because of mass emigration. Between 1876 and 2005, over 738,000 Lucani left the region, many heading north but many more heading to America. Since the population of Lucania now is just under 600,000, it's often said that there are more Lucani outside it than within. And people here are fond of claiming various American icons as their own: the actress Anne Bancroft was born Anna Maria Louisa Italiano in the Bronx, but her parents were from Muro Lucano; Carlo (or Charles) Paterno – whose parents had to leave Lucania in the 1880s because of, inevitably, an earthquake in Castelmezzano – was a property developer responsible for some of the most innovative buildings in Manhattan, such as Paterno Castle and Hudson View Gardens.

But as well as being a net exporter of humans, Lucania has sometimes received them too. Between 1448 and 1532, as the Ottoman Empire was expanding eastwards, large numbers of Albanians found sanctuary in the remote mountains of Basilicata. They were granted lands by the Aragonese royalty on the throne of Naples and settled in two tiny villages in the valley of the Sarmento river. It's a testament to the isolation of those two villages that even today, five centuries after they started arriving, those Albanian immigrants still speak Arbëresh, the old, traditional Albanian. Even the road signs use the old language. Streets are called *rruga* instead of the Italian *via*; a *piazza* is a *qaca*; a *strada*, a street, is an *udha*; the open spaces are called *sheshe*. Even for most Italians, this is a foreign place.

I go first to San Costantino Albanese on the west side of the valley. As you drive in, there's a long mural depicting events in the life of George Kastrioti Skanderbeg. He was the Albanian lord who, having created the League of Lezhë in 1444 to unite the Albanian principalities, for two decades led the resistance against the Ottoman Empire. It's a long, simple mural, but its significance is clear: this is a community that knows its history and its heroes. It's a tiny village and the houses on the narrow streets look very basic: some front doors are just planks nailed together or corrugated metal plates. On one door someone has written 'knock' in paint. Another house has chicken wire over the windows. As usual in these picturesque mountain villages, there are thin staircases falling away from the path at oblique angles. People nod and stare, perhaps surprised that there's someone wandering round their quiet alleys. I get the impression that, within a few minutes of my being here, everyone knows there's a foreigner around. Young kids peek round the sides of houses, giggling at me and disappearing again when I shout '*ciao*'.

On the other side of the valley is another Albanian village. Called Casalnuovo until 1962, when it was renamed Shën Pali Arbëreshë (San Paolo Albanese), it's the smallest *comune* in Basilicata with, at the last count, only 342 inhabitants. It's 800 metres above sea level and, as usual, the view is spectacular: there are birds soaring peacefully way below, gliding in the wide valley of the dry river. On the other side you can see San Costantino Albanese like a thin, oblique slit in the mountainside. You can see the roofs of the houses below the summit and they all have stones placed on the tiles around the edge to keep them from blowing off. Around the walls of each house are huge piles of wood, neatly stacked and ready for what is, presumably, a pretty harsh winter.

I walk around the small settlement, looking for the museum of Arbëreshë culture. I can't find it, but I enjoy the search. I come across a building that obviously has subsidence problems, but instead of rebuilding it thick beams have been leant against it as wooden buttresses. There are six pairs of beams, each pair divergent like open scissors pressing against the ancient wall. It looks odd because the beams, which were presumably meant to be temporary, have been cemented in place and the temporary has become permanent. A patch has become part of the fabric. I've often heard Italians complaining that everything here is *provvisorio*, that everything is provisional, temporary or just an interim solution. They say that nothing ever gets decided, that plans and projects are done on the hoof. But there's something attractive in that improvisation, in that spontaneous adaptability. Looking at this building, it's clear the beams are now there for the duration; judging by their age, they'll need shoring up soon, and so the accretion of patches and improvisation will go on. It's what I've seen described, in a tourist brochure on this region, as 'spontaneous architecture'.

I go and sit in a bar and listen to the men talking to each other. I can't understand a word. I've read that this language retains various archaisms from medieval Albanian. In fact, many modern Albanian linguists come to these villages since they're one of the few places where you can still hear traces of what their language was like prior to the Ottoman invasions. But it's a tongue which varies hugely throughout the many Arbëreshë communities in Italy, and it was, until recently, only an oral language. Without the gold standard of a written version, the language was malleable, accumulating elements of local dialects and mutating from one Arbëreshë community to another.

In a few minutes of eavesdropping I don't hear any Italian and I begin to wonder at the incredible preservation of their heritage: for five centuries this community has lived in a remote village in a remote region of Italy and they're still talking their own language.

They're still considered, by both themselves and by surrounding Italians, as different, as foreigners somehow. They've always aimed at tradition rather than integration, even in the face of fierce opposition. There are similar Arbëreshë communities dotted throughout southern Italy, little pockets of Albanian minorities all over Puglia, Basilicata, Calabria and Sicily. They're very distinct from the 'new' Albanians that started arriving en masse in the 1990s after the fall of communism. If Italy sometimes seems to have had minimal effect on these very traditional communities, the same couldn't be said of the Arbëreshë community's influence on Italy. Many of the best-known Italians of the twentieth century were Arbëreshë, or at least one of their parents was. The father of Antonio Gramsci, the great political philosopher, was of Arbëreshë descent. So too was the father of Enrico Cuccia, the mercurial man at the epicentre of Italian capitalism throughout the First Republic. Francesco Crispi, the Italian patriot who was twice prime minister, was also from the Arbëreshë community, as was Pope Clement XI.

I find the museum eventually, an unexpectedly modern building in the middle of the tiny old houses. Much of the museum is given over to displays showing how colourful clothing was made out of the yellow shrub that covers these mountains: broom or, as it's known in Arbëreshë, *sparta*. I remember vaguely from history lessons past that the Plantagenets used it as their symbol, thus getting their name from the Latin for 'broom' (*planta genista*). Here it's a plant that dominates the landscape, not only turning the sides of the valley a bright yellow, but also, traditionally, clothing the villagers. In March, the men would prune the plants, which were then gathered in July and August. They were made into bunches, boiled, and the fibres extracted from the woody part. The women who, even today, work the plant are identically dressed: white headscarf, white shirt, red dress and blue apron. The fibres were soaked in the river for between eight and ten days before being beaten and dried in the sun. They were combed until soft, spun, coloured and woven. The resulting clothes on display are thick but attractive: waistcoats and jackets and bonnets are brilliantly coloured and often adorned with lace. The *kamizolla* is a red dress with horizontal gold stripes, the number of stripes announcing your social standing.

From the museum I head round the corner to the church. For centuries this tiny community has followed the Byzantine Rite, and the building – although officially affiliated to the Roman Catholic Church as part of the Italo-Greek Catholic Church – looks decidedly Orthodox: there are bright gold icons on many of the columns and walls. Like so much else in this tiny, remote village, it feels as if you're not even in Italy any more. And I enjoy that sense of mild disorientation. Every time I think I'm really getting to know Lucania, it surprises me; every time I begin to feel at home in this primitive, mountainous land, it reveals something new, something unexpected. And perhaps I shouldn't be surprised that the Arbëreshë community has, here more than anywhere else, maintained its cultural traditions for half a millennium: Lucania, after all, offers them perfect isolation.

*

I head west for a couple of hours. The road through the valley of the Sinni river is straight and almost empty of traffic. It's only as I get close to the western coast of Basilicata, on the Tyrrhenian Sea, that the road begins to snake up through the mountains. I head towards Trècchina for lunch, and suddenly, from a dual carriageway, I'm on an unmarked road with patchy asphalt. But it's very picturesque: as the road hairpins upwards, I can see olive groves and vineyards and stacks of timber. In the main square there are plenty of people around, but they're almost unnoticeable. They're chatting quietly in the shade of shop awnings. Many are simply standing next to each other in silence, watching other people doing the same. It's as if the sun has made everyone move slowly, and the only noises I hear are the tinny church bells and the sound of a man trying to sell nets of onions from the back of his pick-up. Not for the first time, I'm made aware of the enthusiastic generosity of this place. As I sit in a bar just enjoying the gentle pace of life, the barman asks me how I like the local wine. He begins enthusing about a little vineyard he's tending and proudly presses a label-less bottle into my hands. It's a deep red colour with a metal cap instead of a cork. I ask what I can give him for it, and he says it's a gift.

*

The Tyrrhenian coastline of Basilicata is entirely unlike the long, sandy beaches of the Ionian coast. The mountains seem almost to lean over the sea, edging right up against the shoreline so that the coastal road has to hug the cliff face. With the mountain range on one side and the crystalline sea on the other, it feels like car-advert country. Every few hundred metres you see a tiny bay or beach, and caves, stacks and small fishing vessels. The coastline here is what they call *frastagliata*, indented or jagged. The road follows the curves of the coastline hundreds of metres below, and at worryingly regular intervals on the metal retainer are bunches of flowers marking the spot where someone, you assume, has fallen to their death. But it's hard not to take your eyes off the narrow road to admire the view. One of the country's most famous writers, Indro Montanelli, wrote of the town of Maratea in 1957 that

perhaps there isn't in the whole of Italy a more sublime countryside and view. Imagine tens and tens of kilometres of cliffs indented with caves, stacks, precipices and soft beaches in front of the most spectacular of seas, now wide open, now closed by harbours as small as basins. It's separated by a chain of dolomites, all rocks the colour of flesh, dotted with half-abandoned villages, with ruined castles and old Saracen towers, a wooded slope broken by streams and torrents and buried under the boughs of holm oaks and chestnuts.

Occasionally there are parking areas on vantage points along the road, and if you pull in you can look back at the dozen bays you've passed and at green, wooded moutains that slowly turn a faint blue in the distance. There's one black beach that looks like asphalt.

Maratea itself is a picturesque place. Full of steep, narrow staircases and pretty *piazze*, it was deliberately built behind Mount San Biagio in the hope that it would be hidden, or protected, from Saracen attack. On the steep, wooded mountainside there are pastel-coloured houses, all seemingly piled on top of each other and struggling for their own view of the beautiful Gulf of Policastro. It's a place that's nicknamed 'the city of 44 churches', and there seems, indeed, to be a place of worship every dozen paces.

It's not a land where the English are particularly fondly remembered. Maratea was one of the few places that resisted Napoleon Bonaparte's invasion. In 1806, a thousand soldiers bravely held out against the French, having been promised that English reinforcements were on their way. The seige lasted for days, until the mayor, Alessandro Mandarini, gave up on the English and surrendered. The walls of the castle were torn down in revenge for his stoical resistance. That old castle is now a ruin. The drive up there is terrifying: the road zigzags on long stilts, swaying over the edge of the mountain so that it seems like you're on a cartoon road, nothing more than a ribbon in the sky. The grey stones of the old castle are crumbling and sprouting grass. Small lizards, green and black, dart all over the place every time you put your foot down. Now, instead of the castle, there's a massive white statue of *Il Redentore*, the redeemer. It's a very clear imitation of Rio's *Christ the Redeemer*, but this one is much less impressive: it faces inland rather than towards the sea, and the arms seem too high and the body too long. It's a mass of white concrete. Under the arms is something that's presumably supposed to be angelic wings or robes, but it looks like the redeemer's arms are webbed. The steel rods of his fingertips are exposed where the concrete has cracked away. But the locals are clearly very proud of the statue, and a nearby kiosk is selling thousands of plastic imitations. On the cage housing the floodlights for the statue dozens of couples have clicked on padlocks, announcing with marker pen on the unremovable metal their undying love. The view from up here, at over 600 metres above sea level and yet almost on top of the sea itself, is stunning.

*

As the train rattles towards Potenza you can see bright red poppies dotted among the fields of yellow corn. They look like drops of blood in the sand. Apart from the wind farms on the rocky, monumental mountains, this place appears largely untouched by modernity.

When you arrive in Potenza, it's clear that it's a strange, sad sort of city. Its centre is huddled on a mountain top over 800 metres above sea level. Edward Lear, in his *Journals of a Landscape Painter in Southern Calabria*, was scathing, calling it 'as ugly a town for form, detail and situation, as one might wish to avoid'. Nor is it a comfortable city to navigate. There's no taxi rank outside the station, and the only way from there to the centre is up a slip road off a dual carriageway. There's no pavement and dense weeds grow along the sides of the road, so you almost have to walk in the middle and take your chances with the oncoming traffic.

The cars here mostly look older and more dented than they do up north. Everywhere I can see evidence of economic depression: adverts for loans or large yellow letters saying '*Compro oro*' – 'I buy gold.' There are fluorescent posters for bargain pilgrimages to Medjugorje or Lourdes. As I walk past the football stadium, I read the insults against the team's owner, Giuseppe Postiglione, who, having allegedly made a lot of money by throwing matches, is now under house arrest.

There are rather ugly escalators to the top of the city. They move slowly through tunnels full of advertising boards. As you step off one escalator you walk towards another, past local artwork, until another escalator at a slightly different angle takes you up again through a tunnel of advertising. It seems, compared to the thin, sweet *scalinate* of most hilltop towns, a strangely lazy, soulless way to reach the top of the city. These, of course, are the escalators that Danilo Restivo claims to have fallen down and cut himself on when they were under construction in 1993.

When you come out at the top you realise how high up you are. This is, apparently, the highest provincial capital in Italy. Way below you can see swallows circling in pairs between rusty aerials. There are pebble-dashed benches with flat, rectangular spaces on the backrests for advertisements. But there aren't any adverts; just a flat space waiting for the next marketeer. People are moving slowly in the sun wearing colours I've only ever seen in Italy: lime-green trousers and custard-coloured jumpers. On one street corner I see an old man, barely five foot and with a dark, wrinkled face like a walnut, selling flowers. I can hear people greeting each other, shouting sawn-off names: '*ciao*, Anto',' '*ciao*, Marce'.'

I walk the short distance to the Chiesa della Santissima Trinità. It's barely a hundred metres along Via Pretoria from where the escalator emerges. The church is just as I've seen it in photographs and news reports through the years, with a *piazzetta* in front of its wooden door. It seems simply surreal that a sixteen-year-old girl could just walk in there and never be seen again.

Coming out of the church I call Gildo, Elisa's eldest brother. He tells me to wait for him in the main square by the City Hall and he'll come and pick me up. I'm apprehensive about meeting him. I've seen his face regularly on television and it has always looked stern. He is, understandably, not a man who suffers fools. But when he rolls up, pulling a helmet off his head, he's immediately smiling and affable. He has gingerish hair and a greying goatee. The skin on his hands and around his eyes is discoloured, as if he's been burnt (later I learn that it's the result of vitiligo, a condition that causes depigmentation of the skin). We shake hands and chat briefly in the *piazza* before he suggests I jump on the back of his Vespa.

'We'll go and talk in my office,' he says.

We career down the road that spirals outwards and downwards from the city centre. It's a ten-minute ride to Gildo's office, a language school called St Andrews. We go and sit in his office, and he changes slightly. As we begin to talk about his missing sister, he goes from having been relaxed to something almost mechanical. He's not tense or evasive, quite the opposite. He's very loquacious and eager to talk about the case. But that face I've seen on television so many times – determined, frowning, frustrated – returns.

'Everything I come across in this case, I have had to break into a thousand pieces,' he says. 'There have been so many silences and complicities.' He tells me about things I have read about, and wondered about, for years: about Restivo's unconvincing alibi, about the lies and half-truths told by Elisa's friends, about the dubious role of Restivo's family, and about the staggering and suspicious incompetence of the investigating magistrate. '*È una pagliacciata*,' he says grimly. 'It's a joke. This case is a manual for all the things that shouldn't happen when someone goes missing.'

He makes it very clear that he's convinced not only that Danilo Restivo is behind his sister's inexplicable disappearance, but that many others are guilty of covering up for him. 'At the moment we're trying to understand not just what Restivo did, but everything else. Because we think there has been so much complicity in this whole thing to allow him to wander around undisturbed all this time.'

As he talks and lists his grievances he puts the fingertips of one hand together, banging them on his forehead before opening out the fingers of his hand as it comes towards you. It's a gesture of the madness of what has happened in all these years. He keeps saying '*Chiediamo . . .*' – 'We ask . . .' – and listing the questions he and his family are posing. It's clear that he's a driven, redoubtable character. 'I've dedicated my life to this story and I can't stop now. I have to understand everything that happened. We'll let no one off the hook. In all this time we've never, ever yielded.'

There will be time, I know, to talk about the ins and outs of the case. But I want to know about Elisa, his sister, the girl whose photo I've seen so many times on posters, on fliers, on the TV show *Chi l'ha visto?*. The photo they usually use is one of her in a baggy white jumper, one arm stretched out so that she's leaning against a wall. She has long dark hair falling on each shoulder. She looks like many sixteen-year-olds: on the cusp of adulthood but still slightly ungainly, as if she has the innocence of childhood rather than the poise of womanhood. I've seen many other photos too over the years: a girl with a carefree smile and large glasses. What strikes me every time I see her face is the fact that she appears so gentle, looking at the camera with an indefinable kind of affection.

Gildo sighs heavily and stares at the table between us. 'I was eight years older than her. Luciano, my younger brother, was four years older than her, so she was the darling of the house. Everyone looked out for her. Losing her has been terrible. She was a very naïve person, very sweet, very affectionate.' Everyone you speak to about Elisa recalls her kindness. She wanted to be a doctor, to work abroad for Médecins Sans Frontières. 'We used to tease her, we used to call her Mother Teresa,' Gildo smiles ruefully.

'She was always lavish with other people, too open. She never saw the bad in anyone, even the worst person. It was something we corrected her on. We said she had to be more careful. In the end she paid for that openness. I think that's what cost her with regard to Danilo because she knew he was a strange boy, but she didn't have any fear. She was just sorry that here was a person who was on their own, who had difficulty forming relationships with other people. He had made a pass at her, and she had said no. He was in love with her and she had pushed him away. But, despite all that, she wanted to offer him friendship at least. She was sorry not to reply to his phone calls . . .'

'What was Restivo like?'

'My younger brother, Luciano, knew him better. He was a strange one. He had some mental problems and a morbid behaviour towards girls. In everyday life he seemed the perfect idiot, struggling to do the simplest things. He had great difficulties in dealing with people, never managing to have a normal relationship. But then, I think, he becomes lucid and very efficient in the application of his perversions. I think he has a schizophrenic personality, that he's unable to control his impulses. I suspect that, since puberty, he's been impotent, that he's unable to consummate a relationship.'

It's interesting listening to Gildo talking about the man who, he's convinced, murdered his sister. He always calls him by his Christian name, Danilo, and he talks about him calmly as someone he has studied, hunted and analysed. He speaks of his nemesis in such a measured way that I'm surprised: Gildo's more clinical than angry.

'I don't have any anger towards Danilo,' he says when I mention the subject. 'Danilo needs to be taken out of circulation, sure, but he's not the problem. I blame his family, who never dealt with his mental condition. I have a terrible, terrible anger about what I assume must have happened, don't get me wrong. I've had to learn to control the anger. We're all angry about the way it's all been covered up, but Danilo . . .' He shrugs.

It's early evening now. Gildo and I are sitting on the balcony of his two-bedroom flat in a block above his language school. We're sharing a bottle of Aglianico and looking at the mountains in the distance, enjoying the sunset and the gentle glow of the dying light. He lights a cigarette and we talk about football and politics and books. He begins to tell me what it was like before 1993. He had been a regional swimming champion, winning the 800 metres freestyle. He jokes, as he pats his stomach, that it's hard to imagine now. There had been traumas before; there were always traumas in this harsh landscape. In 1980, the famous earthquake had rendered the family house uninhabitable and, while his parents lived in tents and containers provided by the *Protezione Civile*, Gildo and his younger siblings had been sent to live with an aunt on the Ionian coast, in Scanzano Jonico. That's when, he says, he got his skin condition.

We talk about Basilicata, about this rugged, remote land. 'It's a place where time seems to have stood still,' he says. 'But we're paying the price of that isolation.' He describes the intellectual emigration of his generation, most of whom have moved north to look for work. 'But all my friends have an incredibly strong attachment to their land. There's something about the simplicity of life here, about the humanity of the relationships between people that you can't find in big cities.'

Back in 1993, Gildo was twenty-three and was only two exams short of graduating in law. Even back then, he says, he was an iconoclast: he never followed any scholastic advice and read whatever he wanted, mainly American novelists – Hemingway, Twain, Hawthorne. He was disparaging about all authority, a rebel without a cause. And then, suddenly, he had one. When Elisa disappeared, he dropped his studies entirely for five years. 'I lost faith in all the values I believed in – justice and so on. I suddenly had too many contacts with that world. I discovered a world that I wouldn't wish anyone to have to deal with. My studies didn't interest me at all. I only did the last two exams and graduated for my mother's sake.' When his younger brother, Luciano, was forced to leave for military service ten days after Elisa's disappearance, it fell to Gildo to battle for justice. 'I completely immersed myself in it,' he says. 'Luciano was working in the background. He has a different attitude towards institutions. He's a policeman now and he always says that I don't make allowances for anyone, that I'm distrustful towards all authority. We've remained a close family thanks to my mother. She receives thousands of letters from all over Italy because people see her courage. She's a real *mamma*.'

I tentatively ask him about his father, a man who, I've heard, has retreated into himself since 1993, someone who has almost not wanted to know about the investigation and the hunt for his daughter. 'He's become enclosed by his own pain. He understood that day that something serious had happened. But he never wanted to talk to the press. He said: "If we do it my way, I'll sort it out. If you want to do it your way, I don't think you'll ever get justice." He wanted to do it his way in the sense that he wanted to go and get Restivo. But we don't talk about it any more with him. My mother's always very careful that he doesn't hear anything on the news. He doesn't speak to anyone any more.'

As we talk, Gildo's phone constantly interrupts us. It's clear that even now he's still completely immersed in it. I listen to him talking to someone, mentioning his latest suspicions and the lack of investigative progress. As usual, he's polite but insistent. He sighs when he hangs up. 'It's not a normal life, this,' he says again.

I wonder how Gildo manages to keep going. 'I made a promise to my sister many, many years ago,' he says. 'I promised that I would bring her killer to court. When you've lived with this thing for so long, it becomes a part of you. It's almost as if you can't do without it any more. In fact, I've a lot of fear about what will happen if, one day, it's all over. Having hunted and battled all these years, it will leave an emptiness when it's all over.'

I quietly wonder whether it will ever be over, whether Elisa will ever be found, if the tragedy will ever come to an end. There are plenty of people who never find what they're dreading: the corpse, the evidence, the closure. He nods slowly, staring into the distance. 'It's terrible living through the disappearance of a loved one. You're in this strange, suspended territory in which you want to know the truth, even if it's the worst you could fear, but you also don't want to know. You can't manage to work through your grief; you never have a full stop. It has been terrible.

'In 2001, I founded the Associazione Penelope for missing persons because I realised that people needed that sort of support. Until you have certainty, until you find the body, there's always the imponderable. There's no mourning, you can't work through your bereavement, you can never metabolise your pain. It's a suspension of life, as if you're always waiting for something, as if you're living from one moment to the next as if something's about to happen. You live just waiting for news. It's strange: you want to know the truth, even the worst, but you don't want to know. These have been difficult years because we've spent so much energy as we know, we intuit that there's a desire not to discover what happened to Elisa. We've just never been able to understand how it's not possible to single out the person responsible when we had so many elements and certainties about the case.'

It's been as if the only people who want to know the truth are the Claps family themselves; as if they have to be the ones to unearth the thing they most dread. It's hard to imagine an agony more acute than that: not only the fear that your sister or daughter has almost certainly been murdered, but also that the onus of fighting, for years, to prove it, to bring the evidence and the guilty before the world is entirely on the grieving family's shoulders. It's a strange, terrible inversion of what life should be.

I slowly say something along those lines to Gildo, who nods wearily. 'This,' he says again, laughing bitterly, 'this isn't a normal life.'

We go inside and eat. His wife Irene apologises for the simplicity of the meal, which seems to me rather splendid. We watch the football on TV as we eat. Later, in the kitchen, I talk to Irene. I wonder what it's like for her having a husband whose life is lived, as he says, 'in suspension', that is dominated by a terrible mystery. Irene lived in Scotland for years, and we talk in English.

'It's difficult for him,' she says. 'Sometimes there are journalists outside the flat, buzzing the intercom all the time. People call him day and night. You've seen what it's like with his phones. At least they don't have our home number.' I realise that Gildo is playing a kind of strategic game with the media: he needs the oxygen of publicity for his battle for justice, and journalists need scraps of information about the investigation. It's a two-way process, and he grants interviews and hands over information in return for keeping Elisa's disappearance very visible on the national radar. That, I know, is why he's been so welcoming to me. He feels it a duty to talk to any journalist who comes knocking. 'I can say it very cynically,' he says, when I ask him about his relationship with the media, 'in all these years I've got to know the mechanisms of the press very well, and unfortunately this story has all the ingredients of a story that will be talked about: a young girl goes missing in a church, a man with a fetish is suspected, and so on.'

When I go to the sofa to watch the rest of the match, Gildo nods his head towards the kitchen. 'I met Irene in 1995, when I was out of my mind, full of anger.' He had, he says, *'perso la bussola'* – 'lost his bearings'. 'She must really love me to have put up with every-thing. I don't know how she's managed.' I gently wonder whether he's ever sought professional help, but he guffaws disparagingly. 'I don't even go to the doctor when I'm ill. No, I'd never seek that sort of help.' He keeps chuckling as we turn back to the game. As it ends, Gildo flicks over to the news. It's the normal, depressing stuff, and he lets off steam. 'This country is ruined, it's in a terrible state. It's a country that has lost so many of its references. There's a failure in the whole system, a degeneration of politics of which Berlusconi is only the synthesis.'

And from there it's a short hop back to the exhausting hunt for the truth. 'Obtaining justice in this country is almost impossible. Perhaps that's why we've become a symbol of tenacity, of determin-ation and of strength in Italy. It's as if Elisa's story is a way for the country to redeem itself. Because if it's not possible to obtain jus-tice for a sixteen-year-old girl who goes missing in a church, well, it means there really is no hope for this country. It's something so big, so powerful that the people feel like it's their story. Not just in this city, but in the whole of Italy people are asking for justice. The longer this mystery goes on, the more Italians seem to identify with us, to express anger and indignation, because it's a story that can't go on like this. There has to be justice for this family that has battled all these years, not just for us but for everyone, because if this is allowed to happen – that with the right connections, the right power and complicities you can remain unpunished despite murder – if this is allowed to happen, it means this country is definitively compromised.'

Three

'La giostra di Via Pretoria
Dopo giri più lenti s'è fermata
E tutto è maceria
Di cose bombardate,
Crepacci di bombe
E fili penzoloni.
Ma l'ombra c'inganna
la tarda memoria.'
Rocco Scotellaro

The new year, 1994, began quietly in the Claps household. Elisa was still missing. In the past, her elder brothers had always taken her down to the courtyard of their block of flats on New Year's Eve to let off fireworks. But this year the brothers sat at home knowing there was nothing to celebrate.

By now, a few months after Elisa's inexplicable disappearance, there was almost a strange pattern to their lives: Gildo was frenetically busy trying to keep media attention focused on the case; his father was retreating ever more inside himself, unable to deal with the enormous pain of losing his beloved daughter; and every time the phone rang there was a palpable tension and everyone stopped to listen, knowing that this just might be the call that realised their greatest hope or fear. The family were still receiving strange calls. Almost every day there would be silence at the other end, as if they were being taunted or as if someone wanted to listen to their anger and pain as they slammed the phone down again.

One day, though, there appeared to be a strong lead. The phone went and, as usual, Gildo picked it up.

'Are they sure?' he said. The others in the house overheard and stopped what they were doing. 'Milan? OK. OK. I'll come round.'

He put the phone down and saw his brother and mother by now gathered around him.

He shrugged, not wanting to betray any excitement or hope. 'That was the *carabinieri*. Someone in Milan thinks they've seen her.'

Gildo looked at them both. They didn't want to betray any hope either, but he could see that they were emotional, desperate for this lead to put an end to their agony. Gildo went round to the *carabinieri* barracks and organised a plan. It was suggested that Gildo and his immediate family were too emotionally involved to carry out an identification, so Gildo's cousin, Pietro, was asked to accompany the *carabinieri*. They left that evening, driving through the night to the faraway city in the north.

That night no one slept much in the Claps house. None of them believed that Elisa would ever have left home voluntarily, that she would have just gone without a word and put her family through so much pain. Gildo, usually the most cynical in dealing with sightings, wasn't optimistic. But even he, sitting up in his room in the middle of the night, longed for it to be Elisa.

The following morning, Pietro phoned from Milan to say they were in position. Hours passed and, as usual, the Claps family felt in limbo, unable to do anything other than wait for news, good or bad.

Eventually the phone rang again. Gildo picked up.

'*Ciao*, Pietro,' he said. He listened for a few seconds and then shut his eyes and slowly shook his head. As he put the phone back in its cradle, he didn't even need to say anything to his brother and mother. They knew from his reaction that it was another false lead. 'Pietro saw the girl in question,' he said. 'She looked similar to Elisa, but . . .' He shook his head again.

[75]

That winter, Luciano spent hours studying old maps of the centre of the city. He had heard that there were tunnels under the main square that led as far as the Chiesa della Trinità. He was convinced that Elisa was to be found within a short distance of where she had last been seen. He tried to gain access to as many isolated corners of the city as possible.

Gildo tracked down Giovanni Motta, the man who had taken Danilo Restivo to hospital on the day of Elisa's disappearance. He told Gildo various worrying details about that day: that Danilo's trousers had dark stains, that he had been sweating heavily, and that Danilo and his father had had a long, private talk in a separate room during lunch.

That winter, Restivo even gave an interview to *Chi l'ha visto?*. He didn't want his face to be shown, which only made his soft, slightly high-pitched voice all the more noticeable. He reconstructed the events of that Sunday morning, mentioning all the details that everyone, by now, knew by heart. He was precise about tiny details, listing with certainty the timings, the streets, his thoughts, his reasoning. And always there was that strange voice which changed tone from one minute to the next: it could be all sweet and innocent and then, suddenly, quite defensive or even aggressive.

But although it seemed clear that Elisa's disappearance must have had something to do with this strange boy with the eerie voice, there were, as in all the best crime stories, plenty of alternatives. To many it seemed that Restivo was certainly socially inept, a slightly weird character with a particularly weird fetish, but perhaps, some thought, he was only a scapegoat for incompetent investigators and a desperate, grieving family. He was the kind of obvious culprit that, were this really a crime novel, would turn out to have been innocent all along, a wronged misfit and nothing more. And those who believed him to be innocent certainly found plenty of other suspects to focus upon. One day, an old woman in the church of San Michele, a beautiful stone church in the centre of Potenza, found a note. Seeing the name 'Elisa' on it, she immediately took it to the Claps family. It was a ransom demand, asking for twenty million lire. The grammar and spelling used in the note were often incorrect and, when an expert examined the handwriting, it emerged that the note had been written, almost certainly, by the strange Albanian Eris Gega. He denied having written the note, but there were other indications that Gega was worthy of suspicion. He had had a white Fiat Uno at his disposition, precisely the car that many witnesses said Elisa had been forced into. Indeed, Gega himself gave a statement saying that Danilo Restivo had urged him, if ever asked by the police, to deny that the two knew each other. Eris Gega seemed, at the very least, to be involved in some way.

Weeks went by during which the Claps family would grasp at any straws. Seers and mystics came forward, offering their magical services to the family. Gildo dismissed them out of hand. He had no time for priests, let alone the whole range of card readers and futurologists who dominated the local TV stations late at night. There had been plenty of stories over the years of such people making millions from selling snake oil, and Gildo wanted nothing to do with them. Only once did Filomena relent. Being a devout Catholic, she was drawn towards a Catholic mystic and seer called Natuzza Evolo. Gildo, out of principle, for once didn't accompany his mother. She went to Evolo's 'surgery', a place where dozens of people were queuing for a brief conversation with the famous visionary. After hours of waiting, Filomena was allowed in.

Evolo was a short, thickset woman with short, dark hair and large glasses. She was gentle but businesslike, cutting to the chase. Filomena watched her as she shut her eyes, trying to see Elisa among the deceased.

'I cannot see her,' she eventually said to Filomena. 'I cannot see her among the deceased, and so she must be alive.'

Filomena looked at the woman before her and longed to believe what she said. She longed for it to be true.

'Soon I hope there will be a sign that will clarify all,' the seer said.

Filomena nodded. 'Thank you,' she said, before being ushered towards the exit.

When she returned home, Gildo could see her relief. Despite his doubts, he was pleased she had gone. But he made her promise that it would be the first and last time that they resorted to such – as he called it – superstition.

*

The phone was ringing. As usual, everyone in the house stopped what they were doing to listen.

'*Sì*,' said Gildo. Then a pause. 'What kind of information?' Another pause. 'You can talk to me.' Then he shook his head impatiently and passed the phone to his mother, who was, by then, at his side. 'They want you.' He pressed the record button on the machine that the authorities had given the family.

For a few minutes she said only 'Yes' and 'No'. When the conversation was over, they listened to her account of what had been said.

'This man says he's got Elisa.' She looked from Luciano to Gildo. Even Antonio, her husband, was listening. 'If we want to see her again we'll have to pay. He'll contact us again in the next few days.'

Gildo, as usual, was sceptical. It didn't make sense that a kidnapper would take a girl from a family with very modest means and then only make contact months later. But, as always, the family was forced to follow every possible lead, however ridiculous or improbable it seemed. There was, inevitably, a permanent injunction against ever ruling something out. The Claps family knew that, almost certainly, there would be no happy ending, but after months of this nightmare they longed simply for an ending, any kind of ending.

The following evening the phone call arrived. The man demanded two million lire for Elisa's return. Filomena asked the man to ask Elisa a question, a question to which only she could know the answer.

'She's not here with me at the moment. I'm simply conducting the negotiation. I'll be able to give you the answer when I've seen her.'

The idea that she might even be close to a dialogue with her daughter gave Filomena a sense of euphoria. They had had their hopes dashed many times before, but this time it seemed different. The following night another phone call arrived.

'Yes,' said Filomena, 'who is it?'

'*Signora*, let's not waste time, you know very well who I am. Are you getting the money ready?'

'Have you asked that thing to Elisa?'

There was a pause. 'I haven't seen her since last talking to you. She's being guarded by other people.'

'Without that reply', said Filomena, a doughty and determined character, 'you won't see a penny.'

'Listen, *signora*. If we don't get exactly what we want we'll send you your daughter piece by piece in the post.' He continued to issue specific threats, listing in minute detail exactly what he was planning for Elisa if the money wasn't forthcoming.

Gildo snatched the phone from his mother. 'Bastard,' he shouted, 'if I ever find you, you'll be the one cut to pieces.'

The line went dead.

[79]

Even though the family by now knew that it was almost certainly yet another scoundrel and extortionist trying to make money, they still couldn't ignore the lead. They agreed that if he called again, they would, to make it appear credible that they really were gathering funds, negotiate him down to one million lire. A few days later, he telephoned and appeared satisfied by the possibility of making such easy money.

The authorities by now knew that the phone calls were coming from a public phone box in Matera. When the final phone call came, Filomena was instructed towards a tiny street in the city. There she was told she would find a note giving her further instructions.

Despite knowing that it was likely to be another disappointment, everyone had a flicker of hope that this might, finally, be the end of the terrible story. Reinforcements arrived from the state police in Rome. Filomena was wired up and a bag was filled with cardboard to simulate the money. Luciano and Gildo stayed in the operations room, listening to what was happening. Their mother had found the note and, whispering into her microphone, was following instructions. It was like a treasure hunt, each message leading to another. The diminutive figure of Filomena Claps traipsed across Matera from one stop to the next, desperately praying that soon she would finally be able to hug her daughter once more. The steely mother kept walking around the famous city, reading each note and letting the police, and her sons back in Potenza, know where she was heading next. The last note she found told her to leave the bag of money in a skip, where she would find directions to Elisa.

Filomena hurried towards the skip, leaving the bag there and reading with excitement that she should go to a small square in front of the hospital. There, in a car with open doors, she would find Elisa. It was a long walk, but she didn't feel tired. She felt as if it might be true, that she was within a few minutes of having her darling daughter back. She kept walking, picking up the pace as she strode towards the hospital.

There was no car with open doors. Elisa wasn't there. Filomena looked around desperately, hoping she had made a mistake. Every time a car door opened she looked closer, praying that Elisa would emerge. It didn't take long for reality to hit. It was, as everyone had dreaded, a wild goose chase.

The police picked up Filomena and the convoy drove back to Potenza. No one spoke. Filomena sobbed in the back of the car. She had dared to hope, and now it felt even worse than before. Not only had she lost her only daughter, but someone was toying with that pain, trying to make money out of it. She moaned angrily at the extraordinary injustice and the horror of what she and her family were living through.

The next morning the police phoned. A man had come in the middle of the night to pick up what he thought was the bag of money. He had been followed in case he was working with accomplices and then arrested. He was a petty criminal called Battente. He had confessed that, seeing the family's desperation on TV, he had decided to make some easy money. He was tried and sentenced to two years in prison.

There were plenty of other false leads. A marshal in the *carabinieri* was aware of a house in a small village near Potenza, in Pantano di Pignola, where young women had been forced into prostitution. After weeks of surveillance the house was raided. There was one woman there and a stack of amateur videos. Only a few other women were involved with the brothel, and only one had been forced into working there. None of them had ever seen Elisa other than during appeals on television.

Other witnesses continued to muddy the waters. One, who wanted to remain anonymous, declared that he had seen Elisa in the company of a young man, walking down the steps that lead from the summit of the city. Next to the statement given by Giuseppe Carlone, the man who lived in the same block as the Claps family and who saw Elisa walking down the steps towards her house, it looked to many as if Elisa had left that famous church alive; that she had voluntarily left home, perhaps in the company of a man. She had, in short, eloped. It was a proposition that made Gildo and the rest of her family furious. The idea of a *scappatella*, an elopement or a casual affair, was inconceivable. She would never have allowed her mother to suffer like this, they said. And yet, for many, those various sightings of Elisa alive had the effect of diminishing their willingness to believe the obvious. How could Danilo Restivo really be guilty of harming the young woman in question if three separate witnesses had all seen her walking away from the city of her own volition?

*

On 14 June 1994, the head of the Potenza flying squad concluded an interim report into the events surrounding Elisa's disappearance. Luigi Grimaldi's eight-page document was blunt. He had gone over the entirety of the investigation and now drew some sad conclusions. He excluded the possibility that Elisa could have voluntarily gone missing. She was a happy, devout girl, someone who didn't use drugs or alcohol, and she wasn't in with the wrong crowd. Grimaldi also excluded the possibility that Elisa had been kidnapped for a ransom. The family wasn't exactly well off and she was hardly likely to be a remunerative victim. Organised criminals wouldn't have operated in full daylight in the middle of the city centre on a Sunday morning. Nor was she, it seemed, kidnapped to be forced into prostitution.

That left Grimaldi with only one, grim possibility: 'It's the conviction of this investigative office that Claps was killed. Murder then. With every probability a sexual motivation. That day,' he wrote in his report, 'Elisa was probably at the centre of a plan which others had organised but of which she was ignorant, an unwitting actress in a performance that had as its dominating motive sexual interests.' Grimaldi thought it inconceivable that a passing stranger would have tried to importune Elisa, not least because she would have been extremely unlikely to accompany someone unknown to her into a hidden corner of the city. He felt it plausible that the most likely author of the tragedy was one of the men who had shown an interest in her, who had been courting her recently and whose 'interest certainly wasn't wholesome and sincere, but spoilt by morbid interests'. That suggestion pointed the finger, fairly clearly, in the direction of either Eris Gega, Danilo Restivo or, indeed, both. Grimaldi wrote of Danilo that he had made false declarations 'consciously, with the lucidity of someone who knows that they have to hide their responsibility . . . This flying squad', he wrote, 'is sure that Restivo has knowledge of the girl's fate and is hiding information pertinent to the investigation.'

Grimaldi identified many inconsistencies in Restivo's narrative of that Sunday. Both of Elisa's friends, Eliana and Angelica, had said that Elisa had told them she was meeting Danilo because he had a present he wanted to give her. He, however, never mentioned any present to the investigators. He merely wanted to meet Elisa, he said, to ask her advice about one of her friends with whom, he claimed, he was in love. Danilo had always said that he and Elisa had been behind the altar, and yet none of the people who were there had seen either him or Elisa. He stated he had previously been at the building site where they were constructing the escalators with another young woman, Paola, but she denied ever having been there with him. The injuries of his supposed fall there were inconsistent: a tiny cut to his hand but no bruises, no other injuries. Restivo, Grimaldi concludes, 'although he had seen Elisa in front of the church, had then led her into another secluded place'.

Grimaldi duly requested that the *pubblico ministero*, the magistrate in charge of the investigation, Felicia Genovese, arrest Danilo Restivo. It was a request that was denied.

*

In the summer of 1994, the Claps family was introduced to a traffic warden from Policoro, a town on the Ionian coast. Called Nicola Sozio, he had a small business selling used cars to Albania. One day, he said, he had heard two Albanians chatting in a bar while reading *La Gazzetta del Mezzogiorno*, the main newspaper of the Italian south. Since it featured a photograph of Elisa, the two Albanians were chatting about the case. Sozio had approached them and got talking. One of them had said that, just a few weeks before, he was certain of having seen Elisa in the Albanian capital.

Sozio was a murky character. Nobody really knew the nature of his business in Albania, and Gildo was, as usual, suspicious. He wore a recording device to their meeting and, on seeing him, was even more suspicious. But Sozio told him something else: that only recently he too had been in Albania, and there he had met many people who were certain that they had seen Elisa and, moreover, heard her speaking in Italian. Gildo, as always, was sharp and asked for the exact date of the original meeting in the bar when, allegedly, there had been a photograph in the paper of Elisa. It turned out there had been no article about her in the period mentioned by Sozio.

But the fact that so many elements in the story pointed towards Albania somehow made the story credible. And, as always, the Claps family could never ignore a lead, however unlikely. The family agreed to meet him again, and this time he told them of another lead: that one of the many traffickers bringing Albanians to Italy's Adriatic coast in the 1990s had, in September 1993, returned to Albania with an adolescent Italian girl fitting Elisa's description. Sozio was sure he was close to cracking the case and asked for just a little advance to make a last trip. All he needed, he said, was two million lire.

The Italian embassy in Albania was alerted. Sozio was interrogated in the Questura. The family had to decide whether to ignore the murky character or give him money, and, in the end, Gildo gave him just over a million lire. Within days, of course, the whole story became international news. Sozio had grandly announced via a local TV station, Telenorba, that he was about to embark on a journey that would bring home Elisa Claps. The national channels and newspapers jumped on the story, and soon everyone was talking excitedly about the Albanian angle. Gildo and his family watched the TV in disbelief. Rather than acting with discretion, Sozio had tried to milk as much money, and publicity, as possible. For a week there were daily updates of the search until, inevitably, the story was punctured and quickly deflated. Elisa wasn't in Albania.

Filomena hit rock bottom once again. It seemed incredible that so many people were prepared to exploit their epic suffering just for a bit of notoriety or cash. She dared to allow her hopes to rise, only for them to be dashed again. And each time they were dashed it was worse than before, a reminder of the dreadful reality that Elisa was never coming home. She would never be found. She wasn't among the living any more, despite what various scoundrels said. Gildo was apoplectic with anger. He drove to Policoro at high speed, tracked down Sozio and screamed at him.

'I don't ever want to hear of you again,' he shouted, as people turned round to see what the noise was all about, 'I don't ever want to hear your name. You're a piece of shit, a miserable piece of shit. You're pathetic, dishonest, a disgrace. You dared to give my mother hope, and now she's weeping while you're counting your cash. If you ever contact us again,' he screamed, 'I won't be responsible for my actions.'

*

A few months later, just two days before a procession through the city to mark the anniversary of Elisa's disappearance, Danilo Restivo was arrested. He was charged not with murder, but with giving false statements. Restivo was held in a cell with Eris Gega, the Albanian who appeared to be involved in some way in the disappearance. The decision was clearly a strategic one and, having bugged their cell, the investigators hoped that the two would reveal something pertinent. Not once did they mention the case and, in fact, the bug soon stopped working. It was while he was in prison that a psychological profile of Restivo was prepared. The experts wrote that:

> One finds in him, in disguised form, a background of inadequacy, insecurity, a sense of inferiority, anxiety, a sensation of scarce acceptance of himself by his peers. The subject tries to confront conflictual aspects between himself and his father, between himself and surrounding reality, by putting into effect defensive dynamisms . . .

*

Within days of Danilo's arrest, his father, Maurizio, had called a weekly magazine begging for a chance to put his family's side of the story. A few weeks later, the article appeared in the pages of *Visto*, accompanied by photographs of the parents sitting at home. 'My son doesn't know how to lie,' Maurizio Restivo said in the interview. 'He's a good boy, normal, passionate about classic cars and motorbikes . . . with women he's pure . . . from prison he's told me that he's serene, to not worry because he's innocent. I say once again that I believe him, and that his father will do everything possible to bring him home.'

It's hard to know how much Maurizio Restivo really believed in that innocence and how much was wishful thinking. Even in that defensive interview he conceded that his son had 'created a few problems', and he recalled the time when Danilo had, allegedly accidentally, cut a boy's neck during a game of Cowboys and Indians. Even Restivo must have known that his son had strange perversions, that he was more than just *goffo*, clumsy. He knew about the hair-cutting incidents. But Restivo publicly maintained that his son was 'pure' and 'good'. It was, clearly, an attempt to defend his son, but it was, equally, an attempt to defend his own reputation. Maurizio Restivo was a powerful player in that small city. He was the director of the National Library, a man who was an accomplished scholar and painter. The subjects he chose – he wrote a tome on female brigands and drew disturbing images of religious rituals – might have raised eyebrows, but he was one of Potenza's power-brokers. He was an intellectual, a rich and cultured man in a country where hierarchy and social position seem far more important than they do in more meritocratic countries. If the Claps family held his son responsible for the disappearance of their daughter, Maurizio Restivo clearly believed that the Claps family was likely to rob him not only of his son, but of his entire reputation. In one, bugged telephone conversation with his daughter Anna, he gave full vent to his fury at the Claps family, mentioning his suspicion that they themselves were involved in Elisa's disappearance. 'They're pretending to be good people,' he said.

Every time that the public appeared ready to believe that Danilo Restivo was guilty of involvement in Elisa's disappearance, something came up which threw the whole logic of the investigation into doubt. It was almost as if those distractions were organised deliberately, and the timing was always suspicious. Restivo had returned to solitary confinement after a brief spell sharing a cell with Eris Gega; it was at that time that Gega's lawyer announced that he had received information suggesting Elisa was in a remote village in Albania. As usually happened, the lawyer, Piervito Bardi, didn't quietly reveal the lead to investigators or the family but went on national television. The revelation came when Gildo, too, was doing a live link for the programme, and his face was twitching with fury as, yet again, the investigation was swung towards the chaotic country on the other side of the Adriatic. The new lead seemed particularly bizarre since Bardi, being Gega's lawyer, should logically have been doing everything possible to avoid the investigation turning back towards Albania. And yet here he was, suddenly relishing the limelight and suggesting, once again, that Elisa was alive and well there. Such a suggestion only heightened suspicions that his own client, being Albanian, was complicit in Elisa's disappearance. A cynical explanation for such extraordinary behaviour was either vanity or conspiracy: either the lawyer longed for fame, or – given that his intervention led directly to the end of Danilo Restivo's solitary confinement – he had been prompted by Restivo's side to distract deliberately the whole investigation. Donato Pace, a policeman from Potenza, went to Albania and interviewed various people. So too did one of the journalists from the *Chi l'ha visto?* programme. There was, needless to say, no trace of Elisa.

*

When the trial did eventually begin in January 1995, the two families found themselves sitting in close proximity.

'Shame on you,' Filomena shouted at Maurizio Restivo as he

gave them a sarcastic smile. 'The truth will come out sooner or later.'

Italian trials start and stop, repeatedly getting delayed and interrupted so that the whole agony and uncertainty is dragged on far beyond what is necessary. Gildo took the stand twice, once to confirm what had happened that Sunday and once to have a direct confrontation with Giuseppe Carlone, the neighbour who said he had seen Elisa on the Via IV Novembre staircase. Mario Marinelli, Danilo Restivo's volatile and irascible lawyer, frequently interrupted proceedings to remind the court that his client was on trial merely for perjury, nothing more.

Restivo himself came across in the witness box as very sure of himself. He was, according to interpretation, either reliable or arrogant. He looked young and fresh-faced; his glasses and soft voice made him appear studious. If he wasn't innocent, he could do a very good impression of innocence. He was little more than a boy, and some watching him almost felt sorry that he had, by misfortune, become connected to such a tragic case. But there were flashes that betrayed something else: the way he got suddenly irritated, the way he smiled at the Claps family as if almost challenging or taunting them.

And it was only in a different, adjacent court that another side of Restivo would emerge. One day, the Claps family arrived in court to be told by an acquaintance of theirs that the trial had been moved to another courtroom.

'That can't be right,' said Gildo, 'I've seen the court listings. It's here.'

'Well,' the acquaintance said, 'I've just seen Restivo and his lawyer, Marinelli, downstairs.'

The family went down to the magistrates' court and listened to proceedings. Restivo was accused of the terrifying molestation of three young students who lived in an apartment opposite his family. For months they had been subjected to the worst Restivo could invent: he had phoned, always anonymously, to describe the clothes they were wearing. He had sent them extremely pornographic drawings. A wooden box with one of the girls' names on had been left on top of their letter box. Inside was a note saying, 'Boom. How long have you got left to live, Giovanna?' They also received declarations of love and letters full of unfettered fantasy. In one, he signed himself 'Giuseppe', claiming that it had been one of his assistants, Vittorio, who had sent the fake bomb and had made the late-night phone calls. 'Giuseppe' told Giovanna in the letter that his parents had died in a car accident when he was ten and that he had to have morphine regularly injected for various pains. He wrote another letter to Sabrina, saying that it was difficult to write about his sentiments because 'I can't manage to focus on them because my illness has never allowed me to meet people of the opposite sex.' They were both bizarre, unsettling letters, clearly full of immature fantasies and false names. Most worrying was the fact that often the phone would ring in the girls' apartment and all they would hear was the music to *Profondo rosso*, a famous horror film. But sometimes all they heard was a bagatelle in A minor by Ludwig van Beethoven, a piece of music known more commonly as 'Für Elise' or 'For Elisa'. This had happened back in the spring of 1993, months before Elisa had gone missing, and it clearly hinted that Restivo had nurtured an obsession with Elisa long before her disappearance.

As had happened before, the Restivo family paid to protect their son from justice. Instead of an eighteen-day custodial sentence for terrifying the students, Restivo was fined 450,000 lire on 23 February 1995. As Marinelli, the Restivo lawyer, left the courtroom, he noticed Gildo and his mother sitting at the back.

'Even here I have to see you. What do you want from me?'

'From you? Nothing,' Filomena said, her eyes glaring at him.

'Nothing from a piece of shit like you. You make money out of keeping a murderer free. You're worthless. Your mother must be ashamed you were ever born.' She kept tearing strips off him, giving him as much of her mind as possible.

The supercilious lawyer tried to walk away, but Filomena followed him, still shouting. He had always treated them with disdain, working himself into a theatrical rage that his client was being so unfairly treated.

'I wouldn't wish that even my worst enemy', Filomena said, catching up with Marinelli and glaring at him again, 'should go through what I am going through, but I hope that if one day your daughter should disappear out of the blue that you'll remember me and that you'll understand what I'm feeling at the moment.'

Marinelli pulled his robe out of her fist and walked away.

Restivo's other trial, for false statements, continued slowly. There, too, there were surprises. One cameraman from the regional TG3 news noticed that Eris Gega, on leaving the court bathroom, had given a thumbs-up sign to Maurizio Restivo. The cameraman immediately went to see Gildo, who went and informed the police inspector present in court. It was an extraordinary gesture: the man who many suspected of being Restivo's accomplice had been seen saying, with his thumb, 'It's all OK.' The implication was, presumably, that he was going to keep his mouth shut.

The verdict arrived on 7 March 1995. Restivo was found guilty and sentenced to a year and eight months. Marinelli immediately announced that his client would appeal, and the sentence was suspended pending that appeal. After the verdict, Gildo made it very explicit that he believed Restivo was guilty of much more than perjury. 'I can't say', he said, 'that I believe Danilo Restivo guilty of anything other than the crime of false declarations. But clearly this isn't enough for my family. I don't believe that it's enough for the city of Potenza, for civil society, to content itself with the fact that Danilo Restivo is judged to be guilty, sentenced, but that he doesn't say the truth about what happened on that Sunday morning. To us a verdict of this sort is of no use.'

Eris Gega was also tried for perjury. He, however, was absolved. Eliana De Cillis, Elisa's friend who had appeared so confused in her descriptions of what had happened, was also tried for bearing false witness. She was absolved in the first trial, sentenced to a year and nine months on appeal (the sentence, again, was suspended), but in the High Court was absolved because she was held to be 'non-punishable': according to article 384 of the penal code, someone couldn't be condemned for committing a crime if they only did so out of fear for their own safety.

That fear was evident in one memorable cross-examination during the trial of Eris Gega. Only once, in all those trials, did she seem to let slip her mask and reveal that she had an inkling of what might have happened.

'You told someone', said the prosecuting magistrate, Felicia Genovese, 'that after the disappearance of Elisa Claps you were worried about your safety, fearing that what had happened to Elisa could also happen to you?'

'Yes,' said Eliana softly, 'I said as much to my friends. I said that if I had found myself . . . that if I had gone with Elisa, then maybe . . .'

'Maybe what?'

'That I would also have been . . . that if I had been, maybe if I had gone with her . . .'

'Where? When?'

'To the date with Danilo, maybe . . . I would . . . it might have happened . . .'

'What? What might have happened if you had gone with Elisa to the date with Danilo?'

'I don't know.'

'Do you think that something happened to Elisa? To have such a worry, you evidently think that something happened to Elisa.'

'I don't know.'

*

Snippets of gossip and information are constantly offered to the Claps family. Sometimes what they hear makes them angry, it's so absurd; other times it merely makes them more worried, as it seems to confirm their worst fears. Urban legends begin to surround the story of the disappearance: like the fact that Elisa was pregnant with the love child of a priest; that stray dogs always gather at a particular point near the escalators where, the story went, Restivo must have buried her; that Elisa had been kidnapped as revenge for the fact that Antonio, her father, was a police informer. Such legends only serve to irritate and insult the already grieving family since they have no basis in truth, but they are repeated and embellished, each time becoming more fanciful and more elaborate. Anonymous letters and tip-offs continue to arrive, sometimes serving only to tease investigators: 'Where is this girl?' asks one. 'She's alive but shuts up, even if by doing so she keeps everyone on edge . . .'

But sometimes what they hear comes from reliable sources. Through an acquaintance Filomena learns that the Restivo family had, in December 1993, withdrawn forty million lire in cash from a bank, money that had arrived by transfer from Sicily. Filomena and Gildo were already convinced not only that Danilo Restivo was responsible for Elisa's disappearance, but also that his family knew as much. Such a colossal cash withdrawal, if true, hinted that they may have been paying someone to cover Danilo's tracks. Suspicions concerning a cover-up only increase when it emerges that, on 11 April 1994, the ex-boyfriend of Anna Restivo, who had been present in the Restivo household that fateful Sunday morning, received a threatening phone call warning him never to consider 'getting something off his conscience' with regard to the disappearance of Elisa. The ex-boyfriend, Giovanni Motta, has no doubts about why he received the threatening phone call: 'The affair is related to the fact that I was going out with the sister of Danilo Restivo.'

But most worrying was the statement given to investigators by a young man called Nicola Sambataro. He was an employee of a sterilisation and disinfestation firm owned by a man who had previously organised the cleaning of Potenza's National Library, of which Maurizio Restivo was director. The owner, Maurizio De Fino, and Restivo were friends. When the firm, called Spix, won a contract for sterilisation work in the Museo Pigorini in Rome in the spring of 1994, Restivo asked De Fino if his son could be employed. Nicola Sambataro was duly asked to share a room with Danilo, and his descriptions of the experience shed a new light on the young man's behaviour. He would repeatedly scream in the night, or he would get up to have long showers, often more than once. He would sweat and have hallucinations and scream for help. He was, said Sambataro, 'extremely abnormal and strange'. One evening, the two were in a car and saw, in the distance, some police cars organising roadside checks on vehicles and drivers. Restivo, Sambataro later told the police, 'began to be agitated and started to make strange gestures, first putting his hands on his face, then bending down almost as if he wanted to crouch on the seat to hide himself. In the end he made me stop and he got out, going on alone.' That evening, Sambataro asks for an explanation from Restivo, who tells him about the disappearance of Elisa Claps. Restivo assures him that he had nothing to do with the young girl's disappearance and that he had left her with an Albanian called Eris Gega. Sambataro is deeply concerned and asks his boss to remove Restivo from the job.

*

By now, the Claps family found themselves in a no-win situation. They were keen for the case to be kept at the forefront of people's minds, and Gildo and his mother felt it their duty never to turn down an interview request. Journalists became regular visitors to their home, some becoming, over the years, very close friends. Gildo would frequently drive for hours to Rome just to have a few minutes on television to renew his appeal for information. But that willingness to stay in the public eye came at a very high cost. Not only were Gildo and his mother constantly being called for updates, being invited to studios and seminars, they were also the channel through which any unscrupulous scoundrel could get on television. Repeatedly in the years after Elisa's disappearance, people came forward with information and seemed to milk the attention it gave them. When that information proved to be false or fanciful, attention turned elsewhere and the family were simply left with their grief and their grievances.

'It seemed', Gildo wrote years later, 'like a game of who could make up the most, often only in order to gain a few minutes on the televisual stage. They never cared in the least that on the other side of the screen were a destroyed mother and father, that every piece of news for them was like the cut of a blade in an open wound, that every time a hope collapsed it was like a torment without end.'

That trouble was exacerbated by the fact that crime reporting in Italy is unlike that in other countries. There are plenty of crimes of passion but also plenty of passion for crimes. Newspapers and TV channels are often full of *cronaca nera*, black chronicles. In the first six months of 2010, for example, the news service of Rai 1 dedicated 431 news items to crime. Between 2005 and 2010, the seven national news channels aired, in the evening news alone, 941 various stories about the Meredith Kercher murder in Perugia, 759 about the murder of Chiara Poggi, 538 about the murder of little Tommaso Onofri and 508 about the murder of Samuele Lorenzi in Cogne. Often studio shows in the afternoons or evenings talk about the ins and outs of these cases for hours, interspersing expert witnesses in the studio with short location reports. And because such cases have one trial followed by another, they last for years and can be forever revisited as the judicial process drags towards a conclusion. They're like stories that never end, either because of judicial uncertainty or because there's no resolution, no conviction, and so speculation and the spectacle of pain can continue untrammelled. One journalist, noting the obsession with crime reporting, once wrote that such cases 'generate anxiety but, at the same time, reassure. They brush up against us, but touch others. It's like leaning over the edge of a precipice to step back at the last moment. You feel giddiness. Anxiety. But also relief. It's a subtle pleasure.'

There's a rather good, if dated, film noir set in Basilicata called *Non si sevizia un paperino* (*Don't Torture a Duckling*). In it the priest blames the media's obsession with crime stories for some of the crimes themselves: 'People watch TV, they go to the cinema, they read newspapers with those scandalous photos . . . and then these terrible facts happen and everyone is astonished . . . and they look for the guilty party and they don't understand that our toleration is to blame . . .' It's true that the media circus that surrounds certain criminal cases only serves to blur them and make it even harder to arrive at a satisfactory resolution, because that circus tends to attract misfits and miscreants onto the stage and suddenly the story is filled with an extraordinary cast of petty criminals and repentant prisoners and seers and soothsayers. It's as if they're all playing a national game of Chinese whispers, and the truth gets mislaid amidst the excitement of the show. And it is, admittedly, a great spectacle, as always in Italy. Each crime story becomes a fascinating, appalling pageant revealing the dark side of the sunny peninsula.

*

Months went by and there was no new lead. The investigation appeared to have petered out. Gildo hated the way that Elisa's absence was starting to seem normal. People were beginning to forget that she was even missing. It was as if the attention of the media had turned elsewhere, to other tragedies, and theirs was gradually being forgotten. His life changed slowly. He went to Macerata, sat his final two exams and, even though he had no intention now of becoming a lawyer, he graduated. He met a woman called Irene and they got married.

On the third anniversary of Elisa's disappearance, in September 1996, Gildo and Luciano put posters of her face all over the city, as they had done so many times before. They decided to put some up under the Restivo family home in Viale Marconi. On driving back that way later they saw that the posters had been ripped off the wall, and Gildo got out of the car and put another one up. As he was doing so, the door to the block of flats flew open and Maurizio Restivo emerged. Immediately an argument erupted, with Restivo demanding that Gildo desist from putting up posters on their front door, and Gildo replying that it was nothing to do with him, unless seeing a photo of Elisa created a problem for him. The two had to be pulled apart, and then, after having tried to rip down another poster, Restivo retreated indoors once more.

'The indifference and haughtiness of that man', Gildo wrote later, 'turned me into an animal. Ever since Elisa's disappearance he and his family had maintained their unbecoming behaviour. They had raised an impenetrable barrier to protect Danilo, and not even for a moment did they appear touched by the tragedy that was happening to our family. That he had actually dared to step forward to impede me from remembering my sister was truly intolerable.' Luciano and Gildo were subsequently denounced by Restivo for threatening behaviour. They were taken to court, but the case was quickly dropped.

*

Just before the appeal against Danilo Restivo's conviction for false declarations, there was another false lead. A man called the offices of ANSA, the Italian news agency, claiming to be a UNICEF doctor in the Horn of Africa. There he had seen three people talking Italian, two strange-looking men and a young girl. On approaching them, the girl revealed that her name was Elisa Claps and that she had been kidnapped a few years before in Potenza. She had, she told the doctor, been taken to Albania and then Africa. She was now being transferred, she said, to the Yemen. The doctor told the ANSA office that he would call back, but was never heard from again. But the call had served its purpose. Once again, attention had been turned away from the man the family held responsible for Elisa's disappearance and on to, instead, some shady, international conspiracy.

Restivo was, however, sentenced to two years and eight months on appeal. His father was furious, screaming at the court that his son was being persecuted. By then, however, four years had passed since Elisa's disappearance and the family were losing hope. Both Eliana De Cillis and Eris Gega had been absolved of making false declarations, and even Restivo was found guilty only of that relatively minor crime. There was no justice and no resolution.

Antonio, Elisa's father, was increasingly closed to the world. He didn't watch TV and rarely went out. He watched his wife and sons running around attempting to find Elisa, or at least her killer, and he felt they were wasting their time. They were chasing shadows. On one occasion his anger, usually so well buried, boiled over.

'It's going to ruin your lives,' he told them at a family meal. 'You can run around from court to Questura for the rest of your lives and never get any closer to the truth. You won't ever get justice. That piece of shit will wander around the world whatever you do.'

'That's not true,' Gildo said, 'we're making progress.'

'What progress? What have you achieved in all this time? What have you managed to do? Nothing. The only right thing to do was to have given Restivo some of his own medicine back then, that same weekend. That's what I would have done, and it would be over.' He moved the palms of his hands together as if brushing dirt off them. 'That's all we needed, but you' – he looked around at his family angrily, as if his predicament were their fault – 'but you forbade it. That first night you absolutely forbade it and now everyone can laugh at us, taunt us, and we'll never know. We'll never know. The only thing to do was to send that piece of shit where he belongs. Only before sending him there I would have made him confess. I would have forced him to tell me the truth. Only then would I have pulled the trigger.'

'If you had done that, we would have lost you as well. They would have put you away.'

'I put myself away a long time ago.'

The brothers and Filomena looked at him. It was true. He didn't seem to be there any more. In some ways, it really was as if he had been taken away, as if his grief had removed him from their midst.

*

False leads, however, continued apace. The boyfriend of one of Elisa's old friends, Silvana Ferrazzano, came forward to report what Silvana had told him: that Elisa was abducted and forced into prostitution in Algeria. It sounded like another fanciful theory, an idea prompted more by paranoia than by fact. But, as always, the authorities were forced to investigate, and they came across some extraordinary coincidences. Silvana, the young girl who seemed to have new information, was repeatedly seen in a Nissan Micra with a Potenza number plate, 331145, a number plate that used to belong to a white Fiat Uno. In a case in which a mysterious white Fiat Uno had been mentioned so many times, it seemed strange. Stranger still was the fact that the Fiat Uno used to be owned by a man who, in 1978, had been found guilty of *violenza carnale*. But, most bizarrely, Silvana Ferrazzano was the owner of a SIM card that had previously been used by Maria Rosa Fontana, the mother of Danilo Restivo. Ferrazzano denied any contact with Danilo's mother, but the episode, like so many others, begged the question of whether investigators were deliberately being misled, whether the case was being *insabbiato*, 'sanded up' with contradictory theories, notions, hunches, guesses and tip-offs.

Sometimes the answer to that question was very clearly 'yes': the investigation was, indeed, being deliberately muddied. Danilo Restivo's appeal sentence had been confirmed at the High Court and he had been sent back to Potenza to serve it in the community. On 23 April 1999, the website set up by Gildo to publicise the search for his sister received an email purporting to be from Elisa herself. 'It's Elisa, I'm in Brazil,' the message said. 'I'm well and I left home voluntarily, tell my family not to look for me, I don't have any intention of returning home.'

The man monitoring the website immediately called Gildo.

'Something very weird has come into the website. There's a message purporting to be from Elisa.'

'How do you mean?' Gildo asked, almost with irritation.

His friend read him the message. 'What do you think?'

'It's bullshit. Can you trace where it came from?'

'Give me a minute.' He put the phone down and ran some checks. A few minutes later he called back. 'Gildo? It came from the Tati Club, you know that Internet cafe in the centre . . .'

Gildo ran down to his car and drove fast through the outskirts of the city. He knew the Tati Club a bit: it was the usual mixture of pool tables, slot machines and computers. He went in and saw a woman behind the front desk.

'Has anyone used those computers?' he asked gruffly.

'I'm sorry?' the woman said, looking suspicious. Then she looked at Gildo again, seeming to recognise him, and she became more open. 'There was a man using the computer, yes.'

'Is that man still here? Which computer?' Gildo asked desperately. 'I need to examine that computer now. Is the man who was using the computer still here?' he asked again.

The woman began to stutter that she wasn't authorised to give out that sort of information. Gildo couldn't hold back any more.

'Someone sent an email from here pretending to be my sister. If you don't let me see the exact list of users right now, the police will be crawling all over this place within minutes. They'll confiscate all the computers, shut you down for days, conduct enquiries into every aspect of your business . . .'

The woman put her hands up to stop him and then reached down below the counter. She brought up a register of computer users that day, opened it at the right page and spun it round on the counter so that Gildo could read the names. There, in clear letters, was the name 'Restivo, Danilo'. He had been using a computer at the exact time, 21.45, that the email had been sent.

Gildo was, inevitably, furious. He thanked the woman and went straight to the Questura to denounce the fact to the authorities. He was ushered in to see Felicia Genovese, the woman in charge of the Elisa Claps inquiry. She, however, didn't seem prepared to pursue the incident and, increasingly irritated with Gildo's forcefulness, informed him that the case was now *archiviato*; it was going to be shelved. There was, she said, nothing else that could be done.

Years later, Gildo reflected that 'it seemed as if a gigantic intrigue had been set up to alter the facts, to mislead the investigation through clever diversions. I thought bitterly that this was a completely Italian peculiarity, the same one that had marked the dark years of the slaughters and the obscure and mysterious black chronicles that remained enveloped in the thickest mystery.' Gildo wasn't the only one who began to suspect that all the sidetracking was somehow orchestrated, that the numerous false leads were deliberate attempts to divert attention from the truth. Indeed, one writer who had studied the case for years wrote that:

> There have been too many Elisas seen in Italy and around the world, too many coincidences and half-truths and half-lies, too many errors and in the end too many oddities that one feels justified in believing a worrying hypothesis: the existence of an occult but organised production room . . . made up of strong but hidden powers . . . which went into action when it was necessary to intervene to defend someone or hide something. As such, the more time goes by, the more one reads and rereads the entire case, the more one is persuaded that, even if the disappearance of Elisa is linked to a tragic but fortuitous and banal incident, the 'hidden world' that went into action isn't at all improvised and casual. Because nothing is left of Elisa, not even the memory, not even the body, not even a trace that could lead one to hope that she's alive or could even enable her to have a tomb where one could take her a flower.

It was often hard for onlookers to understand what was going on. There were, by now, so many stories and subplots that most people were completely confused. That, some thought, was the intention of the *depistaggi*, those red herrings: to sow confusion and complication, to increase doubt and scepticism. The case became, like many before it, a receptacle of hypotheses and hunches, the sort of case about which everyone had an opinion, the more exotic and far-fetched the better. That way it was more entertaining, more breathtaking.

There were continued connections with Albania, Algeria and Africa. There were sightings and suspicions. As often happens in these cases, there was a sense that there was an invisible power behind every visible one, that dark forces were controlling the direction of the investigation. It was noted that Maurizio Restivo was a mason, as indeed was Eliana De Cillis's boyfriend. Then there was a series of fatal car crashes that only added to the intrigue and paranoia. In November 1993, just two months after Elisa's disappearance, a vice brigadier in the *carabinieri*, Pierluigi Tramutola, was involved in a car crash while driving a Lancia Delta on a trunk road, the 407 Basentana. He died instantly on impact. He was an ex-boyfriend of Anna Restivo, Danilo's brother. Most people assumed his death had nothing to do with the Elisa Claps case, but the timing was strange. It wasn't inconceivable, some said, that Anna Restivo might have contacted an ex-boyfriend, a man in the *carabinieri*, in the months after Elisa's disappearance, offering him information or asking advice. Indeed, there were two other car-crash deaths in later years, both victims being peripheral characters in the Elisa Claps tragedy. Massimiliano Carlucci was one of the witnesses who had come forward claiming to have seen Elisa walking away from the city centre, and therefore casting doubt on the theory that Danilo Restivo was somehow responsible for her disappearance. He was twenty-two when he was killed in a crash on the Napoli–Salerno road. Andrea Romaniello, too, later died in a car crash, this time on the Potenza–Melfi trunk road. It was he who had given evidence in court during Danilo Restivo's trial. He claimed that Don Mimì, the priest of the Chiesa della Santissima Trinità in Potenza, had impeded him from conducting a thorough examination of the church. Almost certainly those deaths were nothing more than terrible tragedies, the consequence of dangerous roads and dangerous driving; but to those who glimpsed in the Elisa Claps tragedy evidence of an orchestrated conspiracy, those deaths were linked and far from coincidental.

*

Six years after the disappearance of Elisa, her mother Filomena wrote her an open letter. It was a powerful *j'accuse* against those who had tried, in all sorts of ways, to bury or obliterate the case.

> My dear daughter Elisa,
> At this point I don't have the certainty that you'll be able to read this, but in any case I have the hope, moreover I feel the need to recount to you, to explain to you, what life is like . . . I could talk to you about *omertà*, and not the one in films or newspapers, but that of . . . a part of a city that tries in every way to archive as soon as possible this painful case in order better to guarantee and manage privileges, abuses, cliques and intrigues. I could describe to you the details, the colours of the curtains of the antechamber of the rooms of power, the slaps on the back and the performances accompanied by a simulated veil of tears. Us simple people don't have a right to justice. You will ask why, and what should I reply? Because we're not beautiful, rich or powerful? Because we're not part of any club or association that counts? . . . One thing for me is certain: they've let you disappear twice. You could ask me if I feel . . . the desire for revenge: I can only reply that nausea is stronger than any impetus to anger.

By then, Filomena had changed. She had become battle-hardened. There were dark shadows around her eyes and she couldn't eat much any more. In the evenings she only ever drank a small glass of milk. She had become a familiar presence on television shows, making powerful appeals for information. Her face looked set against the world, her smile more of a grimace.

But when you meet her, the first thing you notice is, unexpectedly, her warmth. She holds your hand in both of hers as you shake hands. And after that first encounter she always greets you with a hug, kissing your cheeks and holding your head in both of her hands as she looks at you. She is, as Gildo says, a typical *mamma*. She asks about your family, about your life, listening carefully to your replies and offering her often forthright opinions. She wants to tell you about recipes and discipline. She's very petite but, no doubt about it, very powerful. She's become almost iconic in Italy, a symbol for long-suffering mothers and a role model of rigour and determination. It's hard not to warm to her, not to want to dedicate yourself to her cause in the same relentless way that she has.

At our first meeting our conversation inevitably turns towards Danilo Restivo. Filomena, like Gildo, subtly changes when the subject comes up. It isn't as if she wants to avoid it; on the contrary, she is keen to have someone listen to her. But she becomes gritty, her face sets into a frown and her lips tighten around her teeth. All her warmth has been replaced now by a focused fury. 'He', she says of Restivo, 'is like a wild beast that grew up in the forest. If he had been brought up in a normal family context, he wouldn't have turned out like that. I feel blind anger right now. If I could, I would tear out his eyes. I would go straight for his eyes. I'd strangle him. I haven't seen him for years, not since that trial a few years ago when he wore that sarcastic smile and treated us with contempt. But I'll pursue him everywhere. That skunk, I could never forgive him, never. No journalist ever asks me that. No, there's no saint that could forgive him. It's stronger than me, how could I? In our house it always used to be a party, that's why holidays and Christmas now are so terrible: there's an emptiness, there's something missing. It's just too sad. We've still got Elisa's bed. Half her clothes are in the countryside house, half are in the city. I just stroke them sometimes.' She looks at me to make sure I've understood. 'I can't leave Potenza. This is where Elisa grew up and this is where I'll die. And when I die I want to close my eyes serenely and say, "I did everything for Elisa."'

I wonder whether the truth will ever come out, and she fixes her glassy eyes on me, as if the question is a challenge to her determination. 'I want the truth,' she says. 'I've always wanted the truth. And I've always been sure about what I thought happened. But the fact that we haven't got to the truth, that you're sure that he's guilty but you can't prove it, that destroys you. I always pray. "God help me," I say. I still have my faith. There is a God. But I don't go to church any more. I can't go in. I don't have any faith in certain members of the church. You just have to brave each day . . .'

I think about my own daughters and try to begin to understand what Filomena's life must have been like these last few years. When we say goodbye, I express the hope that we'll meet again.

'God willing,' she says. 'I always say "God willing" because you never know when you won't see someone again.'

Four

'*Ecco ch'un'altra volta, o valle inferna,*
O fiume alpestre, o ruinati sassi,
O ignudi spirti di virtute e cassi,
Udrete il pianto e la mia doglia eterna.
Ogni monte udirammi, ogni caverna,
Ovunqu'io arresti, ovunqu'io mova i passi;
Chè Fortuna, che mai salda non stassi,
Cresce ogn'or il mio male, ogn'or l'eterna . . .'
    Isabella Morra

From Potenza I head north to Venosa. It's a short drive interrupted by a large flock of goats crossing a roundabout on the slip road off the dual carriageway. I sit watching the animals, not for the first time surprised by the proximity here between ancient and modern. The name Venosa probably comes from the goddess Venus, since the town was dedicated to her and was thus originally called Venusia; others say it comes from the wonders of its wines (Vinosa) or because of the gentle breezes that blow through the town (Ventosa). When the goats move on, I manage to get to the small, picturesque place. There are smooth beige flagstones lining most of the lanes of the historic centre and, opposite the town hall, a large bronze statue of the town's most famous son: Quinto Orazio Flacco, better known as Horace.

It's hard to imagine that this small settlement was once among the leading eighteen cities on the peninsula. Captured by the Romans from the Samnites in 291 BC, it was included almost exactly a century later on the Via Appia. All traffic from Rome to Brindisi duly passed this way, and Venosa grew in stature. It had its own senate, its own laws, its own currency and a flourishing Jewish community. On the nearby Maddalena hill are Jewish catacombs discovered in 1853. Horace was born here in 65 BC, and frequently eulogised the picturesque town and region in his poetry: he wrote of wanting to 'commend my youthfulness to Lucanian girls' and of 'sleeping in boots in the snows of Lucania' in order to eat wild boar. Most of the tiny trickle of tourists that come here do so because of the link to Horace, and the town certainly does its best to promote its famous son. There's the so-called 'House of Horace', though any link to the poet is tenuous at best. And on the wall of one little *piazza* is a tablet with, in Latin and Italian, a few lines from his *Epistles*:

> If you don't know how to live as you should, give way
> To those who do. You've eaten, and wined, and played enough:
> It's time for you to leave: lest you drink too freely,
> And lovelier impudent youth hits you, and mocks you.

It's a beautiful town, august in a quiet way. But it feels, like Metaponto, as if the tide of history receded a long time ago and that only a few ruins remain. When the Emperor Trajan decided to replace the Via Appia with his own Via Traiana, taking traffic through the plains of Puglia rather than across the tough mountains of Lucania, the fate of Venosa was sealed and it began a slow decline. The only hint of that past grandeur is in the archaeological park a short walk outside the centre: there, the amphitheatre and thermal baths and residential complexes have been reduced to ankle-high outlines, like architectural plans in real scale. But when you walk around and see the *laconicum* (the old sauna) and the *domus*, you begin to get a notion of how grand the place used to be. Many of the stones from these buildings were taken to build a large church that was expected to back onto the old church: over the centuries, as Lombards, Byzantines, Normans, Swabians, Angevins and Aragonese took control, each tried to complete the ambitious ecclesiastical structure, raiding the Roman ruins in the process. But even today that church is still called 'the unfinished church', and its random walls stand as a testament to misplaced ambition. It looks like a ruined church but feels different since it has no past; quite literally there's nothing behind it. The grand facades are two-dimensional, their bells hanging there for no purpose. When Edward Lear came here in the mid-nineteenth century, he revelled in this strange place, writing that Venosa 'gave great hopes of employ for the pencil'. He admired the resourcefulness of the locals who had planted a vineyard in the nave of the unfinished church, turning the whole aisle into a 'pergolata walk'. The vineyards are not here any more, but the church is just the same, no nearer completion than it was when he visited in 1852. Next to it is the Abbey of the Trinity. There used to be over a hundred monks living here, but now it's principally a place to admire art and architecture, and for friends to stand before the Column of Friendship holding hands, thus guaranteeing, says the folklore, eternal friendship.

I wander back through the centre and towards the castle. It's an imposing, rather beautiful building with a squat, cylindrical tower on each corner. It was built by Pirro Del Balzo in the second half of the fifteenth century. The Del Balzo coat of arms – a shining sun – is obvious from the battlements of the west tower. There are two grand lions taken from the Roman ruins a few hundred metres away. They stare at you from the start of the bridge which leads over a now-dry moat. The most famous resident of this castle was a Carlo Gesualdo, the prince of Venosa, who was a noted composer of Renaissance madrigals, a man who counted cardinals, saints and popes among his immediate ancestors. He married his first cousin, Maria D'Avalos, but she subsequently began a passionate affair with the Duke of Andria, Fabrizio Carafa. In October 1590, Carlo told his wife that he planned to go hunting for two days in the Bosco degli Astroni. He had ordered his servants to get copies of the keys to his palace made in wood and, returning unexpectedly, he caught the two lovers in his wife's bed. He murdered them both and, with the help of his servants, left their bodies outside as a sign that his humiliation was at an end. As was usual, there were no proceedings against him because of 'the just cause' which had moved him to commit murder. It was only in the last century that Gesualdo's fame as a composer surpassed that of the murderer: his chromatic music has been seen as a precursor to modernist composers, Aldous Huxley even comparing him in *The Doors of Perception* to Schoenberg: 'It does not matter that he's all in bits. The whole is disorganised. But each individual fragment is in order, is a representative of a Higher Order. The Highest Order prevails even in the disintegration. The totality is present even in the broken pieces.'

It's a short drive from Venosa to Melfi. Nowadays Melfi is occasionally mentioned in the news because it has a huge Fiat factory and is often the scene of industrial unrest; or because this is where they filmed the adaptation of Niccolò Ammaniti's book, *I'm Not Scared*. But back in the Middle Ages it was one of the most important places in the peninsula. Five papal councils took place here between 1059 and 1137; it was here that the momentous decisions to launch the first crusade and to impose celibacy on priests were taken. From the dual carriageway far below you can see the famous castle, a tumble of square turrets sitting on top of the grassy hill. It dominates the landscape, a reminder that this was once a frontier town that stood between the Byzantines and the Lombards. And the whole place is certainly built for defence: there's a hefty wall, first started by the Normans, that still circles the entirety of the town and runs for about three miles around its historical centre. But once inside that perimeter, the place feels, like Venosa, august and dignified. There are palm trees, cedars and cypresses amidst the broad boulevards and smart churches. If many of those churches and *piazze* look immaculate, it's because, as usual, many have had to be rebuilt following devastating earthquakes in 1694, 1851 and 1930.

The heyday of this town was in the thirteenth century, when it was used by Frederick II as a summer residence, the perfect base from which to practise his favourite hobby of falconry. Called Stupor Mundi ('astonishment of the world'), Frederick II became the heir to the Holy Roman Empire when he was only three; being the head of the House of Hohenstaufen, he amassed titles and kingdoms throughout his life to become King of Germany, King of Italy, King of Burgundy, King of Sicily, King of the Romans and King of Jerusalem. The fact that Melfi was one of his main residences turned the small town into a big player on the European stage. It was here that the Constitutions of Melfi were promulgated: they became the foundation of state administration in the Kingdom of Sicily for the next six centuries. In many ways, Frederick II was the first person to attempt the unification of Italy. He came close to succeeding but was foiled, as would happen many times in later centuries, by the power of the papacy. Pope Gregory IX excommunicated Frederick and invaded Sicily when he was in the Holy Land. He was foiled, too, by the Lombard League, a federation of towns and cities in the north that was to be invoked in the late twentieth century by the nascent Northern League.

It's very clear, as you walk around, that Frederick II is still, almost eight hundred years since he resided here, a celebrated figure. He was one of the great monarchs of the Middle Ages, and the main road leading to Porta Venosina, the beautiful gate in the old wall, bears his name: Via Federico II di Svevia. But as you go through that gate, across the grass and under a small arch, there's another street bearing the name of another hero: Ronca Battista. He was, legend has it, a simple woodsman minding his own business who, unwittingly, got caught up in the bloody feuds between the French and Spanish rulers who, in the 1520s, were competing for control of the Italian peninsula. In 1527, Charles V's Spanish troops, along with the Lanzichenecchi mercenaries, had sacked the Eternal City, invaded the Vatican and imprisoned the pope, Clemente VII. Following an outcry across the European continent, the French saw an opportunity to send troops to Italy under the command of Odet de Foix. From Puglia they pursued the Spanish troops towards Napoli, arriving at Melfi in March 1528.

So began the Seige (or Sack) of Melfi, also known as the Easter of Blood. The story goes that Ronca Battista was cutting wood near the town when he met an old, frail woman who was collecting dry wood to give to a baker in return for bread. Battista took pity on her, gave her his coat to keep her warm and broke off a piece of his bread for her to eat. She was sufficiently moved that she kissed him on the forehead and blessed his billhook. Battista duly exhorted the Spanish soldiers to defend Melfi and, finding a narrow street, protected it against hundreds of French troops. Legend has it that he killed three hundred Frenchmen before he, too, was killed in battle. The French troops, assisted by the Bande Nere, the Black Gangs, then entered Melfi and massacred everyone they could find. Various sources suggest that thousands were slain.

I walk round the place, enjoying the sense of being in a small town with a long history. Edward Lear described Melfi as a 'perfect tame oasis': 'so many fine features in a circumscribed space it is not common to see, even in Italy'. He admired

> the picturesque buildings of the city . . . the valley below it, with
> its clear stream and great walnut-trees; the numerous fountains;
> the innumerable caves in the rocks around, now used as sta-
> bling for goats, which cluster in swarthy multitudes on tiers of
> crags; the convents and shrines scattered here and there in the

suburbs; the crowded houses and the lofty spires of the interior; and the perfectly Poussinesque castle, with its fine corner tower commanding the whole scene.

Lear saw Melfi, though, before the earthquake of 1851, and much of its antiquity now feels modernised and decidedly done up. The castle, rather than the grand residence in which Lear was entertained, is now a hollow shell, housing a sarcophagus and a museum but little else. As usual with Italian restoration, it looks as if no amount of municipal, or European, money has been spared, and the result is a space that feels peculiarly contemporary. It takes a big feat of imagination to recall that this great hall, now pristine and empty, is where monumental papal councils took place. It's only outside the castle, on the cusp of the grassy hill, that you can get a sense of what this place must have been like back then. Far below is the valley and, beyond that, Monte Stangone; the other side, falling away as if huddling behind this feudal fortress, is Melfi itself.

That night, I sit in my room watching *Tre Fratelli*, a slow-moving but touching film directed by Francesco Rosi. Three brothers return to their home town in Basilicata on the death of their mother and rediscover the simplicity and passion of their homeland. One character, musing on the state of the nation, says: 'Hasn't Italy always been like this: bloody, violent, ferocious? So much for the country of the easy-going. This is a land of abusers, brigands, kidnappers, hired killers and instigators. And where do you put the Mafia? You remember *The Betrothed*? Today, like yesterday, between the institutions, between groups of leaders and the people there isn't any relationship.' It's an arresting line, something that has been suggested, in different words, throughout Italian history. This, people have repeatedly said, is a bloody country, a place where massacres and murders are commonplace. It's not, factually, true: it has a far lower murder rate than Britain or America, for example. But that perception persists, partly, no doubt, because of the fame of organised crime; and also because certain events – like Carlo Gesualdo's jealous vengeance or the Sack of Melfi or the murder of the Count of Matera – are commemorated for centuries in a way that doesn't happen elsewhere. Every Pentecost, for example, Melfi remembers Ronca Battista and the thousands who fell defending their town. The procession through the centre is led by two pages carrying parchments from Charles V eulogising Melfi's fidelity and bravery. It's as if folklore and history and modern pageantry have all combined to remember the spilt blood of centuries past. Perhaps it's not that there's more blood spilt in Italy (as if one could quantify such things anyway); it's just that there's a longer memory about the spilling: there's a desire to commemorate and memorialise all massacres, murders, vendettas and assassinations that elsewhere disappear into the mists of time.

I don't know why I'm always drawn to those stories, but each time I visit one of the magnificent castles round here I look out for the gruesome tale of bloodshed. While in Melfi I hear the story of another castle, a story which, while possibly apocryphal, offers an insight into how Frederick II is remembered. Just over the border, in Puglia, is Castel del Monte, another of Frederick II's great castles. Octagonal in design, with eight octagonal towers and eight rooms on each floor, its symmetry and simplicity and extensive use of marble made it one of the most beautiful castles in Italy. It's so iconic that it's now on the back of Italy's one-euro coins. The story goes that Frederick II sent one of his courtiers to check on the progress of the castle, but the courtier fell in love with a girl in Melfi and never got round to travelling the short distance to Castel del Monte. When he was summoned back to Naples, the courtier assumed the emperor would never find time to go to the castle either and so, when asked about the progress of the building, he denounced the castle's builder as a feckless scoundrel who had done little work. The emperor summoned the builder, who begged for a chance to take leave of his wife and children. Fearing disgrace and ignominy, he then killed his whole family and himself. On hearing of this tragedy, the emperor decided to visit the castle himself, taking with him the duplicitous courtier who had got waylaid in Melfi. Frederick II, on seeing the magnificent castle and realising the tragedy of his most skilful builder's suicide, dragged the courtier by his locks to the top of the highest tower and threw him off.

The story may be little more than legend, but that of Isabella Morra, a poet I've been reading throughout my travels in Basilicata, is more reliable. She was the author of beautiful, plaintive sonnets. Born in 1520, she was one of eight children. Her father, a fervent supporter of Francis I of France, was forced to flee to Paris as Spanish troops slowly took control of southern Italy once more. An educated young woman, living in the remote castle of Valsinni (called, in her day, Favale), she lamented the cruelty of her fate: her isolation, her absent father, the barrenness of the surrounding 'infernal valleys, steep rivers and ruinous rocks'. With all their talk of cruel fate, it was almost as if her melancholic poems – only thirteen survive – anticipated her terrible destiny: she met and corresponded with a married Spaniard, Diego Sandoval de Castro, a man whose nationality would have marked him, from Morra's family's point of view, as the enemy. The exact nature of their relationship is unknown, but Isabella's brothers decided to put an end to it, killing their sister and her tutor when she was only twenty-four and, a few months later, killing de Castro himself.

The antiquated Italian of her verse, the sorrow of both the poems and her life, and the satisfying simplicity of her rhymes make reading Morra very moving. But it's especially so since lines occasionally jump out at you that remind you of why you're here, of why you're criss-crossing this remote land. Because there are lines from almost five centuries ago that seem to talk directly to the Elisa Claps case: 'Tell my dear father of my pain,' she begs; 'what an unheard of thing, to deprive a father of helping his daughter . . . All hope, brother, is in vain.'

*

The next day I drive the short distance to Rionero in Vulture. Nestling on the slopes of Monte Vulture, it doesn't have the grand buildings of Melfi or Venosa. Most of the rectangular palazzi look the same, painted an ochre yellow or rusty red. On each street corner there are almost two metres of small signs pointing you towards local businesses and shops. The main road that brings you into the town from the dual carriageway is called Corso Italia, and there are, as usual, various streets called Garibaldi, Mazzini and Verdi. But the true soul of the place is revealed elsewhere: one side street is named Via del Brigantaggio, 'Brigandage Way', and there's a plaque to a man called Carmine Crocco. This small, fairly nondescript town is where a ferocious insurgency against Italian unification began in the early 1860s, and Carmine Crocco, born in one of these side streets in 1830, was its leader.

For almost a century after Italian unification, the memory of Basilicata's brigands was vilified. The men and women who took to the remote mountains and forests to launch attacks on Italian troops were seen as no better than bandits, outlaws and mercenaries. They were, it was thought, the terrorists of their day, ignoring the rule of law and showing no respect for property or human life. Almost all of the heroic Italian patriots who had battled for unification were bilious in their judgements about the brigands in the south: Luigi Carlo Farini said, 'What towns are these? What barbarousness. This isn't Italy, this is Africa. The Bedouins, compared to these louts, are flowers of civic virtue.' On another occasion he said that 'we'll need iron and fire to extirpate this cancer'. Nino Bixio called the south a place that needed to be 'burnt alive on a slow flame . . . it's a country that needs to be destroyed or at least depopulated and sent to Africa to become civilised'. Cavour called the south 'corrupt to the marrow'. More than terrorists, those brigands were seen as the prototypes of the organised-crime syndicates that would dog Italy for decades to come: as one recent historian put it, 'The way in which it [brigandage] was fought would develop [into] "organised delinquency", and would excessively increase the seriousness of a southern question that was destined to make gangrenous the political life of the country by perpetuating the contraposition of north and south.' Lucanian brigandage was, it was thought, one of the many precursors to the Mafia. But in recent years the rise of the Northern League has allowed southerners to reassess their own secessionist past, and the brigands have been, if not rehabilitated, certainly more intimately understood. The old story of wonderful patriots fighting dastardly, lawless brigands has become much more nuanced and interesting.

The story of Carmine Crocco certainly reads like that of a true folk hero. When he was a child a dog had run into the family's house and attacked a chicken (other sources say a rabbit). Carmine's brother had killed the dog, which, unfortunately, belonged to a local landowner called Don Vincenzo. Don Vincenzo was so incensed that he beat Crocco's pregnant mother, causing her to lose her child. Don Vincenzo was later shot, and Crocco's father, though innocent, was imprisoned. His mother died of her injuries in an asylum. Crocco moved to Puglia aged ten to work as a shepherd. There he saved the life of another rich landlord, and was rewarded with fifty scudi. The stories of fights and scuffles, however, continued. During military service, he killed a man who had accused him of stealing meat in a brawl; and on his return home he had killed another nobleman who had defamed his sister.

He was imprisoned, escaped, joined Giuseppe Garibaldi's army but, disappointed by the new Italian state, set up a rebel army supported, clandestinely, by the deposed Bourbon monarchy and various elements within the Catholic Church.

Rather than outlaws, those brigands saw themselves as *legittimisti*, as faithful subjects who were defending the Kingdom of Naples, and the papacy, from the Piedmontese, from the 'northerners' and 'foreigners' who had no business in, or knowledge of, the south. Indeed, throughout the insurgency there was suspicion that the long hand of the Bourbon monarchy, and of Francesco II's wife Maria Sofia in particular, was feeding the fire (decades later, Maria Sofia was even rumoured to have been involved in the assassination of Umberto I in 1900). The priesthood was, equally, under suspicion. In August 1861, the Italian prime minister Bettino Ricasoli wrote to Italian diplomats abroad that 'it's manifest that the complicity and connivance of the Roman Curia with Neapolitan brigandage derives from the solidarity of temporal interests'. Huge tracts of ecclesiastical lands had been confiscated in the two and a half million hectares annexed by the new Italian state, but the peasants of the south, inevitably, gained no advantage from their redistribution. If anything, their condition was worsened by a tax on flour. Malnutrition, malaria and abject housing created sympathy for those brigands who opposed the apparently rapacious new regime, a sympathy felt not only by the many *manutengoli*, those people who maintained or hid the brigands, but also by the clergy. The Jesuit Carlo Piccirillo in *Civiltà Cattolica* compared the new Italian troops to a 'thief who comes into my house, and in part sustained by the violence of his arms and helped by the betrayal of my servants, cruelly evicts me and seats himself as landlord in my place. What right could he invoke in his favour if later, having rebuilt my morale and strength, I come to assault him in my occupied house, and force him from a nest not his?' It's true, of course, that many of those brigands were indeed the habitual delinquents and petty criminals imagined by politicians in the north; that some merely wanted to settle scores with landlords, to pillage and plunder. But many were fighting the injustice of an invasion that had, they thought, already pillaged their lands and their livelihoods. In a great book about brigandage called *Il sangue del Sud* (*The Blood of the South*), one historian recently wrote that the brigands were fighting for 'land, justice, honour, tradition, pride and the eviction of the foreigner'.

Crocco became a kind of Spartacus, leading thousands of men against far superior forces. In April 1861, he quickly took control of the entire Vulture area, including Lagopesole, Venosa, Lavello and Melfi. Francesco II's coat of arms was once again hung from public buildings. Although the arrival of the Italian National Guard from neighbouring cities forced a retreat from Melfi, the uprising spread to the fringes of Campania and Puglia. With his deep-set eyes, his long nose and beard, Crocco appeared the perfect brigand. He was cunning, determined and ruthless, killing traitors and showing no mercy to the soldiers he captured. By the autumn, the momentum of the revolt was such that the exiled Bourbon government was sending reinforcements from Spain and France, and more villages and towns – Calciano, Garaguso, Salandra, Aliano, Stigliano, Grassano – fell into the rebels' hands. In each they gained new arms and recruits, and by November they were on the outskirts of the province's capital city, Potenza. Only a last-minute betrayal by a former Bourbon aide prevented Crocco from taking the main prize, and he was forced to retreat again, back to the densely forested mountains. Although the initial momentum had been lost, and the Spanish general sent to help Crocco had been executed, for the next three years the brigands continued to fight the Italian National Guard across the south.

There are many gruesome stories from those three years. That of Marianna Oliverio is typical. She had married a young charcoal-burner-turned-brigand called Pietro Monaco. He later began an affair with her older sister, and Marianna duly murdered her in front of her three children with a hatchet. Monaco forgave her and the two became outlaws, part of that grey area between cruel criminality and principled resistance. Marianna's rumoured habit of slicing up the cadavers of her enemies was widely reported, as was the story that she always wore blood-soaked clothes. They kidnapped nobles, priests and children, often managing to earn huge ransoms. The band was dismantled only when three of Monaco's men betrayed him, shooting him at point-blank range. Marianna decided to burn her husband's head, rather than have it paraded by the state troops as a trophy, and the chestnut tree from which she found the wood for the fire has now become an unusual tourist attraction.

Another notorious woman was called Filomena De Marco, nicknamed Pennacchio because she always wore feathers in her cap. Beautiful and fiery, she had killed her aggressive husband when still a teenager, slaying him with a silver pin to the throat. She fled to the mountains, met Crocco's brigands and had a relationship first with the leader himself, and then with two of his men. She became the companion of Giuseppe Schiavone, riding alongside him in guerrilla operations, including the slaughter of ten Piedmontese soldiers in Sferracavallo. Schiavone's former lover, jilted and jealous, betrayed his whereabouts to the authorities and he was captured. His dying wish was to see his pregnant Pennacchio, and he led the authorities to her too, kneeling down, kissing her hand and begging for forgiveness. She was imprisoned, but – since she collaborated and informed on her accomplices – was released from prison in 1872.

The response of the nascent Italian state to such widespread brigandage was to introduce, in August 1863, martial law. The so-called Pica Law stayed in force until 31 December 1865, introducing military courts and executions for armed resistance. There were no appeals against sentences but, anticipating twentieth-century tactics, penal leniency for informers. Twenty newspapers were closed and eighty-nine town councils dissolved. The Bishops of Foggia and Muro Lucano were thrown in prison, as were the curates of Reggio Calabria, Sorrento, Rossano and Capaccio. The Bishops of Lecce, Trani and Avellino were expelled from their dioceses. Enrico Cialdini was sent to Naples and, from there, reported to parliament in Turin fairly shocking figures: 8,968 people executed, including sixty-four priests and twenty-two friars. Over ten thousand people had been taken prisoner, 918 houses and six towns had been entirely burnt, twelve churches sacked, 13,629 people deported and 1,428 councils were under siege. That was in the Neapolitan region alone. The total number of people killed varies according to sources, but it's clear that the brutality of the brigands was matched by that of the Italian state. Some historians in the south calculate that as many as a hundred thousand people may have lost their lives in the ferocious civil war. 'Their hypothesis', Giordano Bruno Guerri wrote recently, 'is certainly closer to reality than the official figures.'

Eventually, inevitably, Crocco was captured. Due to a betrayal within his ranks, many of his followers had already been killed or captured, including his lieutenant Ninco Nanco. Crocco travelled to Rome to seek protection from Pope Pius IX, but papal forces arrested him and handed him over to the Italian authorities. He was eventually tried in Potenza and, on 11 September 1872, sentenced to death for his part in sixty-two murders and thirteen attempted murders. That sentence, however, was commuted to life imprisonment and he lived for another thirty years, becoming something of a folk hero and publishing his rather gripping memoir, *Come divenni brigante* (*How I Became a Brigand*). In it, he defended brigands, writing of the people in the south who had been 'disdained by regal functionaries and the treacherous Piedmontese' and who felt that

> every right had been denied us, even man's dignity. Who could vindicate them if not us, linked by a common destiny? We, also, were peasants, no longer disposed to bow our heads . . . Liberty doesn't mean changing the landlord. It's not a vain, abstract word. It means saying without fear IT'S MINE, and feeling strongly in possession of something, starting with the soul. It means living by what you love . . .

The era of brigandage has always fascinated writers. Alexandre Dumas and Stendhal both wrote extensively about the brigands. Charles Dickens wrote admiringly of Crocco. A biopic was recently made of his life, *Li chiamarono . . . briganti!*, and one of Italy's most famous actors and directors, Michele Placido, himself a native of Rionero in Vulture, claims to be a descendant of Crocco. Every summer in the Parco della Grancia there's a production that recreates the life of Carmine Crocco called *La storia bandita*. Carlo Levi was intrigued by the brigands' legacy, writing that

> their traces are everywhere; there is not a mountain, gully, wood, fountain, cave or stone that is not linked with one of their adventures or that did not serve them as a refuge or hide-out; not a dark corner that was not their meeting place; not a country chapel where they did not leave threatening letters or wait for ransom money . . . every family was at one time for or against them: one of its members was an outlaw, or they took in and hid a brigand, or a wandering band killed some relative, or set fire to their crops. Then it was that the feuds arose which were to be handed down from generation to generation and which rage even today.

Levi saw that the myth of the brigands was very dear to many Lucani, that it represented 'the only poetry in their existence . . . when, after infinite endurance, they are shaken to the depths of their beings and are driven by an instinct of self-defence or justice, their revolt knows no bounds and no measure'.

There are many stories and legends about the brigands, but what's interesting is the insight they offer into the mentality of this mountainous part of the peninsula. One contemporary journalist, the eloquent Ferdinando Petruccelli della Gattina, knew the people of Lucania intimately, having been born in Moliterno in the province of Potenza and having himself lived clandestinely. An Italian patriot before unification, he had gone into hiding in the aftermath of the 1848 revolutions, adding the 'della Gattina' onto his name to confuse the Bourbon police. He described his compatriots as 'taciturn, surly, proud, they instinctively hate any kind of power. Their obedience is a protest, their submission a challenge.' He drew a portrait of a people whose anger could suddenly explode before slowly subsiding, returning to their habitual gruffness and courteous obedience. The more you read about the brigands, the more it becomes apparent that this is a land of rebels: this is where Giovanni Passannante, who in 1878 tried to knife Umberto I, came from. His whole town was forced to change its name from Salvia to Savoia (the name of the monarchy) di Lucania. Even Horace mentioned that 'Lucanian folk threatened violent war.' And what's relevant about the brigands for the sad story of Elisa Claps is that Maurizio Restivo, Danilo's father, is fixated on those knife-happy female outlaws, even publishing a book on them called *Donne, drude, briganti*. Restivo senior had also, on the very night that his son told him about another murder to which he had been linked, ordered a book called *I pugnalatori* (*The Stabbers*), an account of the knifings of thirteen people in Sicily in 1862. Restivo's father's fascination with all things sanguineous persuaded him to organise an exhibition, in the National Library in Potenza, of guillotines. Many people in Potenza had long wondered how it was that Danilo Restivo became obsessed with cutting hair, if not worse; given his father's obsession with bloodthirsty stories from the nineteenth century, some people thought the answer lay very close to home.

I walk towards Crocco's home, a place that is now, appropriately, an armoury. It's a humble house in the middle of a terrace. There's also a small museum commemorating his life. It's strange how remote that bloody history seems now, and it's hard to imagine that this town was once the epicentre of such a powerful rebellion. There are only a few clues dotted around the otherwise patriotic street names: there's a plaque to Crocco and a street named after the emigrants to Argentina. It's estimated that in the decade between 1870 and 1880, in the aftermath of the suppression of the brigands, a million southern Italians emigrated to the Americas, mainly to Argentina and the US. Rionero was, for a long time, a desolate place. Nowadays the area is more famous for its wines made from the black Aglianico grape, to which Edward Lear gave the superlative 'superexcellent'. The wine benefits from the very particular soil here: the rich minerals of volcanic soil and the tufa rock which act as a sponge, absorbing moisture and releasing it in drier periods.

I walk to the cellars of the famous Cantine del Notaio (the 'Notary' wine producer). Given the name of the producer, all the wines have legalistic names: *Il Repertorio* (the repertory), *Il Rogito* (the deed), *Il Sigillo* (the seal), and so on. I taste one or two, and they are extraordinary. But the prices are pretty eye-watering and I can't afford a bottle. The man behind the counter doesn't seem to mind. He just enthuses about the various subtleties of the bouquet – the hints of marasca cherry or liquorice, of chocolate, dried figs or rose petals. As often happens round here, he seems in no rush to do anything else; he's content just to share his passion for this fabulous liquid. I promise to come back one day when I've made my fortune.

From Rionero in Vulture it's a short drive up to the Laghi di Monticchio. These two lakes are all that's left of the volcanic craters of Monte Vulture. It's a beautiful drive, the road snaking around the side of the mountain before dropping down through a dense woodland of turkey oaks and alders. The lakes themselves are wide expanses of water lined with trees whose branches almost seem to be drinking from the still surface. At the far end is the monastery of San Michele, formerly a Benedictine and now a Capuchin monastery. Its large, white walls look almost incongruous against the trees and foliage. The monastery is now besieged by the usual sights associated with a tourist destination: the shores of the lakes are lined with restaurants, kiosks, boat- and bike-rentals, hawkers and pedlars and the like. The place is so crowded that it's almost impossible to walk in a straight line. You can tell by the number plates of the cars that there are plenty of people here on day trips from the big cities, from Potenza and Bari. Children are running around with large helium balloons or new plastic toys. Groups of teenagers are queuing to get on a pedalo to cross the lake.

But once you're on the far side it's quieter, and the shouts and laughter that reach you across the water sound softer, nothing more than a gentle reminder of distant exuberance. I sit there, under the old monastery, watching the couples walking arm in arm along the path. One girl with long dark hair comes into view. Both of her arms are wrapped around the left arm of her boyfriend, and her head is resting on his shoulder as they walk. She looks roughly sixteen, and I immediately begin wondering about Elisa. It seems inconceivable that, in all these years, she's never been found. It must be like living with your life on hold, unable to go forwards, unable to go backwards. Her absence has been haunting me ever since I heard about this story, but I can't begin to imagine what it must be like for her family. Haunting can hardly be the word. At least that suggests some kind of spectral presence. They've had to survive with nothing: no word, no truth, no sign of life, and yet, despite all that, no certainty, no closure, no mourning. And this incredible land of rocky mountains and dense forests, this land that is so powerful and beautifully basic, that has such a rich history and accumulation of culture, must appear to them truly desolate. This is the sort of place where a person can disappear without trace. This is the sort of place where secrets are kept and never revealed. I get up from the small bench and decide that it's time to go back to Potenza.

*

The approach to Potenza is, as usual, confusing. No matter how many times I've come here, I'm still thrown by the road layout. What you assume should be main roads snake between housing blocks and temporary orange plastic fencing. There always seem to be potholes and roadworks. Once again, I have a sense that the *provvisorio*, the temporary, has assumed a permanence, as if this road was never meant to be here but just ended up here. I always get lost on these roads, unable to distinguish one roundabout or bridge from all the others. Dotting each hillock and valley are the huge rectangular blocks of flats. There doesn't seem to be any sense or logic behind where they're built or what direction they face. They've just, like the roads, assumed a permanence, become part of the scenery.

As far back as 1957, a journalist wrote scathingly about the extraordinary appearance of Potenza:

> Only houses and houses and this impression grows as you get
> closer. Going up through the tortuous, if new, streets, between

[126]

the high walls of buildings, it seems as if you can never arrive at the vital nucleus of a city composed only of suburbs. In the end, when you do manage to get there, the centre seems hidden, ashamed of the boastfulness of what surrounds it. Perhaps there's no other city in Italy whose ancient face has been so arrogantly overwhelmed and cancelled . . . perhaps there's no other city in Italy in which the reasoning of urban planning, or even only common sense, have been so completely ignored. You only need to stay for a few hours to realise that wherever there are streets, there's a disorganisation which borders on the absurd. Everywhere agglomeration, overcrowding, upward development of buildings, and all this in the capital of the least developed region in Italy.

Even years later, in 1980, another journalist was lamenting the 'mass of cement boxes which have irreparably marked the end of the historical centre and which reveal the true reality of this regional capital: that is, that it has grown in too much of a hurry, often in the shade of the most shameless speculation, sometimes under the impetus of interests which the man in the street will perhaps never fully understand'. Urban development and rampant house-building are hard to hide. Even if the man in the street doesn't fully understand why his city has been engulfed in cement, he still knows it's so. Anyone with a pair of eyes can see that Potenza has been subject to some of the most relentless, and reckless, building imaginable.

Nor are the reasons so hard to understand. This is a city in which politics and urban planning have always been intimately connected: in the words of one author, in Potenza the cement of power was the power of cement; the way to retain control of the city council was to give the go-ahead to urban sprawl, to green-light as many building projects as possible in order to garner electoral funds. When you read histories of local politics in Potenza (not something, it should be said, that makes exactly gripping reading), a clear pattern emerges: throughout the post-war years, journalists or opposition politicians would denounce the appalling appearance of a city that had been ravaged by cement, and the response was always the same. The incumbent politicians and their allies would portray the criticism as a betrayal of Basilicata, as a denigration of everything local and Lucano. In the fog of controversy, of accusation and counter-attack, the blunt truth about the blighting of the city got lost. A new urban plan would be published, ignored, rewritten, criticised and defended until, by the time of the earthquake in 1980, the city had truly succumbed to cement. When that earthquake did come, on 23 November, many buildings were damaged or uninhabitable, and the whole process began again.

That cosy relationship between politics and property development wasn't, of course, unique to Potenza, but there were certain factors that made it unusual. The first was profitability: property development is a far more lucrative business in Italy than agriculture or manufacturing, but in Basilicata those gains are inexplicably large. Profits from construction in Basilicata are, astonishingly, 37.2 per cent higher than in any other region of Italy. It's probably partly to do with the affordability of labour and the high demand for housing in a region that had precious little modern accommodation for the masses prior to 1945. But for whatever reason, the construction industry in Basilicata was even more remunerative than it was elsewhere. The other particularity of the region was political. Throughout most of the First Republic (from 1948 to 1992), one politician from Potenza was returned to parliament with higher percentages of the vote than anywhere else in Italy. Emilio Colombo was the archetypal Christian Democrat politician: a man intimately linked to the Catholic Church, he was a patriarchal politician who was once described as having a 'persuasive voice and a meaningful smile'. He had thick eyebrows, a bald head and large glasses. Potenza was his fiefdom. He was born here and worshipped at the Chiesa della Santissima Trinità in Via Pretoria, the same church in which Elisa had met Danilo Restivo. He held every Cabinet post possible, becoming also prime minister of Italy and, later, president of the European Union. In the words of the journalist Indro Montanelli, 'He's been a minister, it seems to me, for ever; he was born a minister as others are born albino or hunchback.'

Colombo's unassailable position as the most powerful man in Potenza meant that there was no opposition, no meaningful alternative to what his party wanted. The Christian Democrats decided what happened, and if – under the guise of providing contemporary housing for the masses – they wanted carte blanche for constructors, that is what happened. Colombo was a top-down politician, offering houses like handouts. When he was criticised for that strategic dispensation of favours, one of his allies defended him stoutly, saying that people shouldn't forget that 'here clientelism is a kind of assistance. It's the indispensable, lawful and hoped-for address to underdevelopment. Colombo, therefore, becomes almost an infrastructure of Potenza.' It's a revealing quotation, highlighting the way in which Colombo had become, like an old-fashioned feudal lord, an integral part of the fabric of the city. Many people still admire Colombo for his devotion to Basilicata, for the way in which he battled, for decades, to lift this remote and underdeveloped region into the modern age. His influence in Rome secured huge sums for the region and meant that, in the space of a few decades, almost everyone had access to sanitary housing and laudable healthcare. But he created and perpetuated a system that offered favours in return for political fidelity. No initiative was ever disinterested or unpolluted by some kind of clandestine quid pro quo.

The consequences and costs of that system were stark. As one observer from Potenza wrote in *Il caso Italiano*:

Responsibility doesn't reign, the powerful do, creating relation- ships of dependence, feeding political parasitism, guaranteeing public promotion at every level. Political friendship links, binds, imposes and founds the clans, instituting a fiduciary trust that is social and prepolitical. Who doesn't compromise is out of the game . . . we have devitalising clubs, crowned by squalid political commissions, that dispense public works that produce no benefit and scholarships and money for under-occupied intellectuals.

The hard-working, shrewd peasantry of the past was, in a gen- eration, turned into the passive recipient of state beneficence; and the cost of such lavish gifts – those roads and houses and funds – was political obedience. Many people realised they had to vote, rather than work, for a living. Notorious funds like the *Cassa del Mezzogiorno* (the 'Fund for the South') became, according to one critic, 'degraded to an electoral instrument or, if you prefer, to an administrative instrument for the concession of funds to be lavished as elections approach'. With an average annual budget of what would now be over three billion euros, the Cassa could clearly be a persuasive tool in the hands of shrewd politicians.

Some people who derided the habitual give-and-take of the sys- tem were themselves parliamentary deputies. Angelo Sanza was a Christian Democrat from Potenza, and even he discerned that Potenza 'suffers from an exasperated personalism: the most ele- mentary rights of citizens are conditioned by the need for pulling strings, by the acceptance of a hierarchical order of clientele . . . the denunciation of scandals or corruption often generates only panic, a panic that the high priests of sham respectability transform into *omertà* and indifference'.

All of which have been familiar and habitual laments over recent decades. Many observers have criticised the clientelism of the country, and of the south in particular. Writers like Ann Cornelisen saw, as early as the 1960s, how the recipients of political largesse had been turned into dismayed passivity, reduced to 'stringing and restringing the pearls of their discontent. A hundred years ago,' she wrote, 'such men were brigands. Today they are a castrated menace; they resent, but they are afraid to act.' But if such observations are common to the south, what makes Basilicata, again, unique is its isolation. When you look at a map of the country it's immediately clear that the vast majority of main roads skirt around its border: the A3 runs from Salerno to Reggio Calabria, remaining to the west of the region through the Monti della Maddalena and only briefly entering the region at Lagonegro; the SS106, going from Brindisi to Reggio Calabria, also goes through the region, but hugs the coastline between Metaponto and Policoro; the A16, the old Via Traiana, almost seems deliberately to avoid Basilicata, curving upwards to go outside the area of Monte Vulture before turning down towards Bari. It's not as if there aren't major roads or train lines through Basilicata, but it's not on the way to anywhere. You whizz through it unless you've reason not to. The mountains have always been inaccessible. The roads are, to put it kindly, not great.

That remoteness is one of the reasons the region is so charming. Only here could a mountain be called Dolcedorme, 'sweet slumber'. And when you climb the mountains here you can hear, from the summit, the distant clanking of cow bells, a reminder that this is a place where cattle still range free. There's no sound of traffic or even aircraft. Part of the charm of coming here is the simplicity, the sense that life here is still basic in the best sense of the word. The courtesy and generosity of people not used to tourists, of people who are grateful that anyone should visit the homeland of which they are proud, is astonishing. And that unwitting isolationism of Lucania was one of the reasons that the region perceived itself as an *isola felice*, a 'happy island' in a southern sea of organised crime. This, they used to say, was Lucania Felix. Each of the neighbouring regions had their own infamous mafias – the Camorra, Cosa Nostra, the 'Ndrangheta, the Sacra Corona Unita – but Basilicata, it was thought, was somehow different: this was a region of simple, honest folk, far removed from the horrors of organised crime. 'Until the 1970s, Lucania told itself the fairy tale of the "happy island",' Pantaleone Sergi wrote recently.

> One spoke with warmth of this land that had problems, many problems, but that hadn't known, since the brigandage of the nineteenth century, phenomena of criminal associations . . . the countryside of Basilicata presented itself as a miracle, almost an Eden that had survived in a south that was drifting. Healthy flavours, ancient values, men broken by inclemency, knowledge and strength forged through thousands and thousands of difficulties: a bucolic and Virgilian image useful for tourist postcards.

It's only very slowly that that Arcadian image of Basilicata has been eroded. In many ways it was the earthquake of 23 November 1980 that changed everything. 'The earthquake', wrote a historian of the Mafia in Basilicata, 'distorted in every sense life in Lucania. It reawakened indebted appetites, shook people out of their slumbers . . . Behind the construction, Law 219 foresaw an expenditure of 8,000 billion lire, bulldozers and billionaire business. There were many, not only the Mafia in yellow gloves, that glimpsed an opportunity for speedy changes, for immediate and illicit enrichment . . .' It was in the 1980s that the usual signs of organised crime began to be seen. A former Christian Democrat senator, Decio Scardaccione, was kneecapped. Scardaccione had become the president of ESAB, the agricultural development agency for

Basilicata, and had been trying to introduce more transparency in the awarding of contracts. Another director of the agency, Carlo Cornio, had suffered a bomb attempt outside his house. Basilicata is where there was an attempt on the life of the anti-Mafia judge, Luca Tescaroli. There were various shootings and bombings throughout the decade: a car bomb in Matera, a bomb in Rionero, another explosive device outside a church in Matera. There were tit-for-tat killings throughout the early 1990s as rival gangs fought for supremacy of the lucrative drugs trade. There were attempts on the lives of mayors and priests, anyone who stood in the way of the increasingly confident gangs. Whenever the issue of Mafia infiltration was raised, however, local bigwigs took umbrage, accusing the media of criminalising and insulting a peaceful, contented corner of the country. The size of the problem, however, could no longer be denied, and various investigations – nicknamed, ironically, 'happy island', 'happy island II', 'Siris', 'Medusa', 'Fenus', 'Turris' and 'Oro Nero' – rounded up hundreds of clans and, in the resulting trials, the '*mafiosità*' of those involved was officially recognised. Investigators had unveiled something that local politicians had always denied: the existence of a fifth Mafia on the peninsula, the so-called *Basilischi*.

Long before those trials, however, it was clear to many that Lucania Felix was something of an invention. When you talk to people about the Elisa Claps case around here, many begin to mention similar cases which have never been satisfactorily resolved. Some recall the case of the twelve-year-old girl called Ottavia de Luise. She lived with her seven older siblings in Montemurro. On 12 May 1975 she disappeared. There were stories that old men in the village used to give her coins for lewd reasons; that she had been seen walking towards a farm on the outskirts of town. Over the years, anonymous letters were sent to the family; farms were searched and suspects named. But Ottavia has never been found. There's the case of the so-called 'school teacher of Lagonegro', Maria Antonietta Flora. Married to an Enel employee and with two young children, she disappeared without trace on 10 November 1984. She had left home at 19.00 to have an injection, but was never seen again. Her car was found in a small lay-by on the Reggio to Salerno motorway. It had traces of her blood in it, but she has never been found. Suspicion originally fell on a butcher from Lagonegro, where Maria Antonietta taught: he had been insistently seeking a relationship with her and had even seen her on the evening of her disappearance. But he was found not guilty in court, and attention turned to another man, Domenico Di Lascio. A well-known local businessman, he had apparently had a relationship with the woman and was, it seemed, about to transfer various assets to her. Di Lascio, however, was murdered five years after Maria Antonietta's disappearance. At 23.30 on 11 January 1989, in his study in Nemoli, in the province of Potenza, he was fatally shot, his murder only adding to the sense of conspiracy surrounding her disappearance. 'There have been periods', Maria Antonietta's sister once said, 'in which my family have been scared because something ugly is certainly behind this case.'

Such cases, of course, don't necessarily have any connection to organised crime, but some do. In July 1993, a man called Vincenzo De Mare was working as an HGV driver. He was killed by two shots at his home in Terzo Cavone. The suspicion has always been that he refused to transport or threatened to denounce the trafficking of illegal waste, one of the most profitable rackets for organised crime. Far from being isolated from the various mafias, one journalist wrote a few years ago that 'as soon as you arrive at the top of the steps in Potenza, the "vertical city" as the mayor calls it, you feel sucked into a sinister gothic novel: power, politics, money, speculation, sex and assassins'. One case that seems to have brought all those elements together was that of the so-called 'lovers of Policoro'. A young couple, Luca and Marirosa, were found dead in a bathroom on 23 March 1988. It was immediately assumed that the couple had been electrocuted by a faulty heater in the bathroom, and they were buried without an autopsy. In time, however, it would become one of those Italian mysteries that would provide endless fuel for conspiracy theorists: years later the bodies were exhumed, and it became apparent that both youngsters had been assaulted and drowned. The motive for the attack was, allegedly, to silence a secret: that Marirosa had been a regular at exotic parties organised for the pleasure of powerful politicians and magistrates. Over twenty years later, however, nothing other than the incompetence of the original investigators has ever been proved.

None of which necessarily illuminates the Elisa Claps tragedy. But the crimes offer an insight into comparable tragedies, and into the criminal backdrop of Basilicata. One case, however, really did overlap with Elisa's disappearance, and the connection between both events, while tenuous, highlighted quite how small the strange world of Potenza was and quite how many innocent, or incriminating, coincidences there were in that world. On 29 April 1997, a man called Pinuccio Gianfredi and his wife, Patrizia, were returning home with warm pizzas that they had just bought. In the back of their BMW were two of their three children. Just as Patrizia, their mother, was about to open the gate to their block of flats, two assassins opened fire with a Luger pistol and a sawn-off shotgun. Both parents were killed instantly in front of their terrified children. The two murderers left as quickly as they had arrived. The car fell silent but for the radio and the sound of the windscreen wipers, still moving left to right as if nothing had happened. The windows of the two front doors were shattered, and Pinuccio's head was resting on his right shoulder, his dead eyes wide open. The last of the eight shots had been into his mouth at point-blank range. That same bullet had gone through him and into his wife's thorax. Her head had been blown backwards and she was bleeding from her nose and mouth. The children couldn't even hear their own screams.

It was a shocking crime which, in the words of one author, began to reveal the inner workings of this strange city: 'That evening in Potenza not only was the umpteenth veil of the criminal underworld torn away, but a little edge of the blanket made up of silence and *omertà* that has often characterised this land began to be lifted.' As investigators started to dig into the background of that shocking double murder, Elisa's whereabouts weren't, inevitably, revealed; that new crime didn't explain her disappearance or who had been responsible for it. But it did begin to explain why she had never been found and why the search for her had been so futile.

Five

'We were investigating favourable mortgages,
altered trials, judicial protection and aspects
relating to cases of an unheard-of seriousness, such
as the double murder of the lovers of Policoro,
the disappearance of Elisa Claps and the health
service, of which the husband of an influential
magistrate in the Potenza Procura was a part. I
found myself confronted by an illegal control of
judicial documents and a diffused clientelism based
on familism. So much for Lucania Felix.'
    Luigi De Magistris

A nephew of Pinuccio Gianfredi, the murdered man, was one of
the first on the scene. Vincenzo was a policeman who had been
about to come and say hello to his uncle. On seeing the car, he
immediately realised what had happened. He asked his partner to
look after the children and called an ambulance.

The emergency services arrived almost immediately, but there
was nothing to do. Both Pinuccio and his wife were dead. The
sirens and screams had caused various people to come out onto
their balconies, and they watched as an ordinary part of the city
was transformed into a crime scene: photographs were taken,
witnesses interviewed, police cordons erected. From the balcony
of the Gianfredi family home, Angela – the daughter who had
remained at home because of an illness – heard what had happened and ran downstairs.

It was, it seemed, a professional hit. The speed and ferocity of
the murders suggested that this was a crime linked to gang war-
fare. In fact, the authorities already knew Pinuccio Gianfredi. He
was part of a criminal clan called the Martorano. Rather than the

quiet, serious family man he appeared, he had connections with organised crime in both Calabria and Sicily. He made money out of high-interest loans and the supply of materials – acid and weapons and the like – to his contacts in neighbouring regions. Investigators, however, made little headway: the stolen car without a number plate used for the crime was recovered to the north of the city; and an anonymous phone call to the Questura gave a dubious explanation for the crime ('We made an error . . . we were supposed to hit a state's witness from Turin who has the same surname'). But the identity of the killers remained a mystery.

The killing did reveal, however, how small the city of Potenza was. On 22 July 1997, a few months after the double murder, a well-known doctor called Michele Cannizzaro went to the authorities to declare, for clarity, that he had been to Pinuccio Gianfredi's house the evening before the murder. He had wanted to clarify the fact, he said, because he had heard malicious gossip in the city about the visit. He had merely been conducting house visits, as was normal for a doctor, and had been called to Gianfredi's house to discuss a medical condition. It may have been that, as Cannizzaro said, his visit to the murdered man's house was merely a professional one. But there were plenty of people who doubted it. Vincenzo Bonadies, the policeman who was Gianfredi's nephew, signed a statement declaring that Cannizzaro was a '*mafioso* above suspicion . . . a very powerful and dangerous person'. Cannizzaro vigorously denied the allegation. What was extraordinary was that Cannizzaro was the husband of the woman who was charged with investigating the double murder, Felicia Genovese. It was she who had been in charge of the investigation of the Elisa Claps disappearance. The ways in which the Cannizzaro–Genovese axis appeared to obscure or hinder a transparent investigation became clear through Genovese's subsequent decisions. Police had requested permission to intercept the phone conversations of a nurse from the San Carlo hospital with connections to Gianfredi. Genovese, the magistrate who could authorise such intercepts, said that they were unnecessary since her husband, the director of the hospital, would be able to glean any information in person. That, in itself, was an unorthodox approach to investigation – refusing permission to bug someone's telephone because the man in question was an employee of your spouse – but even greater conflicts of interest were to emerge in due course.

In the autumn of 1998, a man called Rino Cappiello was arrested on suspicion of extortion. A man who had connections to various criminal gangs, he decided to collaborate with the authorities and began providing extraordinary insights into the underworld of Potenza. According to Cappiello, both the doctor, Michele Cannizzaro, and the murder victim, Gianfredi, were assiduous card players and their games often involved huge sums of money. Cannizzaro, moreover, was seen as a guarantor of Gianfredi's immunity, able to lean on investigators in order to take the heat off his friend. He had intervened not only with his wife, but also, as far back as 1985, with another magistrate, persuading him not to proceed against Gianfredi. There were also suggestions that Cannizzaro helped Gianfredi's favoured companies win contracts from Anas, the Italian highways agency. By 1997, however, the heat was such that not even Cannizzaro was able to help his friend, and the two had had a heated argument in a restaurant. Cannizzaro allegedly told Gianfredi that there was nothing he could do to keep the investigators off his back, to which Gianfredi replied that 'if I go down, everyone is coming down with me'. Shortly afterwards he was killed.

The account of the *pentito*, the penitent criminal or 'grass', seemed incredible. The implication of his version of events was that Cannizzaro, one of the city's most powerful men, was intimately connected to a gangland criminal, even implicated in his demise.

Cannizzaro denied any involvement and, indeed, the case against him was later *archiviato*, meaning the prosecution was dropped. But the allegations got even more sensational when Cappiello began to talk about the Elisa Claps case. The *pentito* claimed that an art dealer and family friend, Luigi Memoli, had confided to him that Maurizio Restivo, Danilo's father, had once approached him to act as a go-between in the Elisa Claps case. Restivo wanted an introduction to Michele Cannizzaro in order that he intervene with his magistrate wife to take the heat off Restivo's son. Restivo and Cannizzaro duly met in the art dealer's gallery, and the cost of the doctor's intervention was agreed at one hundred million lira. The investigation into Elisa Claps's disappearance would, thanks to the sinister accord, be deliberately skewed.

Once again, the allegation seemed unbelievable. All those named by the *pentito* – the art dealer, the doctor, Restivo's father – vehemently denied the allegations. In fact, many suspected that Cappiello was strategically slinging mud, sullying the good name of an investigative magistrate and her spouse simply because she had dared to go after local gangs. The declarations of *pentiti* are notoriously unreliable, and Cappiello's reconstructions of various crimes seemed, to some, calculated more to exact revenge than to reveal the truth. Others suspected that he was being manipulated by Genovese's rivals within the Potenza Questura, by those who saw in the *pentito* an opportunity to lay low an ambitious rival. Despite all those caveats, however, it was clear that the Cannizzaro–Genovese axis was hardly conducive to clarity and transparency. And when the authorities looked more deeply into Cannizzaro's past, a worrying picture emerged: in 1992, two *carabinieri* discovered that Cannizzaro was, at his house in Petile di Calanna, entertaining various affiliates of the Greco criminal clan. His brother was deputy mayor in Santo Stefano in Aspromonte, part of a town council which was dissolved in 1998 because of suspected mafia infiltration. There were records of phone calls to Cannizzaro's home phone from Giorgio Ierinò, a noted member of the 'Ndrangheta, the Calabrian mafia. There were two calls between Leonardo Garreffa, another convicted criminal, and Cannizzaro. The accusations against Cannizzaro and his wife were so serious that the entire investigation into Elisa Claps's disappearance was removed entirely from Potenza and put in the hands of the DIA, the Direzione Investigativa Antimafia, in Salerno.

At the height of the scandal the Claps family were invited in to see Felicia Genovese. She wanted to reassure the family that the accusations – that her husband had taken money in order to derail the investigation into Elisa's disappearance – were completely false. She listed all her efforts over the years, and enumerated the actions she had taken in the hope of finally finding Elisa. At the end, looking weary and contrite, she asked Filomena if she believed her.

Filomena stared at her, at the woman who had been so extraordinarily incompetent: she hadn't sequestered Danilo Restivo's clothes in the days after the disappearance, even though they were, according to witnesses, blood-soaked; she hadn't organised a search of the church where Elisa had gone missing. Filomena didn't know how to interpret that incompetence, whether to believe that it was innocent or not.

'I don't know what to believe any more,' she said. 'I only know that my daughter's no longer here and that no one, not you or the others, has been able to bring her back to me or to tell me what has happened to her. I know only that, and that's it. I know that you also have an adolescent girl. Try and imagine', Filomena stared at Genovese, 'just for a moment what a hell your life would be if from one day to the next you didn't know anything more about her. I don't want to believe that a mother was able to impose on another mother such suffering. I hope never to know such a terrible truth. I don't have any more tears to cry any more.'

In due course the accusations against Cannizzaro and Genovese were 'archived'. Rino Cappiello, the man who had pointed the finger at Cannizzaro, was even charged with involvement in the Gianfredi murder himself. He had, it was clear, an obvious motive, having been publicly humiliated and beaten by Gianfredi. But he, too, was eventually cleared of all charges. In one of the legal documents archiving the case, it was written that 'multiple checks have taken place regarding Cannizzaro, from which have emerged . . . sporadic contact with people with criminal records'.

Barely had those charges against Cannizzaro and Genovese been dropped, however, than another scandal engulfed them. Various regional councillors were under investigation for *abuso d'ufficio*, abuse of their office: they had replaced Giuseppe Panio, the director general of the Azienda Sanitaria Locale, the local health service, with someone who was much more politically allied to themselves, someone who was much closer to the centre-left party, Giancarlo Vaineri. It was, according to the accusation, the same old story of jobs going to political cliques rather than to the ablest candidate. Felicia Genovese investigated the accusations of *abuso d'ufficio* and formally requested that all charges be dropped. The request was twice rejected, and it emerged that not only was Genovese a card-carrying member of a centre-left party, but she was hardly disinterested in the goings-on in the local health service: her notorious husband, Michele Cannizzaro, had in fact just been elected director general of the region's largest hospital, the San Carlo, by the very people his wife had dropped charges against. As one journalist put it, 'The essential synthesis is that the husband of the magistrate was promoted by those investigated by the magistrate and for whom the magistrate had just requested that the case against them be archived.' Justice, it seemed, was being manipulated in order that someone's spouse could get the right job. Cannizzaro got the position the month after his wife had requested the case against his 'electors' be archived. It was another of the many coincidences that happened in this small city.

A daring and maverick investigator began an investigation into what he called '*Toghe lucane*', 'Lucanian togas'. Luigi De Magistris was a tall, young and idealistic magistrate, and he didn't spare anyone. It was an investigation that concerned, as he wrote in his memoir, *Assalto al PM*, 'the untouchables: the magistrates . . . it concerned a tangle of power held together by strong criminal interests that involved members of the institutions, of politics, of business and various magistrates. It was an investigation that led me to the heart of the magistrature of Basilicata [. . .] which doesn't tolerate the control of legality upon itself.' In the Act of Conclusion, written as a summary of his investigation, he wrote that 'Genovese and Cannizzaro guaranteed the outcome of penal procedures in which they had interests and those of people for whom they acted as guarantors.' Both Genovese and Cannizzaro denied any such interference. But De Magistris appeared to have revealed that, in the words of one author, 'in Basilicata one finds oneself coming up against a real and proper "system" of crooks, a cupola of power, digging into which De Magistris runs up against a series of ugly crimes, of old stories that have never reached a solution, of real and proper mysteries . . .' Among those mysteries, of course, was that of Elisa Claps.

As often happens to fearless investigators, De Magistris was himself investigated. The case against him was eventually dropped, but by then the great and the good of Potenza had closed ranks and a window which had briefly opened on the strangely interconnected world of Basilicata's powerful was suddenly and brusquely closed. De Magistris went into politics, joining the Italy of Values party before becoming the mayor of Naples. The insight he offered into Basilicata, however, was fascinating: he had shown in compelling detail just how small the city of Potenza was. He had shown the extraordinary overlap of interests which meant that no trial, no appointment and no contract was ever objective or meritocratic. In that tiny, provincial setting, the main players all knew each other, and favours were swapped accordingly. Even an outsider with only a passing familiarity with the place begins to recognise the same names going round: Cappiello's lawyer, for example, was Piervito Bardi, the same man who had defended Eris Gega and who had, with his mysterious leads in Albania, sent investigators on another wild goose chase during the search for Elisa. Even as Bardi's client, Cappiello, was denouncing Cannizzaro, Cannizzaro and his wife were having dinner with Bardi.

Such encounters may have been innocent, but it's hard not to conclude that the city was too small for disinterested decisions to be made. And the closer you look at people's careers, the more you begin to wonder how they got there. Two of the minor characters in the Elisa Claps' story – Giuseppe Carlone, the witness who allegedly saw her descending the steps of Via IV Novembre, and Luigi Grimaldi, one of the original investigators – end up working at the hospital where Cannizzaro was, of course, director general. Conspiracy theorists in Potenza muse about whether those appointments were coincidental or actually part of a darker plot in which a powerful *deus ex machina* was rewarding certain people with certain posts. And maybe, they say, the fact that Cannizzaro was a member of a masonic lodge, the Loggia Mario Pagano, is of consequence; so, perhaps, is the fact that Maurizio Restivo and Francesco Urciuoli, the ex-boyfriend of Eliana De Cillis, were also freemasons. The Claps family were, rightly, demanding an uncompromising, single-minded investigation, but the regular overlap of interests and intrigues suggested to them that the investigation was anything but. It was as if the search for Elisa had shone a torch into the dark corners of this city, and the more corners were glimpsed, the more it was obvious how easily the search for a sixteen-year-old girl could be compromised, sidetracked and distracted.

The scandal of '*Toghe lucane*' also revealed the politicisation of appointments. Potenza was, as it always had been, a *città impiegatizia*, a city of clerical jobs. As the capital of an underdeveloped region struggling with high unemployment, white-collar jobs in various quangos and commissions were highly sought after and were, usually, the reward for political fidelity. As one writer commented years ago: 'In Potenza, no state or state-controlled functionary can stay for long without having a party card.' Felicia Genovese was a card-carrying supporter of a centre-left party, and that political alignment had significant impact on both her and her husband's careers. Without being part of a political pyramid, it's inconceivable that Cannizzaro would have become director general of the San Carlo hospital, able to decide the destiny of multimillion-euro contracts in the local healthcare system. Even more extraordinary is the fact that Genovese was given the post of consultant to the Parliamentary Anti-Mafia Commission in Rome. Despite the very legitimate doubts about the links between her husband and certain gentlemen in Calabria, she was promoted by her political allies as someone who could advise those who were at the heart of the battle against the Mafia. To say the appointment was ill-advised is to be unnecessarily generous. When the scandal broke and Genovese was relieved of her post, the then minister of justice spoke about 'an ugly story . . . a Calabrian family that's trying to increase its influence in Basilicata by exploiting the increased importance of a person [Cannizzaro] linked by family ties to a *sostituto procuratore* from Potenza [Genovese] who was even until a few days ago a consultant of the anti-Mafia'. Even now, the newspaper of the centre-left party of which Genovese was a part fiercely defends her and her husband. It's as if they simply can't see any conflict of interests.

Luigi De Magistris wrote in his memoir that 'the real anomaly of our country is to be found in the ruling class, which is so much more inclined towards illegal behaviour than happens in any other advanced democracy'. When I go and see him in the offices of the Italy of Values party in Rome, he expands on the point: 'The battle for legality is very complicated. Today, illegality, organised criminality and corruption have become a true and proper system. They assume ever more the appearances of the institutions, of politics and public things. Illegality isn't something outside the state like terrorism, that the state can clash with openly; it's on the inside, an interior anti-state that corrodes the democratic institutions. The "Lucanian togas" investigation was emblematic in that sense: it made you understand how corruption is actually within the magistrature, inside the forces of order. And you realise that the battle becomes very difficult because your principal enemy is in the next-door room; the person who should help you is actually the one who betrays you and colludes with external criminal powers. That, today, is the great risk for Italy: that the Mafia, organised crime, gangs and corruption increasingly have the face of the lawmakers.'

I ask him about the Elisa Claps investigation and he winces, as if almost embarrassed by what it revealed. 'It's a very disconcerting case. Frankly it's fairly evident that there certainly was investigative incompetence, undervaluations, omissions. It's easy to see that there were complicities. I've got to say, it's a very worrying case.'

The search for a sixteen-year-old girl has, unexpectedly, led me somewhere completely different. Rather than getting closer to understanding what happened to Elisa, I'm getting closer to understanding why Italy is the way it is and why, perhaps, Elisa has never been found. The generous interpretation would suggest cock-up rather than conspiracy: since there's precious little meritocracy, provincial investigators had been promoted far beyond their capabilities and were simply not up to the job. They were so incompetent that blood-stained clothes weren't confiscated and a presumed crime scene wasn't searched. The less generous interpretation is that of conspiracy, that the Elisa Claps case involved people who felt their position or power were threatened by the investigation and who duly did everything they could to mislead it. The vast majority of people in Potenza, and the Claps family in particular, favour the second, more cynical, interpretation. In some tangential way, the case appeared to touch those who were at the epicentre of power in the provincial city: the director general of the city's hospital, the director of the city's National Library, and so on. And the more the people of Potenza perceived the case as one which was 'hot', the less inclined they were to come forward with information and be dragged through the newspapers and courts. It's extraordinary that, for the first ten years of appeals on *Chi l'ha visto?*, there was only one phone call to the production team. Gildo would, years later, write with understandable bitterness about the city's reticence:

> I'm convinced that it all came down to the fact that the disappearance of my sister had unexpectedly rippled the placid surface of hypocrisy under which the life of this little provincial city moved. The event itself and that which later sprung from it had inevitably interrupted this apparent idyll. Behind the shiny patina of the happy island there was, everywhere, human destitution. What was important was that all that remained hidden behind the mirror of respectability . . . the word *omertà* echoed often in our appeals, irritating the conformists and hypocrites . . . we were guilty of having shed a light on a city that until then had serenely slept lying on a reassuring cushion.

The more silence and *omertà* surrounded the case, the more the conspiracy theorists believed they were correct in glimpsing darker powers at work. It led to that familiar feeling in Italy that there's an invisible power behind every visible one; a sense that anything of any importance becomes part of a battle between political parties that divide up the cake of power according to precise percentages and boss territories as jealously as organised crime; a sense that justice is never done and that nothing is impartial, that nothing is noble and disinterested; that jobs are so scarce that any post is filled not on merit but on recommendation from the powerful, so that favouritism supplants competence and, therefore, even if someone is honest, they might just not be up to the job; and that person, unwittingly incompetent or knowingly corrupt as may be, will always have to show gratitude for that job, and show it in a range of ways that might include turning a blind eye; and the higher you go, the greater the compromises, the greater the gratitude needed until, in the end, the system repeats itself. In among all that, the disappearance of a young girl could seriously upset the apple cart, and few, it seemed, wanted to risk the system to find her.

*

But if the Cannizzaro–Genovese axis seemed to affect the way in which Elisa's disappearance was investigated, there was another institution that behaved in an even more reprehensible manner; an institution that should have opened its doors to the terrible suffering of Elisa's family but which, instead, literally slammed doors in their faces. The Chiesa della Santissima Trinità was the personal fiefdom of a man called Domenico Sabia, known to everyone as Don Mimì. A short, shrewd man with thin, tightly combed hair, he was conservative and haughty. He liked his sermons to last exactly eight minutes. He had left Potenza on the very afternoon of Elisa's disappearance and, ever since, had wanted nothing to do with the family's desperate investigations. When Filomena

organised discreet boxes to be left in various churches in case anyone wanted to leave an anonymous tip-off, Don Mimì refused to
allow one in his church. When bells were rung from church towers across the city on one of the anniversaries of Elisa's disappearance, Don Mimì refused to allow his bells to be tolled. When an
architect, and later an investigator, sought permission to go to the
upper floors of the church, they were both told it was impossible.
He gave the same blank refusal to Elisa's mother, who would recall
years later: 'Don Mimì Sabia never deigned to let me see inside his
church, where I was convinced Elisa had remained: that left in me
a doubt.' Filomena once confronted him, sarcastically thanking
him for all the help he had given in the search for her daughter.
His reply astonished her: 'I don't know Danilo Restivo,' he said,
'and I didn't know your daughter.' The past tense with reference
to her daughter alarmed Filomena and she wondered what the
priest knew to use that tense. His protestation that he didn't know
Danilo was also, very soon, shown to be false, as a photograph
emerged of Don Mimì standing next to Danilo at the time of his
eighteenth birthday party.

Don Mimì's obstructionism had a worrying precedent. Almost
exactly a year before Elisa's disappearance, in September 1992, a
young woman called Cristina Golinucci went to see her confes-
sor and spiritual director, Padre Lino. He lived in a Capuchin
monastery in Cesena, far to the north in Romagna. Cristina's blue
Fiat Cinquecento was found outside the monastery, but Cristina
had disappeared. Her family went to the monastery two days later
with a dog, hoping to search for her, but Padre Lino, amazingly,
refused them entry. Confronted with a terrified, confused family who were convinced the answer to Cristina's disappearance lay
within that sacred sanctuary, Padre Lino turned his back and shut
the door on them. Cristina has never been found, even though the
prime suspect was, it seems, living in the monastery at the time of

her disappearance. The monastery was only searched an incredible five years later, by which time, inevitably, there was nothing to be found.

Faced with the agony of the Claps family, the behaviour of Don Mimì was inexplicable. It seemed to many that he was wilfully obstructing every attempt to arrive at the truth. His sudden disappearance that fateful Sunday afternoon also aroused suspicion. Surely it was inconceivable that he had had a hand in Elisa's disappearance, but some began to wonder if he had knowledge of her fate, of what had happened to her that day. How else to explain his dogged refusals for co-operation and his adamant stance that no one could ever search his church? There's an old saying in Italy that goes '*La Chiesa non si tocca*' – 'You don't touch the Church' – and never before had it seemed so apt. But even if Don Mimì did have knowledge of Elisa's fate, it was hard to understand why he should have constantly thwarted investigations. The most plausible explanation was that he didn't want the sacred space of his church sullied; the more paranoid explanation was that Don Mimì was eminently blackmailable because he had vices of his own and that he was being forced to foil all attempts at the truth. Those vices, alleged one investigator, were hardly original, but they were potentially explosive: Don Mimì had gathered about him various gay men in a study centre on the first floor of his church. The centre was called the Centro Newman, named after the British Catholic convert of the nineteenth century. Don Mimì, it was said, was an active homosexual, one who was, indeed, extremely close to the all-powerful politician from Potenza, Emilio Colombo. Colombo, in fact, worshipped at the Chiesa della Santissima Trinità; he lived a stone's throw away. And Colombo himself had unusual habits: in 2003, two of his bodyguards were arrested for placing regular orders for cocaine. The by then eighty-three-year-old former prime minister and senator for life admitted that the drugs were for himself, and that he regularly used cocaine for therapeutic purposes. It was an extraordinary admission, not least because it came in the midst of investigations into the supply of sex and drugs to high-society figures in Rome.

None of which, perhaps, is particularly illuminating for the Elisa Claps case. The admission that Colombo was, in his eighties, a cocaine user and that Don Mimì wasn't celibate doesn't shed any light on what happened to Elisa. But what it does demonstrate is the anthropological backdrop against which her disappearance occurred; it shows why, perhaps, some people could be leant on to make sure that she was never found. Once again, two of the most powerful people in Potenza had habits they wanted to keep hidden. All of which reminds me of that great comedy set in Basilicata in the 1930s called *Anni ruggenti*. In it an insurance broker is mistaken for a Fascist inspector sent from Rome, and the whole town is suddenly terrified of all the dark secrets the inspector will unearth: 'If an inspector wants to find something that's not right, well . . .' says one character, implying that we all have our weaknesses. Another says, 'I've got a few little sins . . . and who hasn't?' It's a line that is often heard in real life and is, in fact, a defence frequently deployed by Silvio Berlusconi: not that he's innocent, but that everyone else is just as guilty. That's the sense you get as you scratch the serene surface of life in Potenza. Everywhere you look there's some element of institutional life that isn't what it seems or isn't what it purports to be. Those who are supposed to be the upholders of civic virtue appear to have cupboards bursting with skeletons. What they are prepared to do in order to keep those cupboards closed is anyone's guess.

It certainly makes you look at the Catholic Church with very different eyes. Back in the 1960s, Ann Cornelisen spent years in Basilicata and wrote that 'in southern Italy the facts of life are simple: without at least the tacit approval of the Church no outsider will last more than forty-eight hours'. She looked at the 'black-garbed army' and concluded that 'the social and economic force of the Church has never been progressive. Its temporal aim has been the preservation of its own power, and while it has succeeded, it must also take much of the blame for the poverty and degradation of Southern Italy.' She wondered with amazement at how priests could ease 'quietly onto the plateau of immunity that unwritten Southern law allows distinguished personages. Whatever he does will be sanctified by official right and no matter how question-able his methods may be, no one would dare investigate or even complain.'

But if there's one thing I've learnt over the years it's that Italy is a land of contradictions. When you begin to feel confident that you can safely make some assertion, you realise that, weirdly, the exact opposite is also true. And just as I was on the verge of conclud-ing, not for the first time, that the Catholic Church in Italy has a hugely deleterious effect on the civic life of the peninsula, a priest emerged who demonstrated quite the contrary. He was someone who accompanied people through their darkest sufferings, who constantly demanded the truth, someone who never stood on cer-emony but who worked tirelessly for those who had undergone terrible injustices. Don Marcello Cozzi was from Basilicata. He worked for the anti-Mafia organisation Libera. Tall and thin, he was bald and wore glasses. He barely ever wore the livery of a priest, preferring to wear trainers, jeans and a polo shirt. He looked normal, but behind that front of normality was a man who was exceptionally courageous: he had written a book called *Quando la Mafia non esiste* (*When the Mafia Doesn't Exist*), an ironic echo of the old line that in Basilicata there's no organised crime. Cozzi had shown just the opposite and had named names. The Calabrian doctor, Michele Cannizzaro, was inevitably suing him for libel.

Cozzi asked an intermediary, a Rai journalist, to arrange a

meeting with Gildo Claps. Gildo wasn't keen to meet him; he disliked priests and everything they stood for. But he wearily agreed to meet Don Marcello. When they met, Gildo was surprised by the young, lithe priest and the informality of his appearance.

'Let's go somewhere quiet to talk,' Don Marcello said softly.

Gildo looked at his watch, not sure what they had to talk about.

'I won't take much of your time,' the young priest said.

Gildo nodded his assent and followed him into a nearby room with a bare, wooden bench.

'Like many people', Don Marcello began, 'I've followed this case through the newspapers, and now I've felt the need to know another story, that of the family that has been able to support all this for years. I wanted, through you, to know Elisa, what she was like before the whole of Italy could see her smiling face in those photos . . .'

There was something in the solicitous way that Don Marcello spoke that opened the floodgates. Having battled to be heard for years, Gildo finally found himself sitting next to someone who was prepared to listen to everything he said, to take seriously his every suspicion. He sat there on the bench and poured out the years of suffering, the humiliations and heartaches and the indifference of the institutions. Don Marcello simply sat there, asking occasional questions or requesting clarifications. At the end of it, Gildo asked him why he had wanted to meet up.

'What else should a priest do,' he said, 'if not take on the suffering of others and try to alleviate them?'

'How are you going to help us?' Gildo said, straight as ever.

'The only way I know is to walk alongside you. I've had confirmation from your words of something I had imagined, that someone doesn't want the truth to come out, and together we'll do everything to demonstrate how wrong they are.'

It was the start of a long friendship. Don Marcello began, with

Gildo, organising events, meetings and processions. He went on local radio and TV stations to keep the fading memory of Elisa alive. He read and reread all the legal material surrounding her disappearance and contacted people like Eliana De Cillis, pleading with her to tell the truth about that Sunday so many years ago. He even appealed publicly to Danilo Restivo, asking him, too, to reveal the truth about Elisa's disappearance. It was all to no avail.

I call Don Marcello and arrange to meet him in the offices of Libera. They are in a small building down an alley. Inside there are posters of previous campaigns. Don Marcello's own office has a large poster of Elisa on the wall, alongside various commemorative plaques and quotations about the Shoah. He's got the usual rimless glasses and is, unlike many priests, entirely informal. He's wearing a blue T-shirt and sandals.

I ask him whether he's uncomfortable about the behaviour of the Catholic Church towards the Claps family. He nods. 'Without doubt, we should side with those who suffer, with those who have suffered injustices, and that means that we should always accept the truth, whatever the truth, without making allowances for anyone, either for ourselves or for the Church. Truth is more important than the Church. I'm convinced of this: siding with Elisa, and with the family of Elisa, means siding with God, the God of the suppressed. Who hides the truth, even if he's a priest, isn't on the side of God.'

We get to talking about the Claps family, and he runs out of superlatives to describe their determination, their strength and their courage. Filomena, Elisa's mother, 'is an oak tree'. She's small, he says, but has so much inner strength that nothing will get in her way. He describes how much her husband, Antonio, has suffered and details the sheer doggedness of Gildo and Luciano. 'Those brothers', he says, 'have lived a double injustice. Not just the killing – because by now I talk of killing – not just the killing of

Elisa . . . but also the people who covered up, who deviated and sanded up the investigations, they committed a second murder because they didn't allow Gildo and Luciano to live a normal life. They've spent their adult lives looking for a little sister who wasn't there any more. I sometimes wonder how they do it. Elisa's assassin killed only Elisa, but those who came afterwards wounded an entire family.'

Don Marcello makes it very clear that, whatever happened to Elisa, there was a determined cover-up, that many people were colluding to ensure that the truth never came out. 'I'm coming round to the idea that the person who can help us understand many things is Danilo's father. He and Danilo should explain to us what happened that morning, what happened when Danilo returned home, what was said, what they did.' He looks up at the ceiling briefly and shakes his head. 'They'll never do it.'

I ask him what Danilo is like. 'He's a person with multiple personalities, an imbalanced but lucid person. He's too lucid to be mentally ill. And during his trials he was tranquil, even arrogant. He was so arrogant that he allowed himself to challenge the Claps family, to insult them in various ways.' As we talk about the case, I can understand why this priest has become such a close confidant of the Claps family: he's thoroughly informed about the facts, he's amusingly ironic about the ludicrous overlaps of power, and he exudes an empathy and warmth. You can tell from the posters in his office that he has dedicated his life to the underdog and to those who suffer. He shakes his head in dismay as he lists all the tiny details of the case: 'If a film director had had to think of a screenplay of this type,' he says, 'he would never have imagined it as complicated as this story of Elisa. I don't think that even the best director would have ever thought of such a complex screenplay.'

*

As the official investigation was stalling, another man began helping the Claps family. Marco Gallo was a private investigator, someone who had just set up his own detective agency in Salerno. Gallo's 'security and investigations' firm mainly worked for companies concerned about confidentiality and financial security. Gallo himself was charismatic and had film-star good looks: he was young, tall and tanned, like a cross between Bruce Willis and Roberto Saviano, the author of *Gomorra*. He was also idealistic: he had studied theology and was a devout Catholic, albeit one who was often scathing about the Catholic Church. He offered to work for the Claps family pro bono, and they, by now at their wits' end and suspecting that the official investigation would never make any headway, gratefully accepted. Little did Gallo know, when he made the offer, that he would work for the family for over a decade.

Gallo began investigating all the protagonists in the case. He did extensive research into the Restivo family, into Don Mimì, into all the minor characters who had, over the years, led the investigation astray. He suspected, like the Claps family, that Danilo must have killed Elisa and hypothesised that her body might be found in the garden of a juvenile seminary in Viale Marconi. The location itself was suggestive: it was at the exit of the escalator that was under construction close to the Restivo household back in 1993. It was also where Restivo's father's National Library had been housed. It was an area that Danilo would have known very well and, in January 2000, Gallo sought permission to conduct some excavations. After a few days, he discovered what looked like a femur. Gallo alerted Luciano and Gildo to the discovery and took the bone to an acquaintance for further tests. There was a possibility, the expert said, that the bone was human.

However, the investigator and the Claps family now had a dilemma. They had independently conducted their own research

Elisa Claps.

Elisa's mother, Filomena, with her daughter's diary and a lock of her hair.

The Via Pretoria entrance of the Chiesa della Santissima Trinità.

Potenza.

A view of the Tyrrhenian Sea from Monte San Biagio, Maratea.

Heather Barnett.

Danilo Restivo.

Police cordon outside Heather Barnett's flat.

Gildo Claps putting up posters in memory of both his sister and Heather Barnett.

Gildo Claps talking to reporters outside Winchester Crown Court.

Professor Francesco Introna oversees the removal of Elisa's remains from the church.

Elisa's funeral, 2 July 2011.

Elisa's white coffin.

and, now that a possible piece of evidence had emerged, they knew that they had to hand it to the authorities. No one trusted the Potenza Questura any more: they had been shown to be completely incompetent, if not actually corrupt. So Gildo decided to take the bone to Sabatino Riccio, a man who had previously been extremely courteous and diligent in his investigations, but who had now been transferred hundreds of miles to the north, to Forlì. Gallo duly gave Gildo the bone, wrapped in cellophane. It was a strange object: Gildo didn't know whether he was holding in his hand the last, earthly remains of his sister or if this was, again, just another red herring. He didn't know whether to hope it was her or not, whether to hope for certainty or to hope, against all odds, that she was still alive.

Gildo phoned Riccio, who invited them to Forlì. He drove through the night with Luciano and their lawyer, arriving in the town at sunrise. When they told Riccio, however, about the bone in their possession, he became anxious.

'Don't get me wrong,' he said, 'I'm proud of the trust you have shown in me by coming here. During the short period I was in Potenza I must have evidently done my duty. But you must understand I'm in a difficult position. I can't take the responsibility of keeping this bone. I'm not even in charge of the investigation into Elisa's disappearance, and even if I was I would be obliged to inform the judicial authorities.'

Gildo stared at the carpet. He had driven all through the night only to be told, effectively, that he should go home. The three got back in the car and started the long drive back to Potenza. On the way, they called Inspector Pace and alerted him to the discovery. Once back in the city they handed over the bone and signed statements. The next day the Procuratore Generale heavily criticised the brothers and Gallo for conducting autonomous research and for failing to hand over evidence immediately. It was clear that there was no longer any trust on either side. Only weeks later were they informed that the bone wasn't human but, in all probability, bovine. 'It was difficult', Gildo reflected years later, 'to say whether it was a relief or a disappointment. But that interior conflict mirrored exactly the state of mind we were living in those years: on the one side, hope – like the flame of a candle which flutters with every gust of wind, bends, and when it seems as if it's about to go out, it revives unexpectedly; on the other hand, the knowledge, dictated by reason, that the person you love is no longer living, united with the terror of finding yourself in front of that truth.'

*

Salerno is a big, bustling city on the Amalfi coast. It was, briefly, the Italian capital during World War II, when the Italian monarchy fled south from Rome after signing a peace accord with the Allies. There's a long walkway along the sea, a boulevard between mature trees. About a hundred metres from the shore are large, concrete dice, all lying at odd angles to protect the marina from the sea. There are a few bathers on the narrow strip of sand between the road and the boats.

I turn away from the sea and walk up Via dei Principati, one of the main roads that runs perpendicular to Corso Vittorio Emanuele. This is where Marco Gallo, the private investigator, has his offices. Gallo welcomes me in: he's got a five o'clock shadow, and the skin to the sides of his eyes creases when he smiles and shows his perfect teeth. He's wearing a white linen shirt and a silver necklace with a crucifix.

His office is deliberately set up to look almost like a policeman's: there are Italian and European flags behind his green leather desk. There are plaques and certificates, but also the gadgetry of the private investigator: a lot of screens, suitcases, phones and a memory stick disguised as a fountain pen.

We talk for four hours. To begin with, he's formal and cautious, slowly going through the case bit by bit, listing all the dead ends and diversions over the years. But the longer our conversation goes on, the more animated he becomes, until at the end he is freewheeling, letting off steam as he narrates, with disbelief, everything he has seen.

'This story is a disaster,' he says passionately. 'It's a complete, tragic mess. You never touch the bottom.'

'How do you mean?'

'Potenza is a very small city, but it's the regional capital. All the most important jobs in the province are there. And there is a handful of people who all know each other, who handle power, and they have the opportunity to manage the whole region. All the European finances go through Potenza; that is where all the commercial activities pass through, both clean and dirty. That knot of power isn't in the hands of two or three hundred people, as it would be in Rome, but just a few. It allows an exaggerated control of the territory: sooner or later anyone who wants really to work has to refer, directly or indirectly, to those people. The whole city is monopolised by very few people. There's a state within the state, a very strong association between people not for criminal reasons – these aren't people with criminal records, but important people with money. These people have a huge power and they form a group in which, if someone needs to ask for help, they can receive it in a very discreet way. And if they want to get in someone's face, they can. It's silent, intelligent, astute. It's a reality that doesn't appear in the newspapers, but it's a reality that everyone knows.'

'What's all that got to do with Elisa's disappearance?'

Gallo puts the fingertips of his right hand to his forehead, then opens out his fingers, a gesture to express his incredulity at what went on. 'You've got a missing person, and the last person to see her alive declares that his clothes had blood on them. What should you do? You arrest him, interrogate him, search his house. That's the basic ABC of any investigation. It's very strange that that wasn't done that day. There has been a series of cover-ups and deliberate false leads at various levels. Then there's a big, big question mark against the priest, Don Mimì, because it's come out from various investigations that he isn't a clean priest. He takes care of the great and good of Potenza. His church is a church of the elite, and it is frequented by the most powerful people in Potenza. They would certainly have had an easy job of asking Don Mimì to turn a blind eye because he was very blackmailable. Scorching truths have come out about him . . .'

Gallo mentions the priest's sexual vices, something I've heard elsewhere. He also says that Don Mimì is someone whose point of reference was the Vatican, not the local bishop. He is, says Gallo, a person who can be cantankerous, but who is cultured, very prepared, really intelligent. 'He has an image to maintain,' says Gallo, explaining why Don Mimì may have become complicit in a cover-up. 'If it had come out that he was homosexual, that he notoriously did things that were "unpriestly", everything he had constructed would have collapsed. He couldn't allow such a very serious thing to happen, to the point at which he kept within himself such a monstrous and incredible thing. It's ugly that someone who should help people with a spiritual discourse hides the truth and allows a family to suffer.' In his research, Gallo has obtained samples of Don Mimì's handwriting and taken them to a calligraphic expert. Gallo said nothing by way of explanation; he simply asked for an interpretation. For those who believe in such things, the expert's response was categorical: 'This person is keeping', they said, 'a very large secret.'

'The realisation', says Gallo, 'that not only the priest, but many people on other levels were ready to help a friend even when there was something so serious to hide causes me great suffering. It's not a problem linked to Potenza, to the people of Potenza, but a much wider, national problem that puts at serious risk all those values in which Italy has always believed. It's incredible: it makes you understand how much our social system has been undermined. By insisting that recommended people get the jobs that count, you end up losing your compass and the measure of life. It's shameful and dirty. The Claps case is a problem that belongs to everyone. It's not a case linked to a territory that begins and ends there, it's got the power of something much, much bigger: it represents one of the few violations from which civil society can be reborn.'

For Gallo, the Claps case is clearly a keyhole through which one can glimpse the dirty laundry of not just Potenza, but the whole country. 'Italy', he says, 'is a completely atypical country. What amazes me is the downturn we're now making. While in the past there were great statesmen, points of reference for the forces of good who established a minimum of decency, now there are very few figures who emerge from political intrigues. It's a very, very dark time and many people are leaving because they can't put up with all these shady deals.'

His fiercest criticism, however, he reserves for the Catholic Church. He has written to various top-level priests to persuade the Church that it should come clean about what it knows about the Claps case, but has had no response. 'I wrote to them', he says, shaking his head, 'to ask them to give me a hand to make the crystalline truth come out. They did nothing. We can't be content with the simplistic response that the Church is made up of men. In continuing to hide the truth, they only show how very little of anything spiritual there is in the Church. Don Marcello Cozzi is the only priest who's putting himself against the local church.

He's the only person who's giving hope to that family and to many youngsters. He's a person of great depth and courage.'

*

The hunt for Elisa continued in vain. Thirteen years after her disappearance, the city council erected a plaque commemorating her. A small rectangle at the top of the Via IV Novembre staircase, where Carlone had claimed he saw Elisa, simply read: 'Along this route on 12th September 1993 Elisa Claps disappeared. At a distance of 13 years, the city remembers Elisa and awaits the truth.' Years later the plaque would become something of an embarrassment: intended as a well-meaning gesture, it came to seem nothing more than a monument to disinformation. Elisa, it would later turn out, could never have been on that staircase, and putting a plaque there was akin to memorialising not Elisa but the *depistaggi*, the deliberate derailings. But that discovery was still four years away.

A year later, on the fourteenth anniversary of Elisa's disappearance, there was another false lead. The TV programme *Chi l'ha visto?* interviewed an anonymous source, an entrepreneur from Potenza who said he had vital information about Elisa. The man claimed to have heard six years ago a confession from a drug addict with AIDS who had himself heard what had happened to Elisa. She had been taken to a building called the Palazzo Loffredo, a place that was still, more than a dozen years after the 1980 earthquake, under reconstruction. The man who had taken her there made some unwelcome advances and, in the course of the ensuing struggle, she accidentally fell and fatally injured herself. The man in question asked his family for help and they, in turn, asked help from a *personaggio eccellente*, a wealthy man with masonic and Mafia connections. Elisa's body was dissolved in acid. It was another incredible, improbable story that was completely unaccompanied by any evidence or factual support. It briefly held the attention of both the public and investigators before, like many before it, being proved to be false.

The Claps family, however, constantly had to put up with having salt rubbed in their wounds. Phone intercepts from De Magistris's investigation into *'Toghe lucane'* had revealed the contempt that certain investigators felt towards the Claps family. The head of the Potenza flying squad, for example, was heard to suggest that Elisa had definitely run away from home: 'I too would have run away from a family like that. An non-existent father, two brothers and a mother who are all obsessive, who could have put up with that house?' She said Gildo was *pazzo* – mad. When that woman, Luisa Fasano, was openly criticised on *Chi l'ha visto?* for her contempt towards the Claps family, she sued the programme for 200,000 euros in damages. It was the umpteenth example of the complete inversion of logic and ethics: the person who had gratuitously insulted the Claps family felt insulted by the representation of her own insults.

By then an extraordinary forum had taken off online. In 2007, a thread had been opened on a website called *Popolo della Rete* ('The People of the Net'). Called 'So many doubts about the Elisa Claps case', the thread quickly became a repository for every conspiracy theory and complex explanation for Elisa's disappearance. Everyone had their own version of what might have happened; there were over three thousand posts, many of them essay-length monologues containing ideas, hunches, suspicions and accusations. Everyone had a new idea or angle. Over 350,000 people had read the forum. What was intriguing was that many of the posts were vehemently defensive of Danilo Restivo: they suggested that the Claps family were organising a witch hunt against him, that he had been beaten up by police who had lost vital evidence to confirm his alibi, and so on. When Gildo, tipped off by the private detective Marco Gallo, visited the forum, he quickly realised that Danilo Restivo was behind at least one of the nicknames. For months Gildo and Don Marcello used the forum too, hiding behind other nicknames to provoke and contradict Restivo. It was, in a way, a virtual game of cat-and-mouse; a sign of how little hope Gildo now had that he was prepared, for hours every day, to read a paranoid forum full of blind hunches and disinformation in the hope of glimpsing a tiny element of truth.

And the truth about Danilo was, albeit slowly, beginning to emerge. He had become the archetypal drifter, shunned by people in each place he went. They called him *imbranato*, awkward or clumsy, and a *tontolone*, a dimwit. Various incidents had revealed his strangeness. He had made anonymous phone calls to friends in Rimini. Having failed entrance exams to become a fireman, he had started a fire near his house in order to show that he was capable of putting it out and being a hero. But the fire got out of control, and he had frozen, standing there – according to a witness – 'shaking like a leaf'. Everywhere he went there were reports of young women having their hair cut. It emerged that he collected photographs of missing women, including that of a young girl, Erika Ansermin, a woman who had disappeared on Easter Sunday 2003. A psychological profile suggested that Restivo had an antisocial disturbance. It was typical of people with such a disturbance, the authors wrote, that

> they can't conform to the social norms according to legal behaviour, they don't respect the desires, rights and feelings of others. They're often dishonest and manipulative in order to obtain personal profit or pleasure. They can repeatedly lie, use false identities, trick and simulate. Decisions are made on impulse. Individuals with antisocial disturbances tend to be irritable and aggressive and can commit acts of physical aggression . . . another element to consider is that of hair-cutting. Subjects

affected by fetishism use various objects or parts of the body, including hair, to reach sexual excitement. The forms of fetishism that involve open cruelty towards others are often present in people with antisocial personality disorders . . .

His family, too, began to appear troubled. There were reasons, it seemed, for his mother's worried, weary appearance. Her husband, the man with the heavy, serious face and thick eyebrows, was obsessed by Nietzsche and the bloodthirsty acts of female brigands. When police had searched the Restivo family house they had found various sex toys. One young girl recalled going to the Restivo house one evening, where a group of friends were playing the adolescent game of 'spin the bottle' in which chance dictates which couples kiss. Both of Restivo's parents were playing the game with the young adults. The *pubblico ministero* in Salerno who had taken charge of the case would write of the Restivo family that it had 'elevated an impenetrable, protective barrier' around Danilo.

*

By then, however, I felt I had got as far as I ever would with the story. That 'impenetrable, protective barrier' seemed so complete that I began to doubt that any truth would ever come to light. And I felt ready to go home, to move back to Britain. I had lived in Italy for many years and, having long been fascinated by the mysteries of the country, I was now becoming jaded. I didn't find them exciting or exhilarating any more, only frustrating. It seemed as if Italy was a country struggling with an absence of the truth. It was as if you were inside the most fantastical crime novel imaginable, but that there was never any denouement. No case ever seemed to reach a satisfactory conclusion in this country of smoke and mirrors. There were suspicions, but never convictions; there was much smoke, but you could never find the fire. Nowhere was that more true than in the Elisa Claps case. It appeared blindingly obvious to all concerned that one man was responsible for her disappearance; it seemed simply inconceivable that this strange, troubled fetishist wasn't somehow to blame. But various people appear to have muddied the waters, deliberately making what should have been an open-and-shut case amazingly *ingarbugliato*, tangled. If you picked up those tangled threads, they led you into the dark corners of the country, to places where the powerful seemed to gather, whispering to each other in discreet huddles. The threads led you into masonic lodges, into the secretive cloisters of the Church, to the fringes of organised crime. As ever, it was impossible to assert that those corridors had any part in the original crime, but it was, to say the least, coincidental that so many threads always ended up there. I could begin to empathise with the fury of the Claps family: it must have appeared to them, during more than fifteen years of looking for Elisa, that the powerful were constantly conspiring against them. The disdain and arrogance and incompetence of the investigators was one thing; but the deliberate sidetracking and derailing of the investigation was even worse. I had become good friends with Gildo and his family and, without being too emotional about it, I was sickened by what they had had to put up with. Elisa's disappearance seemed emblematic of a deep, deep malaise in the country, and – after five years of working as a reporter in Italy – I longed to go home.

But there were other reasons I wanted to leave. By then the country was under the control of a media magnate who was part clown, part godfather. A vain, womanising, sinister politician, he was – through his business and his media outlets – turning the country into something far removed from the generous, refined paradise I thought I had found when I first moved there in the late 1990s. There were, admittedly, all sorts of little things that irritated me about the country, but Silvio Berlusconi was worse than an irritation. I felt he was annihilating all that was best about Italy. He was slowly turning the country into a videocracy, a land where one person could spread disinformation and lies to millions of passive spectators who were hypnotised by the flashy, false glamour of television. Every month there seemed to be a new scandal, but nothing could bring him down: not the stories of bribery or of prostitution, not the gaffes or toe-curling vulgarity for which he was famous. There was no depth to which he wouldn't sink. But none of it made any difference: he was ferociously defended by his mediocre political allies and by his hirelings in the media. The man who had, in 1993, seemed to offer so much optimism for the country had unashamedly turned the Second Republic into something far worse than the First. There wasn't a trace of statesmanship or gravitas; there wasn't a hint of honesty or dignity. It drove me nuts and, having done my bit to warn of the danger by writing a book about him, I now yearned to go home.

So my Italian wife and I packed our bags and headed back to England. She perfected her English and learnt about the bizarre delights of snooker and cricket and country pubs. We had children. I was still writing and teaching. We bought a ten-acre woodland in Somerset and ran it as a shelter for people in crisis. We started the long, slow process of learning about forestry and about animal, and human, husbandry. Years went by and the details of the Elisa Claps case became a distant memory.

But Italy, like Al Pacino says about the Mafia in one of the *Godfather* films, just keeps dragging you back in. I had been spending a lot of time on the Dorset coast since I was a trustee of a charity down there. Like any self-respecting journalist, I would usually pick up the local papers when I went there, just to flick through them and see if there was anything of interest. A few years after leaving Italy, I was sitting in a cafe in Dorchester reading the Bournemouth *Daily Echo*. I suddenly saw a face I recognised next to an article about a new lead in the brutal murder of a young mother from a few years before. Heather Barnett was a seamstress who had, in 2002, been hit over the head with a hammer-like object. She had been dragged to her bathroom, her bra had been cut between the cups and her breasts had been severed. Bizarrely, strands of hair had been left in both of her hands. She had been found by her two young children, aged only eleven and fourteen, when they returned from school. They had run out of the flat screaming, calling for help. They were comforted by their next-door neighbour, an Italian who lived opposite. His name was Danilo Restivo.

I stared at the newspaper, unable to believe that a story that had started over a thousand miles away at the far end of Italy had followed me home to south-west England; that a story that had obsessed me for so many years, that I thought I had left behind, had now reappeared on my doorstep. Danilo Restivo was, obviously, the new lead in the murder investigation. I studied his face: the young, clean-cut man I had seen in the trials for false declarations in the 1990s now had receding hair and his cheeks were much more jowly. It looked like he had let himself go. His eyes appeared more bulbous than ever.

I put the newspaper down and looked out of the cafe window, going through a range of contradictory emotions: dismay that the incompetence of the Italian authorities had, apparently, left Restivo free to kill a young mother; astonishment that he had ended up here, on the damp Dorset coast; disappointment that I hadn't followed him, and the story, more closely in recent years; and – I'm rather ashamed to admit it – excitement that the story was now even more extraordinary than ever. In the years that I had been planting trees and rearing pigs, a tragic story from the Italian deep south had become an international one. I paid for my tea, got straight in the car and headed for Bournemouth.

Six

'Yet this one curl, untouched of time,
Beams with live brown as in its prime,
So that it seems I even could now
Restore it to the living brow
By bearing down the western road
Till I had reached your old abode.'
    Thomas Hardy, 'On a Discovered Curl of Hair'

Bournemouth is a genteel town on the south coast of England. It was called 'Sandbourne' by Thomas Hardy, who famously described it in *Tess of the D'Urbervilles* as 'like a fairy place suddenly created by the stroke of a wand and allowed to get a little dusty'. He wrote that it was 'a Mediterranean lounging place in the English Channel'. When Angel Clare first sees the town, he 'could discern between the trees and against the stars the lofty roofs, chimneys, gazebos and towers of the numerous fanciful residences of which the place was composed'.

Although it now looks rather august, it was only founded in 1810. Until then it hadn't been much more than unimproved heathland overlooking the sea, an area used mainly by smugglers and turf-cutters. But nineteenth-century town planners saw an opportunity and quickly built parks and pavilions and mansions. Sitting at one end of the so-called Jurassic coast, with its rich heritage of fossils, Bournemouth quickly became a gentrified seaside resort to rival Brighton and Torquay.

When you walk around it today, it appears a tranquil, cheerful place. It likes to present itself as the 'English Cannes', a place with its own beach culture, its own sand and surf. And it does, in a way, feel unexpectedly cosmopolitan: amidst the many pensioners are hordes of foreign students, there to improve their English.

In a recent survey, Bournemouth was found to be the happiest place in Britain, with 82 per cent of interviewees expressing contentment with their lot. What it lacks in excitement it makes up for in peace of mind. It's perhaps not surprising that Bournemouth was the first place in the UK to deploy CCTV cameras for urban surveillance. The place sometimes feels fairly sedate, which is why, possibly, it has attracted some melancholic, and surreal, writers. It's as if the facade of civility is so comfortable that writers are tempted to tear it away. Bournemouth has cropped up in books by Douglas Adams, James Herbert, Roald Dahl and Andy McDermott. This is where Robert Louis Stevenson wrote *The Strange Case of Dr Jekyll and Mr Hyde*. J. R. R. Tolkien holidayed in Bournemouth for three decades, and eventually retired there. It's also the resting place of one of Britain's most successful literary families: Mary Shelley, the author of *Frankenstein*, is buried in Bournemouth, as is the heart of her husband, Percy Bysshe Shelley, who drowned in Italy. Both of her parents, the radicals Mary Wollstonecraft and William Godwin, are also buried in the town.

None of those writers, however, could ever have invented the real-life, gothic horrors of what happened here in 2002. The Charminster Road area of Bournemouth is a typical strip of shops and cosmopolitan eateries: there's a restaurant offering Berber cuisine; a US diner; Ahmed's food store; a Japanese restaurant, the Nippon Inn; a Lebanese restaurant; and, inevitably, an Italian trattoria, Lorenzo's. In between those restaurants are various shops: a big bed store, a tropical-fish shop, a DVD outlet.

Tuesday 12 November began more or less normally for the Barnett family. Heather Barnett, known to everyone as 'Bunny', had got up at 5 a.m. because the old cat had been sick in the bedroom she shared with her daughter, Caitlin. After that, it was the usual rush to get the kids up, breakfasted, dressed and off to school. Heather was forty-eight. She had short, reddish-brown hair and worked as a seamstress, taking commissions for upholstery, dresses and curtains. She was raising two children by herself. Terry and Caitlin were fourteen and eleven respectively. The three of them lived in a peaceful, suburban street called Capstone Road. It joins Chatsworth Road just before the two reach Charminster Road. Their flat was on the ground floor of a petite, red-brick house, one of a row of identical houses. A white-gravel side alley led down to the entrance to the flat. There were small conifers in pots and old, vertical drains stained orange by the years. Just beyond the entrance door was a black metal gate into the garden that had been covered with vertical branches of willow for privacy. Facing the road were two windows: the bay window that was the bedroom Heather shared with her daughter Caitlin; and the frosted glass of the bathroom.

The children were running late and it was raining outside, so Heather decided to take the car and drop them off at school. In the car on the way home she listened to the radio. The news, as always, was depressing. The US seemed to be upping the pressure on Saddam Hussein's Iraq, with George W. Bush suggesting that war was likely before Christmas. Another Osama Bin Laden tape was broadcast. Firemen appeared to be about to strike. Sven-Göran Eriksson confirmed he would remain as England football manager. Police in France stormed a church near Calais where over one hundred asylum-seekers had been sheltering. A gunman had gone on the rampage in an Israeli kibbutz, killing various people, including two children. Only a few days before, a two-year-old boy called Nafez Mishal had been shot dead by an Israeli soldier in the Tel-al-Sultan refugee camp. Heather had no idea that tomorrow she would be the main story on the news. She parked the car, let herself back into the flat and sat down to work. She had barely begun when there was a knock at the door.

That afternoon, her two children came home from school. They shouted their usual 'Hi, Mum' as they walked in but got no reply. She was normally there when they got back from school and they both felt anxious at the lack of response. The radio was still on, the sewing machine was in the usual place, plugged in, but it had been knocked over. Terry walked into his room and put his bag down, while Caitlin wandered towards the sewing area, looking for her mother.

'Have you seen Mum?' she asked her brother when he came back into the lounge.

'No.' He shook his head.

They walked back into the little kitchen. She wasn't there. It felt strange. Caitlin went into the bedroom she shared with her mother and still couldn't see her. She began to sense that something wasn't right. The bathroom was the only room they hadn't checked.

'Terry,' said eleven-year-old Caitlin, 'I know something isn't right.'

She knocked on the door, but there was no answer. She pushed it open and began to scream. Terry pulled her back and went in himself. It was a moment that would scar both children for the rest of their lives. Their mother was lying there covered in blood. She had been horribly mutilated. Both children felt dizzy with terror and despair.

'Mum,' Caitlin screamed, 'Mum.' She didn't answer. Their beloved mother, they knew instinctively, was dead. They were sobbing, sent suddenly into a frenzy of shock.

Terry went to call the police and was kept waiting on the line for what seemed like a quarter of an hour. 'Come on, come on,' he said, trembling. 'Pick up the call, my mum's been murdered.'

When they did eventually answer, Terry stammered the details. 'My mum has been murdered. This is not a joke. She has had pieces cut off her – she is dead.'

Then both children ran out into the street, desperate to get out of the house they could never call home again. They were still shaking, screaming at the horror of what they had witnessed. A car pulled up across the road. It was Fiamma Marsango, the expat Italian who lived opposite them. Large and arthritic, she was slow getting out of the car, but her partner was quicker, coming up to them and trying to understand what the children were saying. He hugged them and brought them across the road to sit in his house while waiting for the police. He was a tall, bulky man they knew only as 'Danny'. It was Danilo Restivo.

*

Even the most experienced, world-weary police officers found the crime scene shocking: it appeared from the objects that had been knocked over that Heather had probably been in her sewing area, possibly sat down when she had been attacked. She had been hit over the head with a hammer-like object, then apparently dragged to the bathroom, where both her breasts had been severed and placed on the floor beside her. Most bizarrely, strands of hair had been ritualistically placed in both of her hands. Despite those strands of hair, it was a crime scene that offered few clues to police. It was what they call a 'cold start case', with almost nothing to go on.

A forensic pathologist, Dr Allen Anscombe, arrived at Heather Barnett's house at 20.45 on the day of her murder and pronounced her dead shortly afterwards. Her legs were stiff with rigor mortis, and he took the temperature of the deceased from the armpit. Rather than a normal body temperature of about 37°C, hers was 26°. The room temperature was 15°. He calculated the time of death as being between eighteen and twenty-two hours previously. Since Barnett had been seen shortly after 08.30, a little over twelve hours earlier, the pathologist concluded that the time of death was 'likely to be much nearer 8.30' than the time at which she had been discovered, shortly after 16.00. That suggested time of death was later substantiated by the fact that four calls made to Heather Barnett's landline between 10.56 and 16.16 went unanswered.

The post-mortem that Dr Anscombe conducted the following day underlined the gruesome nature of the attack. Scattered over the top and back of the head were deep scalp lacerations, the largest of these – a laceration measuring four by two and a half centimetres – was almost triangular in shape and had penetrated the skull. Brain tissue was visible at the base of this wound. Across the front of the neck, from two centimetres below the right ear to just below the left ear, an incised wound had cut through all the tissues down to the spine, completely cutting across the airway. The arteries had also been cut through. A knife had been used to remove the breasts, although Dr Anscombe didn't think that any degree of skill had been used. A shallow knife cut continued vertically down the abdomen for twenty-four centimetres. These were not random slashes; they displayed care and control. The dry, parchmented, yellowish appearance of the skin, combined with the surprising lack of blood, suggested that many of the cuts had been made after death. Although the jeans had been unfastened and pulled slightly down, there were no injuries to the genitalia. Heather Barnett's hands displayed lacerations, bruising and fractures typical of self-defence injuries. Dr Anscombe listed the localised skull fractures and noted that there was blood in the windpipe and infra-alveolar bleeding, suggesting that blood had been taken into Barnett's lungs as she took her last gasps. His conclusion was that Heather Barnett died as a result of head injuries, the likely weapon being of 'high input energy', probably therefore 'some form of hammer'. The whole attack, he thought, would probably have required no more than a few minutes.

Geoffrey Robinson was a forensic scientist also called to the crime scene at 211 Capstone Road. Bald on top with white hair at the sides, a short white beard and glasses, Robinson was precise and methodical. He examined every inch of the flat, noting that there was a lot of loose hair around the premises. The doors were totally intact. There was nothing, he reiterated, that suggested a forced entry. Nor, he thought, was there as much blood as might have been anticipated from looking at the wounds. Like Dr Anscombe, he thought it likely that the mutilation had occurred after death and that, given the relatively little blood present, Mrs Barnett had been subdued very quickly.

Robinson examined what bloodstaining there was, however. Blood that falls vertically leaves circular stains, but that which flies from a body because of an impact can cause a spray effect like that caused by the wheel of a car in a puddle. It's called spatter. Spatter stains are projected through the air, leaving elongated shapes like teardrops that then allow the investigator to understand the direction of travel of the droplet. Such staining is likely to occur when a hard object has hit wet blood, sending it flying. Through analysing such spatter staining, Robinson concluded that the likely position of Barnett when she received those blows would be somewhere close to the floor. She wasn't standing up. An upturned stool suggested that she may have fallen off it as the attack took place. The sewing machine had also been knocked over. The fact that there were no bloodstains of the type caused by vertically falling drops of blood certainly suggested that Heather Barnett wasn't standing at the time of the attack; and the damage to the back of the heel of her left-hand shoe was consistent with her being dragged.

Robinson concluded that at some point after being disabled, Mrs Barnett was dragged through the remainder of the workshop area, alongside the settee, with bloodstains forming on the throw.

She was then pulled through the short hallway and into the bathroom. He suggested that blood on the top of the side panel of the bath was probably a result of the severed breasts being placed there before being put on the floor. He noted a discoloration on Barnett's knickers. The stains were contact stains that were more pronounced on the inside than out, suggesting that they had been formed by the insertion of something blood-soaked. From microscopic examination of those stains, Robinson was able to ascertain that they displayed a patterning consistent with having been created by a knitted garment. In fact, fibres within the bloodstaining on the knickers matched five fibres embedded in blood on the bathroom-door handle. It was made, he thought, by a dark, blue-black acrylic textile. His hypothesis was that a bloodstained glove had been placed inside the knickers. He noted that Barnett's bra had been cut or ripped at the front, between the cups, and that hair had been left in both of her hands.

That hair was duly examined by two further forensics experts. Human hair grows from within the skin. When you pull hair out, you can sometimes see a white blob at the end – the root sheath material that is the nutrient. Under a microscope, that appears like a spring onion with the roots cut off. Each hair has tiny little scales that can't be seen by the human eye. These scales always point in the direction of the tip, so forensic scientists know which way up a severed hair should be. The section towards the root displayed sharp cuts, suggesting that a sharp-bladed instrument had been used. The DNA was extracted from those hairs by washing them to remove extraneous substances and dissolving them in a series of chemicals to release the DNA. That DNA was then taken and amplified so that the mitochondrial DNA sequence could be obtained. The hairs in Heather Barnett's left hand, given the tag PJB25, were clearly shown to have come from Barnett herself; mysteriously, however, the hairs in her right hand, given the tag

PJB6, provided no match. Those hairs had, it seems, been brought to the scene of the crime by the ritualistic assassin.

Another forensic scientist and crime-scene investigator, Philip Webster, examined the bloodstained footprints in the house. Luminol is a chemical used to identify minute traces of blood; it can detect as little as one part per million, causing a faint blue glow when a reaction occurs between the iron peroxide in the haemoglobin of the blood and the Luminol itself. The glow lasts for between eight and thirty seconds. Webster covered up all the exterior windows with black plastic, mixed up fresh Luminol, placed it in a fine aerosol mist dispenser and moved from room to room observing the reaction with possible bloodstains.

The results obtained showed that there was a fine spray of blood by the patio doors, an effect compatible with someone receiving a very fast, heavy blow. There were strips of blood from the patio doors to the bathroom which were compatible with the dead body being dragged. Bloodied footprints then emerged from the bathroom, the imprints of blood becoming slightly reduced with each step until, back in the sewing room, various bloodied footprints were superimposed. That superimposition, and the fact that the bloodstained footprints then stopped altogether, implied to Webster that the shoes had then been taken off and replaced with another pair. There was no trace of blood found in the hall leading to the front door. Andrew Sweeting, another forensic scientist, took impressions of the footwear from the lino, onto which he had placed a protein dye to enhance the marks. He was then able to identify the shoes as being a model of Nike footwear and estimated the UK size as between nine and eleven.

*

Despite all that forensic evidence, however, it was a case that baffled the Dorset police. Detective Superintendent Phil James was in charge of the investigation. A tall, thin man with a short beard, he has a rich West Country accent and the sort of dispassionate professionalism typical of a long-serving police officer. 'This murder is unique,' he told me. 'Normally murders are quite straightforward: a husband kills the wife, or vice versa. They're normally fairly simple and easy to comprehend. It's rarely ever so complex and difficult to understand. My first reaction was, "How bizarre." Effectively you had a murder for which the motive wasn't obvious. The offender had mutilated the body and had brought with him the weapons, hair and a change of clothes. You can't get more complex and incomprehensible than that. It demonstrates a high level of planning. Our immediate suspicion was that it was something to do with the family, and something to do with Mr Marsh [Heather's estranged partner]. He remained a suspect for a good few months.' Marsh appeared to be unreliable and uncooperative, leading police to suspect him of involvement in the murder.

That fixation on Marsh, however, led them to overlook some startling clues. The day immediately after his mother's brutal murder, her son Terry gave an extraordinary interview to police. The fourteen-year-old was dressed in black trousers and a black T-shirt, and spent most of the interview leaning forward with his chin on his left hand. Considering it was less than twenty-four hours since he had discovered his mother's cadaver, he appeared surprisingly composed and at ease, occasionally smiling and joking with the policewoman who was gently questioning him. He still talked about his late mother in the present tense, as if he still hadn't absorbed the fact that she was dead.

Terry painted a picture of a family that lived very frugally. His mother, he said, didn't watch much TV as she didn't want to waste electricity. She and his sister shared a bedroom. He described coming home from school and the strange silence in the house. 'I thought there's something wrong here,' he said. It was 'one of those feelings in our guts'. He and his sister went through the house until, eventually, his sister knocked on the door and went in the bathroom. 'She went absolutely ballistic. I saw my mum's legs and I thought, "Oh shit." I wasn't scared, I knew something had already happened.' He moved his sister away and then went into the bathroom, where he saw his mum lying on her back with 'blood everywhere'. When he phoned the emergency services, he was 'so calm it was almost unreal . . . more calm than I've ever been'. As he and his sister then ran out into the street, they saw Fiamma and the Italian man arriving home. Restivo hugged them as they both cried.

The vital clue came later. Terry said that his mother was obsessive about locking doors because 'she hasn't really got the money to replace anything if it did get nicked'. She 'tries to keep it locked all the time', he said of the front door. She was security-conscious, not least because when she was younger, in Sturminster Newton, a house fire had consumed many of her possessions. As the policewoman was asking the obvious questions, something emerged: the locks to the front door had been changed just one week before. Terry explained the reason: he had forgotten to take the spare key to school, so, to remind her to hide it under the carpet mat before he came home, his mother had hooked it over the door handle. But then that day a neighbour had come round asking her to make some curtains as a surprise for his wife, and, when he left, his mother couldn't find the keys. With the benefit of hindsight, it's a chilling, revealing insight. Terry describes the man who had come to ask for curtains and who he thinks might have inadvertently taken the keys: an Italian man, 'Danny', who lives opposite with Fiamma. 'The spare key is over at Fiamma's,' Terry says.

Indeed, after Danilo Restivo's visit to his neighbour to ask for curtains, Barnett even wrote a note to Fiamma, politely suggesting that Danilo had inadvertently taken her spare key. On the afternoon of 6 November 2002, she had put the note through Fiamma's letter box, saying: 'Fiamma, Dan popped over to see me this morning regarding a surprise for you. Don't ask questions and spoil it. I had a spare door key for Terry out on a table and I think Dan must have picked it up inadvertently as I've turned the place upside down and can't find it anywhere . . .' The key ring was distinctive enough: it was red plastic with 'ICE' written on it. That same night Heather sent an email to a friend saying that her spare key had gone missing. She also changed the locks. The fact that the strange Italian man opposite had seemingly taken her keys was a vital clue that the police missed.

Other evidence was presented to them but wasn't acted upon. Five days after Heather Barnett's murder, police were obtaining DNA samples for elimination purposes and visited 93 Chatsworth Road, where Restivo lived with Fiamma. Both Italians provided samples of head hair, mouth swabs and fingerprints. The police officer then asked what footwear Restivo had been wearing on the day of the murder. Restivo showed him to the ground-floor bathroom, where he indicated a pair of grey Nike trainers in the bath tub. They were soaking in bleach, something that was well known to eliminate any evidence of blood. The police officer took possession of the trainers, but that suspicious behaviour was barely noticed. The main suspect was still, it seemed, Mr Marsh.

Restivo was also ignored as a suspect since he appeared to have a solid alibi. He was able to produce a bus ticket that he had bought for the number 30. It showed the time 08.44 on the morning of 12 November, and was from the Richmond Park Road stop. He had gone, he said, to Nacro, a crime-reduction charity that works with offenders and those at risk of offending. Restivo had been studying there for some time and had, he maintained, stayed at the Nacro building until 15.45. Heather Barnett's white Fiat Punto had been seen on jerky CCTV footage returning from dropping her children off at school at 08.37 (the time on the CCTV camera actually said 09.25, but since the clock was forty-eight minutes fast, the real time was 08.37). So the purchase of that bus ticket only a few minutes later appeared to clear Restivo. He was never even a suspect, despite the fact that Rodney Brown, a bookseller who had previously been in a relationship with Barnett, had told people that she was scared of him.

Ten days after the murder, Heather's best friend, Marilyn Philips, made an appeal to the public for information about the murder. The following month, traders in the Charminster Road area of the town began collecting money for the two young children who were about to suffer the trauma of their first Christmas deprived of their mother. But despite the publicity surrounding the case, little progress was made. At the start of 2003, the Crimestoppers Trust offered a £10,000 reward for anyone offering information that could lead to the arrest and conviction of Heather's murderer. The response, as it would be throughout the long and meandering investigation, was disappointing.

*

In February 2003, three months after the brutal murder, police released an e-fit of a man they were keen to talk to, saying, in standard parlance, that they would like to 'eliminate him from our enquiries'. The man in question was thought to be between thirty-five and forty, clean-shaven, with pale skin and short hair, possibly receding slightly at the front. He was wearing a black leather three-quarter-length coat, jeans and black leather gloves. He was also carrying a black leather bag. One witness suggested that the man was sweating and had an unusual coloured splash below the knees of his jeans: an orange streak which, police hoped, would be fairly distinctive. By then, they also had CCTV footage of the man they were hunting. The image was taken from the same camera outside the Richmond Park Road pub that had captured the last image of Heather Barnett alive as she turned left into Capstone Road. The road was wet with rain and tree branches were being blown in front of the lens. But at 09.23 a man is seen leaving Capstone Road. He appears bulky, possibly wearing a hood or a hat. The camera zooms in on the man in the last frame, as he stands by a lamp post, but it's almost impossible to recognise any of his features. He is, at best, a blurry blob. The problem was that the CCTV camera was part of a 'multiplex' system, meaning that several cameras recorded their images onto the same device, swapping between one camera and the next to create a continual image of an area; there was no continual footage from one camera. Sometimes there were as many as thirty seconds missing from one camera, meaning that the one mounted outside the Richmond Arms pub didn't pick up the 'outward' journey of the mysterious man seen at 09.23.

That same month, on 7 February 2003, Heather was finally cremated. Against a backdrop of rising fear, police issued an appeal to taxi-drivers for any information. The local newspaper, the Bournemouth *Daily Echo*, published 400 posters that were put up around the town. 'Help Find Her Killer,' they said in large letters underneath a photograph of the deceased woman.

The lack of police progress was particularly worrying, as the normally tranquil Bournemouth had seen other brutal murders in 2002. It felt as if the relatively safe city was suddenly dangerous, especially so when the authorities were unable to identify, arrest and try any suspects. In May 2002, a fifty-six-year-old woman, Jean Rhoda Kenaghan, had been found slumped on the pavement, again in the Charminster Road area of Bournemouth, having been fatally stabbed. In the early hours of 12 July 2002, just four months before Heather Barnett's murder, a student from South Korea, Jong-Ok Shin, was walking along Malmesbury Park Road in the suburb of Charminster after a night out with friends. 'Oki', as she was known, had been in Bournemouth since the previous November, and her English, after eight months, was slowly improving thanks to a course at the Anglo European School of English. Just the week before she had celebrated her twenty-sixth birthday, cooking a Korean meal for the family who were hosting her in Shelbourne Road. Walking home on the night of her death, she was stabbed repeatedly from behind. It was a few minutes before 03.00. She collapsed to the pavement, with blood slowly draining from her body. When she was found, an ambulance was called and she was rushed to Poole Hospital, where she died shortly afterwards. The only details she had been able to pass on about her attacker were that he wore a mask and that he had surprised her from a narrow side street. The following Saturday Oki was laid to rest in the town's Roman Catholic Sacred Heart church. Her parents, relatives and friends filled the church as the bilingual service remembered her short life. At the end, many mourners left chrysanthemums on the coffin, which was then taken to Bournemouth crematorium. Oki's ashes were then flown back to South Korea with her relatives. It was a terrible transformation: a young human being had turned into nothing more than an urn of dark grey dust. No one noticed it at the time, but Oki had been – like Heather and like, one guessed, Elisa – killed on the twelfth of the month.

But if the Dorset police were struggling to make progress on the Heather Barnett murder, they were making suspiciously rapid progress on the murder of Oki. The force were under unprecedented pressure from the South Korean authorities to solve the murder; local businesses, too, knew that a quick, convincing conviction was vital if Bournemouth was going to be able to continue to attract the huge numbers of foreign students who flocked to the south-coast town to learn English.

The conviction they ended up with, however, was neither quick nor convincing. A young woman called Beverley Brown, a drug-user and prostitute, had been picked up for suspected shoplifting in the town and was taken, not for the first time in her life, into custody. Having been involved in petty crime for many years, she knew that she now faced a possible prison sentence and the loss of her children. PC Fen Luckham started questioning her, and slowly the interrogation took an unexpected turn. PC Luckham began asking the suspect if she knew anything about the murder of the twenty-six-year-old South Korean girl. As one police spokesman said years later, 'She tried to help by putting us on the right line.'

Brown's story was incredible: she spoke of driving to the murder scene with three characters called Omar Hussein, Big Mike and Darius. She said that Big Mike had an afro, a Jamaican accent and a gold tooth. She claimed to have seen the fatal stabbing of the South Korean student and then, she said, the men had returned to the car and raped her. Each time she told her version of events, names and details changed until, in late August 2002, police arrested Omar Benguit and, subsequently Nicholas Gbadamosi. When first questioned about the murder, Benguit didn't even know if the victim had been male or female: 'Is it, I mean, is it a woman, it's a bloke?' He had no clue who he was accused of murdering. Neither Benguit nor Gbadamosi had an afro, a Jamaican accent or a gold tooth. The mysterious Darius disappeared from view.

The first trial of Benguit and Gbadamosi took place in July–August of 2003. The case against them was always shaky to say the least. No forensic evidence was ever presented to link them with the crime. Many other suspects had been arrested and released before police detained Benguit and Gbadamosi. Even though Oki's last words, to both police and medical staff, were that a 'man in a mask' (presumably a balaclava) had attacked her, no mask or balaclava was ever presented as evidence in court. One was handed in by a teacher, Catherine Taylor, on 2 August 2002; she had found a green balaclava and blue zip-up trousers and duly handed them in to police, but no mention was ever made of them in the subsequent court case. Other clothes found in the River Stour were tested for traces of DNA but no link was found with either Benguit or Gbadamosi.

The entirety of the prosecution's case relied upon one witness, a heavy drug-user who mentioned the murder, and her own rape, only when she had been picked up for another crime weeks later. Both Benguit and the witness were regulars at a well-known crack house at 47 St Clements Road. What was extraordinary about the witness's statement was the clarity and detail she was able to offer, whereas many other heavy drug-users struggled to distinguish one day from the next. Mary Sheridan, another user and habitual resident at 47 St Clements Road, said in a statement to police:

> There was always a constant stream of visitors to the flat day and night. Many I cannot recall, even who they were or what their names are. I am a crack cocaine and heroin addict myself. Due to my habits, days and months roll into one and I cannot recall many things that have occurred. I have been questioned as to my whereabouts on the evening of the 11th of July. I can honestly say I have no recollection of that night, where I was or what I was doing.

The contrast between Sheridan's honest confusion and the suspiciously precise details offered by the state's only witness was stark. Many suspected that the pressure on the police from the South Korean authorities was steering the case. There was even a member of the South Korean embassy present at all three of the subsequent trials. And the unreliability of the state's witness was underlined when a large part of her testimony – that she had subsequently been raped by the perpetrators of the murder – was revealed to be entirely false. Indeed, many began to suspect that she was a manipulative fantasist: when she was placed in a witness-protection scheme she falsely accused her bewildered neighbours of paedophilia. She accused the police of harassing her, raising the suspicion that she was being 'coached' by them; they could only refute the allegation by claiming that she was, indeed, a fantasist who had invented their visits, a denigration that was hardly the ideal presentation of a supposedly reliable witness. Her testimony in court was described by Oba Nsugbe, Benguit's then lawyer, as 'bitty, incoherent, inconsistent and at times very vague. In a nut-shell, it is very unsafe.'

Towards the end of the first trial, concrete evidence emerged that the witness was entirely unreliable. Although she claimed that Gbadamosi was in her car, CCTV images were found that flatly contradicted her version. Nick Gbadamosi had been snapped on camera in his own car in another part of town. And there were plenty of other suspects that police might have turned their attention to. Oki's friend, Sueem Keem, worked with her part-time at a cleaning job at the Chase Manhattan bank. She recalled that Oki was being harassed by a young Korean man who would wait for them when they finished work. He had round glasses and wore his long, curly hair in a ponytail. The man in question, Sang Kyun Choe, was revealed to be a very volatile, strange character: he had already been evicted from his class in 2002 for aggressive behaviour towards female students. He was arrested and interviewed twice, but subsequently released without charge. Another South Korean man called Lee had had a brief relationship with Oki, but the woman had subsequently ended the relationship. It was possible that the man was resentful about the fact, and, indeed, a member of the family that was hosting Lee, Paul Durden, noticed that a kitchen knife went missing on 12 July 2002. He used to sharpen them regularly as that had been part of his job when he worked on a fish farm and, being one of a set, Durden noticed its absence. The knife reappeared in the top tray of the dishwasher on 14 July. Lee was interviewed and released, and subsequently returned to South Korea later that year. Both he and Sang Kyun Choe denied any involvement in the murder.

Jurors were understandably unconvinced by the prosecution's case against Benguit and Gbadamosi. Nicholas Gbadamosi was cleared of twice raping the Crown's key witness. But after deliberating for over twenty-one hours, the jury was unable to reach a verdict regarding the murder of Oki. Mr Justice Michael Morland called it 'the most difficult murder case I have had to try'.

By the following spring, the retrial of Omar Benguit and Nick Gbadamosi was taking place. The by now familiar version of events of the state's witness was rehearsed again, and once more the result was merely a mistrial. On 29 April 2004, a jury of six men and six women discussed what they had heard in court for eleven hours, but were unable to reach a verdict. They were, as in the previous trial, unconvinced by the evidence presented by the prosecution.

The Crown Prosecution Service finally secured, at the third attempt, a conviction for the murder of Jong-Ok Shin. On 31 January 2005, a jury of eight men and four women at Winchester Crown Court found Omar Benguit guilty of her murder. It had taken them five hours to come to a conclusion. 'I'm innocent, I didn't do it,' Benguit shouted from the dock when the verdict was read out. Marika Henneberg, a senior lecturer in Criminal Justice Studies at the University of Portsmouth, would later comment: 'It's a disgusting case. I can say without a shadow of a doubt that Omar didn't commit that murder.' Many of her colleagues were equally unconvinced and, when the verdict had been announced, journalists in the press box had looked at each other with bemusement, astonished that a jury could convict a man on such flimsy evidence.

In July 2005, Benguit appealed against his conviction, but three judges at the Court of Appeal rejected his bid. A petition to the House of Lords was also refused. Ironically, the attempt to clear his name fell on the third anniversary of Jong-Ok Shin's death. It was only years later that another possible suspect would enter the frame.

*

The breakthrough in the Barnett investigation had come in May 2003. Surprisingly, it had taken police that long to look closely at Barnett's computer. When they did, they finally discovered her email, the week before her murder, describing to her friend the fact that her keys had gone missing. 'We didn't find those emails until May 2003,' Detective Superintendent James told me, 'because you have a team of people working on an inquiry and there's masses and masses of work to do, and you have to prioritise that, and in the first instance you have to prioritise what you think will solve the case. Originally, looking at Heather's computer wasn't something that I imagined would solve the case.'

From there, they realised that the Italian living opposite needed to be looked at much more closely. Danilo Restivo had met Fiamma Marsango online. She was an Italian expat who was living with her two sons, and she was more of a mother figure to Restivo than a partner: she tried to help him learn English and scolded him for his endless childish fibs. Their house was slightly grander than the flat across the road: a semi-detached property, there was a tall hedge in front and an open drive that went through to a largish garden behind. It all looked very normal: there were compost bins and water butts and flower beds. The living room on the second floor overlooked Heather Barnett's bedroom and the frosted glass of her bathroom.

Soon after realising that Restivo was 'of interest' to the inquiry, one officer did an Internet search. As soon as he saw the results, and the endless articles about Elisa Claps's disappearance, he went straight to Phil James.

'Hey, boss,' he said, waving the printouts of the Italian articles he had found online, 'there's something else about Restivo. You've got to see this.'

James held out his hand and skimmed through the sheets. He didn't understand much of it. It was all in Italian, but he recognised the photo of Restivo that accompanied many of the articles.

'He's the main suspect in a missing-person case out in Italy. Young girl of sixteen went missing,' the officer explained.

James looked at the photo of Restivo again and suddenly understood that, finally, he had a serious lead. When he dug further and the story of Restivo's hair fetish came out, many of the team felt sure they had their man. Until then, as James told me years later, Restivo was seen just as a bungling man who spoke little English. 'I was led to believe', James said, 'that he had an alibi and was at Nacro.' Police quickly began to realise that behind Restivo's bungling, awkward front, however, there was a clever, calculating criminal. His well-practised persona – a bit dippy, rather pathetic, slightly childish and very hypochondriac – was nothing more, they began to think, than an elaborate disguise. It had fooled them at first sight and, until May 2003, they had never given him a second thought.

From there the investigation snowballed. At Nacro, there was a log book which was used by students to sign their floppy disks in and out. The original time that Restivo had logged out his disk on the morning of Barnett's murder was clearly 10.28; it had subsequently been crossed out and replaced by 09.00. It was, it seemed to police, as if Restivo had written the real time at which he had entered Nacro that morning, realised his mistake, and then tried to amend it. Police began to surmise that the bus ticket bought by Restivo on the morning of the crime had simply been purchased to shore up his well-planned alibi. An officer walked the route back to Heather Barnett's house as if Restivo had got off the bus after one stop, and it took only eight minutes. If he had chosen a long way round to avoid being seen, it would only have taken eleven minutes. He could easily have been at the flat by 09.00 that morning.

In the autumn of 2003, the Dorset police went public with some astonishingly detailed forensic analysis of the nine-centimetre-long strands of hair that had been found in the right hand of Heather Barnett. A senior lecturer in environmental radioactivity at Reading University, Dr Stuart Black, had conducted a detailed chemical analysis of the hair, and the results offered a tantalising glimpse into the life of the person from whom it had been cut: they had lived in the UK but had travelled to Spain (between Valencia and Almeria) or possibly southern France (between Marseille and Perpignan) about seventy-eight to eighty-four days earlier. And between eighteen and twenty-six days before the hair had been cut, the person involved was in the Tampa area of Florida. The person in question had also twice changed their diet. With that much detail, the police felt confident they would be able to trace the person involved and, they hoped, prove a link between that person and the perpetrator of the horrific murder.

On the anniversary of the death of Heather Barnett, detectives made public the details of the print of the trainer found at Barnett's house in Capstone Road. Police officers had flown to America to identify the trainer from which the print originated: it was, they thought, a Nike Terra Part Stormy. They hoped that the trainer would greatly narrow down the search for the murderer as only a thousand pairs had been sold in the UK. The trainers had been produced in four colours: white, black, blue and red.

All those details gave the police optimism that they would net the culprit. Indeed, they already had experience of capturing a murderer through a bloodied trainer print. Back in 1999, a thirty-one-year-old DJ called Adam Shaw had been stabbed almost a hundred times in his sex shop off Old Christchurch Road in Bournemouth. A footprint from Shaw's kitchen was identified by forensic analysts as being from a size-twelve Adidas off-road shoe, most of which had been sold through the Great Universal catalogue. Detectives searched the list of purchasers in Dorset, which led them to the home of Terry Gibbs, a troubled teenager. There were splashes of blood on his clothing and there was a positive match between material found inside Gibbs's jacket and material on Shaw's corpse. Gibbs was arrested, and he quickly confessed. He was later jailed for life at Winchester Crown Court.

This time, however, the police appeal was unsuccessful. Although the police were, as they said with characteristic understatement, 'interested' in Restivo, they could find little hard evidence to link him to the crime. His alibi had collapsed and his past had emerged, but there was nothing concrete they could confront him with: no murder weapon, no forensics and, certainly, no comprehensible motive. Months went by without any breakthroughs. Heather's former husband, David Marsh, now no longer a suspect, made an appeal. Police made public the grisly details of the crime scene, revealing the mutilation of Barnett's breasts in the hope that someone's memory or conscience might be jogged. This time there was almost a breakthrough. A woman called the police saying she had information about the murder. Immediately intrigued, they prepared to record the conversation, informing the witness of the fact. She immediately hung up, never contacting them again.

Police subsequently appealed for her to call again, insisting that they wouldn't record any resultant conversation, but to no avail.

By spring of 2004, however, the police were convinced they had their man, if not the evidence. Having placed Danilo Restivo under surveillance, they followed him to an attractive, isolated spot on the outskirts of Bournemouth. Throughout late April and early May, Restivo would aimlessly walk around the park between Throop Mill and Pig Shoot Lane. It's a secluded area: there are swans and ducks in the water and tall pylons overhead. There are a couple of ponies in the next-door meadow. The grass is long and willow branches rustle in the wind. Police observed him from behind a one-way mirror in the back of a white van. They could see Restivo wearing round sunglasses, his characteristic bushy black hair and narrow mouth with thick lips immediately recognisable. He had parked his white Metro on a gravel-covered dead end on Pig Shoot Lane and was seen engaging in unusual behaviour: putting on and taking off gloves, wearing his hood tight around his face. On 11 May, he was filmed as he took off a shirt by his car's boot, only to change into a shirt that appeared exactly the same as the one he had just removed. He changed his shoes, too, and was seen observing women from a distance. Restivo was looking around furtively, bending down as a woman walked past, then just standing aimlessly with his hands in his pockets. He seemed to be constantly on the look-out, either to see if he were being watched or to see if there were anyone he could watch. It was, to say the least, strange behaviour. It was also a warm, summer's day, so the use of a hood and gloves seemed particularly suspicious.

The next day, the 12th, was a day of the month on which Restivo appears to have acted out his brutal fantasies in the past. On that day he was seen wearing waterproof trousers and walking around the same park. The surveillance team were so alarmed by his behaviour that they sent in uniformed officers. One of the officers, PC Ian Fryett, saw that Restivo was sweating profusely, with drops falling from his nose and his face. 'I had to calm him down as he was quite agitated,' PC Fryett would later say. In the boot of the car, PC Fryett found a number of jackets and bin bags. In the footwell behind the driver's seat was a black holdall that contained 'a large fillet-type knife and a packet of tissues'. He also found a pair of gloves and a balaclava in the pockets of one of the hooded jackets in the boot. In the driver's door pocket were two pairs of scissors, one black, the other orange.

When he was asked why he had the knife, Restivo claimed that he had found it in the park and that, seeing young children playing near by, he had picked it up in order to prevent them from getting hurt. It was hardly a credible suggestion: it was a school day and at no point in the continuous filming of Restivo did police cameras ever see any children or witness Restivo bend down to pick up the knife. He had clearly come equipped with it, a fact that was underlined when a knife block from his own kitchen was shown to be missing exactly the knife that he claimed to have found.

He had done nothing illegal: there was no law stopping him from watching women while being equipped with a filleting knife, balaclava, scissors and so on. But it was acutely worrying behaviour and it convinced police that Restivo was extremely dangerous. He was arrested a month later. For three days – 22, 23 and 24 June – police officers quizzed Restivo about hair-cutting, the Elisa Claps disappearance, his whereabouts on 12 November 2002 and his recent behaviour at Pig Shoot Lane. As he had done in the past, he stuck exactly to his previous version of events. Often he refused to reply, saying only 'no comment'. To their great frustration, police felt they didn't have enough evidence to press charges. They were left with no alternative other than to release him.

*

For years Gildo Claps had started every working day by doing an online search, typing in 'Restivo, Danilo' and trying to uncover information about his nemesis. In June 2004, he decided to conduct a search solely of English-language sites, and he was astonished at what emerged: an article from Bournemouth's *Daily Echo* recounted that Restivo had been arrested on suspicion of the murder of Heather Barnett. As Gildo sat in his office in faraway Potenza, he couldn't believe that Restivo was apparently, once again, caught up in a shocking crime; a crime which, he felt, wouldn't have taken place if only the Italian authorities had been more thorough in their investigations a decade earlier. As he read the gruesome details of Barnett's murder, his mind inevitably turned to his missing sister, and he began to wonder what on earth that beast might have done to her. Gildo phoned his brother Luciano, who repeatedly asked him if he was sure of the information. Gildo read out a few sentences in English and assured him that, yes, Restivo had been arrested. Then he got up, left his office and went straight to the Questura, to inform them of what he had found. He wrote years later about his amazement at now finding himself in a story which 'with its intrigues and *coups de théâtre* appeared ever more like the plot of a novel'.

The authorities in the Questura, however, already knew all about the Barnett murder. Indeed, the British police had contacted them via Interpol, and they had supplied information on the fetishist many months ago. Gildo was furious that, not for the first time, investigators had withheld vital information about Restivo from him. For months they had known about the Heather Barnett murder and hadn't even thought to inform the Claps family of the strange coincidence. Gildo decided to tip off the press, but, aware that he was about to leak the story, investigators themselves leaked it to local journalists and, from there, it became a national story. He contacted his friends at *Chi l'ha visto?* and decided, with them and his wife Irene, to go himself to Bournemouth.

He met Detective Superintendent Phil James, and the two effectively quizzed each other, sharing as much information as possible about Restivo. Gildo learnt that, just a few days before, Restivo had married Fiamma, the woman with whom he had been living for almost two years. Gildo immediately realised that, since in English law a person can't be forced to testify against their spouse, it might have been a marriage of convenience.

After the interview, the journalist from *Chi l'ha visto?*, Franco De Chiara, drove Gildo and his wife to the Charminster suburb of Bournemouth. They found Restivo's house, and Gildo got out to ring the bell. A student opened the door and explained that he was merely a lodger and that Danilo was out. Just then a car approached, and Gildo recognised immediately Restivo's profile. Restivo, too, recognised his nemesis and got out of the car, running round to the back of the house and closing himself inside. Gildo and Fiamma started shouting at each other. Restivo had retreated up to the first floor and, frightened like a child, was watching the scene from an upstairs window.

'Run away, run away as much as you want,' Gildo shouted. He could feel a decade's anger rising up in him and he gave full vent to his fury. 'Get it into your shitty head that you won't ever have a place to hide. You've seen how far I've come to find you? I've come to remind you that you'll pay for what you did to Elisa.' De Chiara, the Rai journalist, had by now jumped over the hedge and was pulling Gildo away. Within minutes there was the sound of police sirens. Danilo and Fiamma had called the police.

Soon afterwards Phil James and his team came to Italy again to compare notes with the Italian authorities. They took DNA samples from Gildo. Marco Gallo, the private detective working pro bono for the Claps family, also made contact with the British detectives, making available all the information he had gathered on Restivo. By now, everyone involved in both cases seemed convinced that, astonishing as it seemed, the disappearance of sixteen-year-old Elisa in Potenza was linked to a forty-eight-year-old murder victim in faraway Dorset. 'The person who took my little girl away from me eleven years ago', Filomena said to reporters, 'also took Heather from her children. I wish I could see them. When I heard of her death, my first thoughts were for the children, because they found her. I can imagine what they are going through. I think I can understand how they feel having lost a loved one, just like me. I feel a bond with them.'

Despite the conviction, however, that Restivo was responsible for both crimes, the investigation in the UK, just like that in Italy, began to stall. After Phil James's initial excitement at discovering the link, months went by without any further evidence coming to light. Summer turned into autumn, and Heather's sister, Denise, expressed her sadness that her sister's killer was still at large. It was, by now, two years since the brutal slaying of Heather, and the case was no nearer a satisfactory conclusion. Two years later, in November 2006, police almost acknowledged that the investigation had stalled when they publicly appealed for help in tracing Heather's distinctive key ring, the one with the word 'ICE' that had gone missing after Restivo's first visit to her house. Senior detectives travelled to FBI headquarters in Virginia to ask behavioural scientists to help them create a profile of the killer and his motives. 'There was a theory', Phil James told me, 'that Restivo wanted to kill somebody else, but couldn't and was too frightened. The hair placed in Barnett's hand was from the person he wanted to kill. He made Heather Barnett that person.' The trouble was, of course, that detectives could never identify the mystery owner of that hank of hair found in Barnett's hand. Even the FBI, according to James, shrugged their shoulders. 'They said', James recalled, 'that while they had some really strange people, they didn't have anyone like that. They didn't have any more understanding of it than us.'

The case featured on the BBC's *Crimewatch* in September 2006, resulting in 485 calls to the programme. It featured again in a follow-up in November that year. One of the people to come forward was Claire George. She had watched the mystery man in the CCTV footage shown on *Crimewatch* and thought it was Danilo Restivo. She knew him well: she had worked in the same Bournemouth pharmacy for twenty-two years and knew both Restivo and Heather Barnett. When she had first seen the clip she had said to herself: 'It looks like someone I know.' George told police that she could often recognise people by their posture, by the way they moved. He was also wearing a hat, and Restivo, she said, wore a hat practically all the time. The trouble was that police realised George wasn't an ideal witness: she already knew Restivo was a suspect. She had read press reports two years before stating that he had been interviewed under caution. In fact, a friend of hers, her daughter's dance teacher, Sonia Taylor, had had her hair cut surreptitiously on a bus, and so George had printed off material from the Internet about the local Italian man with a hair-cutting fetish. In short, she knew about Restivo and her identification wasn't entirely objective.

Over the years many people had come forward to testify that Restivo had cut their hair on Bournemouth buses. Sonia Taylor, the dance teacher, had been twenty in December 2002. She had been coming home from a morning shift at Topshop and had got on the number 31 bus that went along Charminster Road. At that time her hair, tied in a ponytail, went down to the small of her back. Shortly after she had boarded the bus she noticed a man get on who was asking passengers if they had change for a ten-pound note. Not long afterwards she felt a tug on her hair and thought it was caught in the metal bar above the seat cushions. 'It was quite strong, it hurt,' she would say later. She turned round and saw the man who had been waving the ten-pound note sat behind her. He had said 'Sorry' to her, and she realised much of her hair was falling out. Some of it was on the floor, but by then the man had got off the bus. She later identified the man who had cut her hair as Danilo Restivo.

Other victims of Restivo's hair-cutting fetish came forward. Holly Marie Stroud was seventeen and had been studying for her A levels when she had taken the number 31 bus from Charminster just before 08.00. It felt as if somebody were pulling her hair, as if individual strands were being pulled. Her hair, back then, had been very long, almost all the way down her back. When she felt a particularly hard tug, she turned round to see what it was. She thought it was maybe some child from school playing a trick on her but instead she saw a grown man. His hands were on the back of her seat and she could see his face staring straight at her. Stroud later noticed there was something sticky in her hair. There was an unusual smell, 'like menthol'. At school she washed her hair in the sink and saw cut sections of her hair going down the plughole. She noticed that the strange smell was also on her coat. 'It reminded me of Olbas oil,' she would say later. In June 2004, she identified Danilo Restivo as the man who had been behind her on the bus. In November 2005, after Stroud had left school and was commuting to Southampton, she saw Restivo again at the railway station, on trains and in Southampton itself. The implication was that he may have been following her.

Katie McGoldrick was another Bournemouth woman who had suffered a similar fate. An attractive girl with long, dark hair, when she was in year eleven she had caught a bus that travelled along the Charminster Road. A man got on and sat behind her. She could feel her hair being tugged and tried moving it, but then heard something that sounded like fabric being cut. There was a man right up against the back of her seat. The man got off at the next stop, at the Richmond Arms, but then stood and stared at the girl from the pavement. She later realised that about two inches of her hair had been cut. In June 2004, she was asked to look at photographs, and she picked out Danilo Restivo.

Mark Goddard had seen something analogous happen in early 2003. He had been working with the Crown Prosecution Service as an administrative assistant when he had got on a bus on Hendford Road in Bournemouth. He had sat on the top deck of the bus, on the right. There was a girl opposite him, aged seventeen or eighteen, with long, dark hair below her shoulders. A man got on who Goddard thought had a very strange appearance. It was a wet day, and the man was wearing a green and blue anorak. Goddard described him as having bulbous eyes, spectacles and dark hair. The man had sat behind the young girl and pulled some of her hair under the metal handrail of the chair in front and towards his lap. The hair and the man's hand were both under the anorak, which he had taken off, the clear implication being that the man was masturbating. In all, thirteen women from Bournemouth came forward to say they had had their hair cut.

The police decided to search Restivo's house. On 21 November 2006, Detective Constable Michael Davies, a tall, bald man with a tough, boxer's face, spent all morning combing through the house. He had arrived at 08.30, and it wasn't until 13.20 that he found something significant. At the bottom of a chest of drawers, in a plastic bag containing photographs, he found a lock of brown hair, tied together with green cotton. Those hairs, given the tag MJD2, were passed to Carole Evans for forensic testing. She had DNA samples from Luciano, Gildo and Filomena Claps; from David Marsh, Heather Barnett's estranged partner, and Heather herself; and from Fiamma Marsango, Restivo's wife, and Restivo himself. Those hairs, however, offered no match.

Despite overwhelming evidence that Restivo was bizarre, even dangerous, police still didn't have enough evidence to charge him with murder. They again appealed on *Crimewatch* in December 2007, but to no avail. They also made public appeals on Italian television: twice they went into the *Chi l'ha visto?* studios, hoping to trace women in Italy who had suffered the same hair-cutting treatment as those in Bournemouth. Various women came forward from Potenza, Rome, Milan, Rimini and Turin, and police took DNA samples from fifteen of them, still hoping that one of them would provide a link to the mystery hank of hair in Barnett's right hand. None of them did.

By 2009, Restivo was living a bizarre life. Under constant surveillance by Dorset police, who were convinced he was a dangerous murderer, he was also, allegedly, being threatened. In October of that year, he revealed that he had received bullets in the post. Two six-centimetre brass cartridges and an accompanying letter had been sent to his house. Restivo immediately accused Gildo of making threats against his life, something Gildo denied. By then, Restivo's house had become something of a fortress. There were two CCTV cameras outside it, one mounted on a tree by a bird box and another on the corner of the house. Every few months, when the Barnett murder became news for whatever reason, journalists would arrive to record a news item outside Restivo's house, and every time Restivo would deliberately start mowing or strimming, making as much noise as possible so that any recording was almost impossible. He wrote angry letters to niche newspapers back in Italy in which he made paranoid accusations and threats. He was surrounded, but police seemed unable to collar him.

There were, however, three vital pieces of evidence that, police felt, were very convincing. For years they had held onto the trainers that Danilo Restivo had soaked in bleach in the days immediately after Heather Barnett's murder. They were eventually passed to a forensic scientist called Claire Stangoe. There was no visible blood on the shoe, so she used a chemical called Leuco-Crystal Violet, a colourless substance that reacts with trace amounts of blood to produce a purple colour. Positive reactions were obtained from the inner sole of both trainers and the inside upper-toe area of the right shoe. The distribution of blood staining far inside the shoes suggested that someone wore the shoes with trace amounts of blood on his socks, and that that blood had been transferred to the trainers when they were put on. It was compatible, it seemed, with the hypothesis that the killer had walked back to the sewing area in bloodstained shoes and then changed into a new pair, hence the lack of bloody footprints leading down the short hall and out of the front door. It was impossible to obtain any DNA from the trainers, not least because bleach is known to have a deleterious effect on it. In fact, even Danilo Restivo's wife didn't appear to believe his story that he had placed the trainers in bleach simply because they were smelly. In a covertly recorded conversation on 17 October 2009, Restivo said weakly to his wife: 'I did not know maybe that bleach is *la varecchina* [the Italian term for bleach].'

'And what did you think it was?' Fiamma asked sceptically.

'Soap . . .'

'Oh, come on! You could have smelled it . . . Here it says "Fiamma", it doesn't say "stupid". Please don't go down that road, OK?'

Police had also confiscated the hard drive of the computer that Restivo claims to have used at Nacro on the morning of the murder. A forensic computer expert conducted an 'evidential capture' on it, and found that the computer had been powered up at 08.35.32 on 12 November; it stayed idle until the administrator logged on at 09.08.03 using the password 'Bethune'. Shortly after, an application appeared on the desktop of the administrator; the application was called Spondi Superbi and it had been downloaded the day before, at 09.52 on 11 November, from an Italian website. It had run automatically once the administrator had logged on and was deleted from the system that afternoon. Apart from that application, there was evidence of modem activity but no Internet activity, suggesting that the computer's modem was being accessed by another computer on the network. But between the time of the administrator log-on and 10.10.28 there was no evidence of any user activity. It was only at ten past ten that a user had employed a particular link to start an application, that being the first time since log-on that there had been any work done at the computer. At 10.33 there was the first evidence of Internet activity, as the user accessed an Italian website. Restivo's claim that he had been sat at that computer, working away, suddenly appeared very far-fetched. Moreover, the hard drive revealed that the computer had been used to search for updates about the Heather Barnett murder inquiry. The forensics expert had found 'unallocated clusters' relating to the news articles on the case. On 18, 21 and 22 November 2002, and on 3 and 7 January 2003, the computer had been used to view web pages relating to the investigation: police descriptions of a potential witness, the appeal to raise money for Heather's children, the £10,000 reward offered for information, and so on.

Even more telling was a green towel that had been found on the chair seat below the sewing machine on Heather Barnett's work table. Seventy-five by forty-five centimetres, the green towel had bloodstains on it, and the DNA profile from the blood matched that of Heather Barnett. There were also very weak reactions indicating the presence of saliva, and that possible saliva was submitted for DNA profiling. That sample, too, appeared to come from Barnett. How the blood had got onto that towel was a subject of conjecture: it was resting on a cream-coloured fabric that was also bloodstained, but the quantity of blood on the towel suggested that it hadn't become stained merely by being in contact with that fabric; and the fact that not all the bloodstaining on the towel was on exposed surfaces suggested that the towel was placed, or fell, onto the chair after staining. Since it was found away from the main areas of bloodstaining, it was thought that it might have been used by the killer to wipe blood from his face or hands, and it was therefore subject to extensive tapings: in 2008, those original tapings were examined for flakes of skin and submitted for DNA profiling. A mixed profile with contributions of DNA from at least two people was obtained: the DNA profile of Heather Barnett was recovered, but so were minor DNA components that matched the corresponding components in the DNA profile of Danilo Restivo. Claire Stangoe, the forensic scientist who had also examined Restivo's trainers, was asked to calculate the probability that those minor DNA components *hadn't* come from Restivo. She estimated that it was approximately one in fifty-seven thousand. It was as close, police felt, as they would ever come to a clincher.

But they still didn't feel they had quite enough to charge Restivo with the murder of Heather Barnett. Trace elements of DNA and bloodstains that were invisible to the naked eye weren't thought sufficient to convince a jury to convict him for the seamstress's murder. And so Danilo Restivo, the troubled, childish, spooky fetishist, was still at large in the spring of 2010. It was then that an extraordinary discovery was made in Potenza. Sixteen and a half years since she had first gone missing, the mummified body of Elisa Claps was finally discovered. It had been found in a garret at the top of the same church where she had met Danilo Restivo all those years ago. Finally the net was closing in on the 'barber of Potenza'.

Seven

'In the small circle of pain within the skull
You still shall tramp and tread one endless round
Of thought, to justify your action to yourselves,
Weaving a fiction which unravels as you weave,
Pacing forever in the hell of make-believe
Which never is belief . . .'
    T. S. Eliot, *Murder in the Cathedral*

The seventeenth of March 2010 seemed like any other day to Gildo. It was so long since Elisa had gone missing that he could sometimes get through a whole hour or two without thinking about her, without thinking about her presumed assassin or wondering where she lay. Her absence, terrible as it still was, had become normal. Even the many false leads and deliberate red herrings seemed to have subsided. The huge interest in the case that had been reignited by the murder of Danilo Restivo's neighbour in Bournemouth appeared to have petered out and the 'Elisa Claps case' had been relegated, once again, to small paragraphs deep inside provincial newspapers.

Gildo was driving back from a business meeting in Napoli when his phone started ringing. It was Fabio Amendolara, a young journalist from the Basilicata desk of the southern newspaper, *La Gazzetta del Mezzogiorno*. Amendolara's office was a stone's throw from the Chiesa della Santissima Trinità.

'Gildo? It's Fabio. Are you in Potenza?'

'No, I'm in the car, just driving back from Napoli. Why?'

Fabio paused, not knowing what to say. He had heard something, but didn't want to pass on gossip and hearsay to someone so directly affected by it. 'I just thought you should know . . . there's a lot of movement around the Chiesa della Santissima Trinità. I'll let you know if, you know, if there's any news.'

'OK. *Ciao*, Fabio.' Gildo put the phone down, assuming that the authorities were merely conducting some kind of inspection. Even the mention of that church gave him a pain in his stomach. It had always been the centre of the mystery, and each time he heard about it or drove past it he felt sick.

His phone started ringing again. It was Don Marcello, the kind priest in Potenza who had been one of Gildo's closest friends through the dark years of the last decade.

'*Ciao*, Gildo. Are you in Potenza?'

'No. Why?'

'Where are you?'

'I'm in the car, I'm driving back from Napoli. What is it?'

'Can you pull over?' Don Marcello's voice was serious. Gildo pulled onto the hard shoulder sharply, a chorus of horns cackling at him as he cut across the traffic.

'I've stopped,' he said.

'Gildo,' Don Marcello said softly, 'they've found Elisa.' He paused, allowing time for the news to sink in. 'She was in the attic of the church. She's been there all these years.'

Gildo could barely breathe. 'That cursed church,' he thought, 'that cursed church.' All the anger and sadness of almost two decades rose up in him and he collapsed forward, resting his forehead on the steering wheel. He described it later as a trance, a maddening rerunning in his mind of all the years spent running around, of the vain searches, the furies and battles, the desperation to persuade the world that Elisa would never have willingly left home of her own accord without a word. And all that time she had been there, in that cursed church which they had never even searched.

'Gildo, I'm so sorry,' Don Marcello said.

Gildo picked up his phone from his lap. He had forgotten Don Marcello was still on the other end.

'Are you OK to drive?'

'Yes,' he said mechanically. 'Who found her?'

'A worker. They had someone in there who was trying to find the cause of a leak in the roof. He had gone into a cramped garret using the light of his mobile and . . . well, he found her remains. That's all I know at the moment.' Don Marcello paused. 'What about Filomena? It's going to be public knowledge very soon, and someone should tell her first.'

'I'll deal with it,' said Gildo, the thought of his mother causing his strength to return. He called his brother Luciano and told him the news. Luciano was silent, absorbing the horror of what he had heard. Then he, too, asked what they could do about their mother. He was far from Potenza as well, and couldn't go round there. Irene, Gildo's wife, was working. Luciano said that he would send his wife, Caterina, around.

They both drove as fast as they could back to Potenza. Gildo's phone kept ringing incessantly. Clearly journalists had all heard the news. Federica Sciarelli, his old friend from *Chi l'ha visto?*, called him. She told him how much she loved him and then gave vent to her fury. As she angrily reiterated the facts – that Elisa had always been in that church, that she had never left it alive – Gildo felt the shock of the news giving way to anger too. For seventeen years he had travelled all over Italy trying to find clues and chase leads; he had driven thousands and thousands of miles to talk to people, to give interviews, to support families in similar situations . . . and now his sister had been found in the same, stupid church where she had last been seen alive. He put his foot hard to the floor, speeding the car across the flyovers and ring roads until he reached his parents' house.

His mother came towards him, sobbing. They held each other. In the end, Caterina hadn't got to the house in time and, despite Federica Sciarelli trying to keep Filomena on the phone, she had heard the news from two policemen who had come to her door. Now, though, both of Filomena's daughters-in-law were there. Everyone seemed in an incredulous trance. 'She was always there,' they were saying to each other, shaking their heads. 'She was there all along.'

*

Gildo and Luciano decided to walk up to the church. Already there was a crowd of journalists and members of the public, all pressing around the entrance waiting for news. Various policemen ushered the brothers into the cool church, a building Gildo hadn't set foot inside since 12 September 1993. They spoke to the investigating magistrate, Rosa Volpe, who told them that the removal of the body wouldn't start until the following day. They were asked, however, to go with their mother to the Questura, where they were shown photographs of various objects. Filomena recognised the images of the white top that she herself had knitted for Elisa; she recognised the glasses and sandals.

The next morning the brothers returned to the church. They had to wait for hours until, eventually, they were ushered upstairs. It was only then that they realised the extraordinarily labyrinthine nature of the interior of the church. Accessed either from behind the altar or from an external door on a side road, there were five staircases with ten steps each that led to a recreational area where the Centro Newman used to meet. From there, another staircase led to a small wooden double door that had been locked. Through that door was a cramped staircase leading to a tiny metal door with two locks, one on the inside, one on the outside. That door led to the roof. From there they could see the whole of Potenza. It was next to the base of the bell tower, and it felt as if they were at the apex of the city. Gildo thought sadly that this must have been the last daylight, the last view, that Elisa had seen before her death.

Between the bell tower and the sloping roof there was a narrow passage which led to the garret where Elisa was found. Across its entrance was a large wooden beam that anyone going in would have to clamber over or under. There were three more horizontal beams in there, about sixty centimetres from the ground, meaning that any movement was extremely tricky. In all it was roughly eleven metres by twenty. On the ground was what forensics would later describe as 'amorphous residue': woodchips, bird droppings, dust, and so on. The metal coils of an old mattress were also in there.

Inside it was dark. Only a halogen lamp powered by a noisy generator gave off any light. As soon as he stepped inside, Gildo had to leave. He couldn't cope with the nausea, with the thought that in that dark, dank place was his sister's mummified body. He retreated, leaving Luciano to go in alone. When he came out, the two brothers merely hugged each other in silence.

Gildo still had to confront old enemies, however. On the narrow steps leading down from that tiny garret, he met Mario Marinelli, Restivo's lawyer for the last seventeen years. The man who had worked himself up into a theatrical outrage at the accusations against Restivo way back in the 1990s, shouting absurdly at the court room in indignation, was now silent. His hair had gone grey and he had lost his triumphalism. Gildo watched him traipsing up the stairs, even now unable to offer condolences or sympathy. Then, having ducked past the large crowd outside the church, Gildo was walking home when he saw, by coincidence, Felicia Genovese walking along the same street. She had been the first magistrate in charge of the case, the one whose inexplicable errors had, he felt, allowed Restivo to remain at large and Elisa's body to remain undiscovered. She crossed to the other side of the street, then turned back towards Gildo. She asked after his mother, and he replied, with heavy sarcasm, that if Elisa's body had been found earlier, perhaps her pain would have been eased by the passage of time.

'My conscience is clean,' she said. 'I did everything I could.'

Gildo looked at her and smiled with derision. 'I asked you over all these years to give us explanations for all your failings, which, even today, I struggle to understand. I'm convinced that if you had believed us from the beginning, we would, in all probability, have found Elisa within a few days . . .'

That afternoon all the TV stations showed the images from Potenza of Elisa's remains being removed from the garret. From them it was possible to see forensic scientists in white overalls and, on a zinc stretcher and covered with a sheet, the fragile remains of a sixteen-year-old girl who had disappeared so long ago. When the stretcher reached the ground, there was spontaneous applause from the crowd that had gathered. From there her remains were taken to Matera for a scan and then on to Bari, where Professor Francesco Introna would perform an autopsy.

The reaction of the city of Potenza to the discovery of Elisa's body was one of disbelief and anger. The Saturday after the discovery over ten thousand people joined a procession: they wanted not only to express solidarity with the Claps family; they also wanted to express their own anger that Elisa had been in that church all along. They wanted to reject the suggestion that Potenza was a city of silence, that it was a place that didn't care. At the front of the procession, as always, were Filomena and Don Marcello Cozzi.

'The discovery of Elisa', Don Marcello said, 'represents a great opportunity for Potenza to be reborn: it's a city that won't stop until all the truth comes out. In the story of Elisa, there have been seventeen years of cover-ups, deviations, *omertà*, complicit silences and indifferent silences.'

It slowly became apparent how the discovery had come about.

The company of an entrepreneur, Antonio Lacerenza, had been called by the church to fix a leaking roof. The priest of the church, Don Ambrogio, had gone onto the terrace with Lacerenza and the bishop himself, but they hadn't noticed anything. A week later Lacerenza was called again because water was coming directly into the church. A Romanian worker, Corneliu Todilca, was instructed to go into the *sottotetto* – the attic or garret – and there, using his mobile in front of him for light, he saw her corpse.

Within days there grew up around the now-closed church a so-called 'Garden of Elisa': on the steps and pavement outside people placed teddy bears and pot plants and bouquets. I saw one cyclist get off his bike to put a pot plant upright again, as if even the fact that it had been knocked over was an insult to Elisa. People stopped to read the notices and inscriptions. Many of the inscriptions were particularly angry, calling for justice and truth. '*Non metteteci una pietra sopra*,' said one note, meaning, 'Don't bury it under a stone.' There were the names of other missing girls, Padre Pio candles, gnomes, plastic flowers. 'Silence and cleanliness are signs of civility,' said another note.

*

It's as if the city is in deep shock. The discovery has been, locals tell me, even more shocking than her disappearance years ago. It means that she has been there all along, forgotten and slowly decomposing in that dark attic. Within metres of her people had sauntered around, drunk coffee, eaten ice creams. Underneath her body people had been married and baptised. But, most of all, the people of Potenza are in shock because it means, bluntly, that she was never properly looked for. In the last few days the city has been on the front pages of all the Italian newspapers, as well as many foreign ones, and has been portrayed, unfairly but inevitably, as a place that washed its hands of an innocent sixteen-year-old girl, that looked away, that crossed over to the other side. As one local says to me, 'The city feels wounded, humiliated and offended.' The little garden is one way for the citizens of Potenza to express their indignation at what has happened. On one wall I see a piece of graffiti that is a melancholic play on words: the priest of the Chiesa della Santissima Trinità was Don Mimì Sabia; *sapia* is dialect around here for 'knew'. So someone had scrawled on a wall in big letters, 'Don Mimì Sapia' – 'Don Mimì knew,' it says.

I go and see Don Marcello Cozzi again, and he sums up the sense of disorientation in the city. 'This is a city that doesn't accept the fact that someone didn't look for Elisa, that the church wasn't turned upside down.' It's clear that Don Marcello, too, is deeply moved by the fact that the church he serves has been for so long the sepulchre of the young girl. 'I'm living through this story with suffering for the fact that Elisa was found in a church, and for the fact that inevitably there could be suspicions about men of the Church simply because she's been found there. Maybe they're not involved, but inevitably if they find a body in your house, you're the first suspect.'

Don Marcello explains the impact of the discovery on the family. They have, he says, 'been through great suffering. They've been violated in their emotions. To find the cadaver of her daughter in the church has been a laceration to Filomena's heart. Because she's a woman of faith. She went to that church, went there to pray to the Eternal Father that she should find her daughter, and all the time, in that church, Elisa was up there. You can imagine the storm in the heart of her mother. I understand the reaction she has had towards the Church. Suffering can make you say things you wouldn't want to say.'

Much worse was to come, however, and it started to seem, as Marco Gallo, the private investigator, once said to me, that in this case you never touch bottom. As if it wasn't bad enough that Elisa's body was found in the church, it slowly emerged that she had almost certainly been found months, and possibly years, before, and that the shocking discovery had been hushed up by the Church authorities. The seventeenth of March 2010 was, it seemed, nothing more than an unveiling of her cadaver, a staged presentation of it. The most telling evidence was the fact that many witnesses claimed, over the years, to have worked in the garret and hadn't ever seen her: in the corner where she had been found, they said, there was simply a huge pile of tiles, planks and other material. Now, however, there was no evidence of that material. As far back as 1996 the roof of the church had been repaired, and workers had been inside that garret, within metres of where Elisa's body lay. They had seen nothing other than a lot of rubble. Don Mimì had died in 2008, and a Congolese priest, Don Guy Noel Okamba, had been given the job of being the interim official until a full-time priest of the church was nominated. He was in place from March 2008 to October 2009. Don Guy had asked workers to remove the building materials from the terrace outside the *sottotetto* where Elisa had been found. It was surely then the case, Gildo reasoned, that Elisa had been found two years previously, shortly after the death of Don Mimì.

It was a hypothesis that received confirmation from various scientists working on the case. A botanical expert, Alessandro Travaglini, examined leaves and maple seeds that were present on Elisa's remains and estimated that they dated from approximately two years previously. Indeed, various witnesses came forward to say that they had seen a skip on 22 May 2008 outside the infamous church. Till receipts and ballot papers dating from 2008 and 2009 were found in the garret, yet another clue that people had been there in the years between Don Mimì's demise and the official uncovering. There were also two Peroni glass beer bottles, a length of electric cable and a wooden-handled paint brush. Another forensics expert, Eva Sacchi, also suggested that Elisa's remains had almost certainly been covered with tiles and rubble. Why they weren't present when she had been discovered was a mystery.

Even more astonishing was the revelation, which emerged soon after the 'official' discovery, that two cleaners had seen Elisa's corpse back in January 2010. Don Ambroise Apakta, better known in Potenza as Don Ambrogio, was by then the priest in charge of the church; his assistant was a young Brazilian called Don Wagno Oliveira e Silva. The two cleaners, Margherita Santarsiero and her daughter, Annalisa Lo Vito, had seen the corpse while cleaning the garret and had told Don Wagno. He in turn had alerted the bishop, Monsignor Agostino Superbo, of the presence of a cranium. When the story came out in the press, both the cleaners, the priest and the bishop started making half-admissions, denials and accusations. The bishop said that he had misunderstood Don Wagno, who didn't speak very good Italian, and that instead of 'cranium' he understood that the priest had found a 'Ukrainian'. None of them had thought to notify the authorities of the presence of a corpse, even though, surely, they must have known that it was Elisa. Another disconcerting revelation emerged: the beams immediately above Elisa's body had been sawn cleanly through, creating an opening through which the miasma of her decomposing body could escape. It seemed to everyone that such a tidy, deliberate opening must have been the work of someone attempting to disguise the murder.

Understandably the Claps family were, by this point, incandescent with rage. It seemed as if there were no end of salt to rub in their wounds. Every time they thought they were approaching the truth, they came up against deception and silence. They issued a statement that didn't pull its punches:

We ask with indignation: is it possible that the priest didn't immediately refer the facts of the discovery [of Elisa's corpse]? And if he did, to whom did he refer it? To the bishop or to higher ecclesiastical authorities? Seventeen years of pain haven't impeded that, once again, silence, *omertà* and the tutelage of interests that have nothing to do with Christian values prevail over the piety that one should have for a lacerated corpse. We believe that this havoc definitively puts an entire community – a community that only last Saturday was supporting our family asking for truth and justice – on its knees.

*

I find myself struggling to comprehend the lies that surround the discovery. Even one of my young children could have come up with a better excuse than confusing 'cranium' with 'Ukrainian'. And yet I'm finding it hard to believe, despite the overwhelming evidence, that priests or workmen or cleaners would keep quiet about such an explosive discovery. All of them must have known that this church had, for years, been at the centre of a missing-person investigation that had dominated the news, and yet they appear to have hushed up everything. It seems absurd, a terrible example of the lack of truth at the core of the case. Don Marcello patiently outlines to me a possible explanation. He's interesting to listen to because, being from Basilicata and being someone who has, with the Libera organisation, battled the various mafias for years, he seems to understand how things can sometimes work around here. He suspects that even Danilo Restivo and his family would have been shocked by the discovery of Elisa in the *sottotetto*, that they didn't know she was still up there. In the trial for perjury back in the 1990s, the Restivo family employed an architect to analyse the layout of the church and to investigate its dark corners.

Access was denied to him, of course, by Don Mimì, but the fact that the Restivo family had sent him there suggested to many that they had no knowledge the body was there. Don Marcello explains the possible mechanism: 'Danilo is the assassin and he tells his accomplice what has happened. His accomplice sends him to hospital to create an alibi, while he calls in help to cover up the fact. The accomplice calls someone, and that someone calls someone else: "You remember I did you that favour, remember . . .?" It's a question of blackmail. "Now you have to do me this favour. Go there, see what has happened." More people join the chain, each one asking a favour. Maybe the accomplice, assuming he was the first one to take this step, doesn't know who went up there to do the dirty work, he doesn't know who commissioned the work; he only knows the friend he turned to. And that friend didn't tell him, "I'm going to call so-and-so"; he said, "I'll sort it." Maybe that friend turned to someone else.

'Someone arrived up there, saw that there was the cadaver, but knew that they couldn't take it down. If you take it down, everyone will see you. At the most you put it in a corner and then you tell whoever has commissioned the work – the accomplice or someone – you say, "Don't worry, Elisa's not there any more." Why would they say to you she's still up there? The one who did that work was the only one who knew that Elisa was still up there. The one who commissioned it was calm. Danilo was calm, even arrogant. So arrogant that he allowed himself to challenge us, insult us in various ways. Where does that arrogance derive from? From the fact that he was 100 per cent sure that he would get away with it because Elisa wasn't there any more.'

That all makes sense, I suppose, but why would ordinary members of the public not denounce the presence of a corpse, I ask him. Someone who was involved in a cover-up would obviously keep their counsel, but ordinary folk would surely report the presence of a dead body. Don Marcello stares into the distance, reluctant, it seems, to insult or judge. 'There's a provincial mentality,' he says. 'It says, "I'll mind my own business." Not because they're evil, but because that's the provincial mentality. "Why should I put my nose in the business of others?" Silence comes from that provincial, closed mentality . . .' I can see, though, that by his high standards the behaviour is inexplicable, that even he struggles to understand the silences that surround the case. 'Why not say something?' he asks. 'Why not? I don't know . . .' It sometimes felt as if many people must have known where Elisa was. Only a year before some graffiti had appeared in the toilets of the Gran Caffè, the most central and most frequented bar in Potenza: 'Elisa Claps is in the Trinità,' it had said. It was as if someone truly knew her whereabouts and wanted, anonymously, to declare the fact.

I go and see Marco Gallo, the private detective who has worked on the case all these years. Despite being a devout Catholic, Gallo is scathing in his analysis of the ecclesiastical authorities. 'The most likely thing that happened is very simple. It was all complicated by a series of stupidities committed by the priest. I'm 90 per cent sure that Don Mimì knew that Elisa was dead and that her body was in the church; 100 per cent sure that he knew she was dead. He goes away from Potenza, goes to the spa, saying, "Look, I'm not interested. In the next few days do me a favour and sort everything out." Someone had the job of making the body disappear, but they couldn't because the city had already been mobilised, something that took them by surprise. Since these people had already taken the money, they could have said, to either Restivo's accomplice or to Don Mimì, "OK, we've made the body disappear." And in the meantime they've hidden it very well, not just well. The priest', said Gallo, looking at me and shaking his head with disdain, 'was certainly involved.'

What happened in 2008, says Gallo, 'is very simple. Sometimes reality is simple. As soon as Don Mimì had died, the church was entrusted to a priest from the Congo, then afterwards to Don Ambrogio and Don Wagno, both of them also foreigners.' He expresses surprise that such a central and coveted church was entrusted twice to foreigners, the suggestion being that it was easier to lean on them, to make them play along with the ecclesiastical authorities who needed, finally, to clear up the mess. 'When I take possession of a house,' Gallo says, 'I go and have a look, even in hidden rooms. Soon afterwards they had seen all of the church, a church of a thousand hidden doors. They go into the *sottotetto* and discover the body. But as this whole thing involved very important people, it was handled in a certain way.' It was, in short, hushed up. The Church didn't want the body, the hypothesis goes, to be discovered by a priest; they wanted external workers to chance upon it so that the Church authorities could then feign complete surprise at the news.

As he's talking I begin wondering whether all these theories aren't merely the fruit of an overactive imagination; whether all the suggestions and conspiracy theories that are flying around in the aftermath of Elisa's discovery aren't simply the result of the usual yearning to glimpse dark and hidden powers where they don't really exist. I often wonder whether I'm too credulous and, in a dull, Anglo-Saxon way, too willing to believe the official line; I wonder whether most Italians have too much fantasy, and too much fun making up these stories; or whether actually they really are right to pour scorn on an official version that appears to have more holes than a *scolapasta*, a colander. One of the paradoxes of living on the cusp between Britain and Italy is that the British always say to me that Italy surely can't be all that complicated; and Italians always say, when I guess at what's been going on, that actually it's not as simple as all that. Isn't it just possible, I ask Gallo, that the simplest truth is that Elisa really was discovered on 17 March, that that was the first time she was found?

He shakes his head slowly, smiling indulgently at my gullibility. 'Absolutely not. And the proof that a very senior priest knew is the fact that he was called on his mobile while going with two priests to a meeting. They call him saying, "They've found a body." If I hear that for the first time I would rush round there. I would turn the car round. Instead, he says, "OK, all right, I'll come later." That person knew already.' He swears in disbelief. '*Cazzo*, what meeting is so important that you don't turn round for something as serious as the discovery of a cadaver? No, the whole discovery had been organised. Some tiles had been deliberately broken to give the excuse that there was a leak in the church. The only reason, the only explanation, is that they wanted the body to be found.'

*

On 19 May 2010, the Claps family were shocked to hear that Danilo Restivo had been arrested by police in Dorset. Just when it seemed as if the Italian authorities had everything necessary to issue a warrant for Restivo's arrest, they had been beaten to it by their colleagues in England. There had been, according to one policeman I spoke to in Dorset, 'a certain competitiveness' to arrest Restivo first. The discovery of Elisa's body was enough for the Dorset police to act, but it left the Claps family frustrated once again. The fact that he had been arrested in England inevitably meant that it would be a long, long time before he ever faced trial back in Italy. What else, they wondered, had the Italian authorities needed to find before arresting Restivo? Were they waiting, Gildo asked sarcastically, for a signed confession?

The day after the news, Antonio Claps gave a very rare

interview. He had never spoken with reporters before; he had left the whole campaign to his wife and sons. He had closed himself within his own sorrow and had almost rejected the outside world. Now, though, he felt as if the whole attempt to bring Restivo to justice was a waste of time. 'I don't believe in justice any more,' he said with bitterness. 'Ours is a country of buffoons, my dear. Of clowns and jokes. If they had left it to me seventeen years ago, justice would have arrived, and how. Things should have been done then, not now. Instead, everything took another turn. And now the truth doesn't count any more. Of what interest is it to me? She, Elisa, isn't here today. I'll tell you now: I won't go to her funeral. I will stay here, to mourn her alone.'

Exactly a week after Antonio Claps's melancholic words, an arrest warrant was finally issued by the Procura di Salerno for Danilo Restivo. At last, the Claps family thought, it looked like he was going to stand trial for murder.

*

As details emerge from the forensics reports, it's slowly possible to guess at what might have happened all those years ago. Stones were found trapped in the tread of Elisa's sandals, stones which matched some of those present in the garret at the top of the church. 'The position of stones found deeply inserted in the grooves of the heel', one of the forensics experts wrote, 'lead one to presume that such a positioning could have been reached during normal locomotion . . . It's thought, therefore, that it's equally probable that the insertion of the stones happened in the *sottotetto* during the last moments of the victim's life.' In short, only the downward weight of Elisa, still standing, could have caused the introduction of the stones into her sandals; and the conclusion, therefore, was that she had been walking normally when she went into the garret.

The suggestion that Elisa was alive when she went inside is troubling for Gildo and his family. They struggle to believe that Elisa would have accompanied Danilo voluntarily to any secluded spot, not least one which was so cramped and dark. If it's true, as the stones in the sandals suggest, that she was indeed alive when she entered the garret, Gildo is convinced that she can't have been alone; that she would only have gone to such a place if accompanied by someone. Filomena is equally convinced that she would never have gone somewhere like that alone because, for all her innocence, she was scared of Danilo. 'What could be the most believable hypothesis?' Don Marcello asked himself. 'That Eliana went up there with Elisa and Danilo and possibly someone else, possibly Eris, and that Eliana and this other person then left. It's an ugly story,' he says, shaking his head. And as we speculate about who, if anyone, might have accompanied Elisa up there, the mystery of her key returns: a few days after her disappearance Eliana had given Gildo Elisa's single key, saying that Elisa had given it to her because she didn't have a bag. Gildo thought at the time that it was odd, because it was a single key that could fit in a pocket and because Elisa never used a bag anyway. Why did Eliana have her key?

Marco Gallo, the private investigator, was also certain that Elisa didn't go into the garret alone. One theory he puts forward is that 'Elisa certainly didn't go in alone but rather with other people. Probably with Eliana and perhaps [Eliana's boyfriend] Francesco Urciuoli, who then [both] went away without ever thinking that something could happen to Elisa. They left her alone with Restivo, who wanted to make a pass at her.'

What happened thereafter was painstakingly reconstructed by Professor Francesco Introna, a professor of legal medicine at Bari. He deduced that the two circular stains on the wall against which Elisa had been found indicated that decomposition had indeed taken place in the garret. Hair radiating out from behind her head and the raising of the right trouser-leg above the knee suggested to him that the body had been dragged into that position. The waistband of those trousers, too, was hitched up above the waist. In a detail that appeared strikingly similar to the Heather Barnett murder, the zip of the blue cotton trousers had been lowered and the jeans opened, and the bra had been unfastened and lacerated in front, between the cups. The knickers, too, had been cut.

He suspected that a sharp and penetrating injury to Elisa's left scapula implied that the attacker was right-handed and had stabbed with a downward motion from behind. He analysed all the bones and found other lesions to the ribs and vertebrae. He recorded the position of each cut or notch in the bones by placing coloured stickers on a skeleton. Of the twelve injuries he could identify, nine were made from behind and three from in front, although the assailant may still have been behind the victim as he pulled her head back and inflicted the injuries to the breast and neck, arriving as far as the anterior part of the thoracic verte-brae. The presence of red blood cells, indicating a haemorrhage, enabled Introna to ascertain that those stab wounds were inflicted when Elisa was alive. He also hypothesised that the throat injury may have been caused by a pair of open scissors. The ripping of the knickers and bra, the lowering of the trousers and the presence of haemorrhages in particular parts of the corpse – the upper thigh and breast areas – led him to conclude that there may have been a sexual element to the attack. Those haemorrhages occurred very shortly before death because her body hadn't had enough time to produce the fibrinogen necessary for clotting to begin.

Introna's most remarkable discovery, however, involved the many filiform structures that were recovered from the garret. These turned out to be fragmented, thin and often tangled pieces of hair. Under microscopic examination, it became apparent that some clumps of hair had ends that were extraordinarily square: the cut was perfect, a straight line through various hairs. Even hair cut by a hairdresser never achieves that degree of uniformity. Baffled by how the cut could be so clean and linear, Introna and his team conducted various experiments. They took some hair, cut it and then soaked it in blood; they also soaked some hair in blood and then cut it. On both occasions, the result was still irregular. Only when they soaked hair in blood, allowed it to dry completely and then cut it was the result completely compatible. It was as if the hairs were as one, glued together by the dried blood. It led Introna to conclude that Elisa's hair had been cut when certain strands were stuck together, and that required a certain amount of time: he estimated that approximately twenty minutes would have been required for sufficient coagulation to occur. He also concluded that Elisa had reached the garret alive. It would, he thought, have been impossible for any aggressor to carry a woman up the very narrow and steep stairs and through the narrow door leading to the roof. The knife used in the attack, he suggested, would have had a single blade and was possibly small – a minimum of 5.5 centimetres – but very strong. Introna didn't believe, however, that any rubble had been placed on top of the body. If the body had been obscured by rubble, it must have been in front rather than on top of her.

Another striking similarity to the Barnett murder emerged from Cristina Cattaneo, a professor of forensic medicine at the University of Milan. She had extrapolated evidence from the desiccated, mummified hands of the corpse. She had tried to reconstitute and rehydrate the hands with distilled water, and was thus able to identify a number of 'defence wounds' incurred during the attack. They were caused, she said, by the passage of a blade. But most telling was the discovery of 'piliferous formations' in both of Elisa's hands. They were, it seemed very likely, fragments of hair. Exactly as had happened in Bournemouth, Elisa's assassin appeared to have left hair in her hands as some kind of macabre, ritualistic signature. Reiterating the hypothesis of Professor Introna, Cattaneo thought the lesion on the first thoracic vertebra had occurred either through two separate stab wounds produced by a single-edged blade or, possibly, by a single blow from an open pair of scissors.

*

Towards the end of June 2010 another revelation put the Elisa story back on the front pages. A red button had been found under her body that was described as *rosso porpora*, purple red. The colour also denotes a cardinal, since the phrase '*essere elevato alla porpora*' means 'to be raised to the dignity of cardinal'. *Porpora* is shorthand for the higher echelons of the Church, and the discovery of a button that colour in the immediate vicinity of where Elisa had been found was explosive. Immediately newspapers began speculating about whether the button belonged to Don Mimì. One sharp journalist looked at an old publication, *Don Mimì Sabia, storia di un curato di città* (published by the now infamous Centro Newman, the cultural association that Restivo and others used to frequent). In that publication there was a photograph of Don Mimì with a button missing from his soutane or cassock. Inevitably there was frenzied speculation about whether that absent button was the one found in the garret. *Chi l'ha visto?* broadcast the photograph, zooming in on the buttonhole with the missing button behind it. Church authorities, meanwhile, rushed to clarify the fact that only cardinals wear the colour *porpora*; for a bishop or archbishop, they declared, the standard colour was *paonazzo*, meaning 'purple' or 'violet'. The forensics expert examining the button then called its colour closer to *rosso ponsò*, meaning 'poppy red'. For a few days, not only in Potenza but across Italy, anyone who had followed the case appeared to be debating the subtle hues of purple and the ecclesiastical implications of each shade.

The feverish speculation died down soon afterwards. Don Mimì had left his soutane in his wardrobe, expressing his desire that the next incumbent of the Chiesa della Santissima Trinità that became, like him, a Monsignor should inherit it. Dr Eva Sacchi, the forensics expert responsible for examining both the button and the soutane, excluded that the two were linked: the other buttons were, she said, 'not compatible from a structural point of view' with the one found under Elisa's body. She did, however, also conclude that 'assuming that the colour (as seems probable from the composition of the fibre) hasn't undergone a variation, the button could have belonged to a cardinal's cassock'; she added that Don Mimì's soutane was 'worn and many times repaired', and that 'the condition of the buttons lead one to maintain as possible the fact that the buttons had been replaced'.

More revelations only increased the Clapses' dismay. It emerged that there was a mattress in the garret that had undergone tests. Preliminary results suggested that there was semen from two different men on it. The *sottotetto*, it seemed, had been used as a place for carnal encounters. There was also DNA from semen on a dishcloth or duster that had been found near by; that third semen sample matched the DNA of one of the two from the mattress. The dates on which the semen had been deposited weren't clear, but it was obvious that the church wasn't exactly a holy, sacred space; that it had, in fact, been a squalid and secretive one.

Once again the Claps family were, understandably, outraged. They issued a press release that summarised all their disgust at the church:

We ask with dismay how much disgrace and hypocrisy we'll be forced to witness and how many times the memory of Elisa must be offended and soiled? Evidently in parts of the church any-thing could happen without people batting an eyelid: from bar-barous murder to sexual acts consummated a few metres from the poor remains of Elisa. But what fills us with indignation more than anything else is the constant and hypocritical defence of the image of the church and of the Newman Centre.

*

A few months after the discovery of Elisa's body, I go and talk to Gildo. The World Cup in South Africa is in full swing, and there are tricolour banners and flags hanging from balconies and lamp posts. Gildo invites me to his flat: there are two goldfish in a tub on the floor named Dora and Diego after the characters in a children's programme; in Gildo's office there are hundreds of old *Tex* comics and lots of model cars: and in the corridor, on a shelf, is a photograph of Elisa, smiling happily at the camera. I meet his two-year-old daughter, Federica. She's a strong character, demanding attention and toys and running around and making us laugh. We're sharing a bottle of Aglianico again and watching some random match from the pool stages of the tournament. As we laugh at his feisty daughter, the whole tragedy of Gildo's sister seems far away. One of the remarkable things about him is that he's great company, making you laugh with anecdotes and stories and guffawing loudly when something, in turn, amuses him. But Elisa is always there in the background. Even the name of his girl is a reminder: she's named after Federica Sciarelli, the host of *Chi l'ha visto?*. As the little girl toddles off with her mother, our con-versation inevitably turns to recent events.

Even now, three months after the supposed discovery of the body, there's little clarity about when Elisa was first found. 'Nothing is clear,' he says angrily. As usual, his voice has subtly changed. Gone is the good humour and he's now, once again, got the bit between his teeth. 'Nothing about the circumstances of the discovery is clear. There have been silences and complicities on the part of the church.

'I didn't sleep for three nights after reading the medical examination. The idea that it took her half an hour to die . . .' He shakes his head. He talks bitterly about how his family had always been right: that, as they had always maintained, something had indeed happened to Elisa, and that Danilo Restivo had been responsible. 'To discover, today, that we had been right all along and that she had never left that church, a church that was never searched . . . it gives me a terrible, terrible anger.' He winces, his face looking weary now, but he starts to offer me his reconstruction of events, starting back in September 1993. 'He managed to convince her to go to the top of the church. The experts hypothesise that she went alone with him into the *sottotetto*, a suggestion that perplexes me. She had concerns about him. The murder happens. That afternoon the priest, like Danilo, leaves the city and the church is closed. Anyone with a key could enter and sort everything out. The first big doubt I have [about the official version of the discovery] is the idea that a priest who controlled everything was unaware that there was a cadaver.

'The body was discovered a few months after the death of Don Mimì. It's possible he confessed to somebody and they didn't know what to do. The discovery of a body by a member of the church signified the risk that people would gossip about the complicity of the church, saying, "So Don Mimì has died, he must have known . . ."' Gildo is convinced that the recent discovery is merely a *mise en scène*. In 1996, he says, workmen were working in the garret reinforcing the floor. They were working within centimetres of the body and they didn't see anything, only that pile of rubble. It was perfectly covered by tiles, so for that body to now be completely uncovered, with Elisa's glasses perfectly folded by her feet, makes him very suspicious.

That's why, Gildo says, the cleaning ladies were sent up there, to make the discovery. 'They had to find it because [the Church authorities] wanted it to appear that everything had happened purely by chance.' But the cleaning ladies, says Gildo, understood the game and didn't want to play it; they didn't want to be the ones who made the discovery, and instead they kept quiet. 'They could at least have called my mother,' Gildo says, incredulous at the lack of civic spirit. 'We'll never forgive them. Mamma went round to their house and said, "You make me sick," and they ran away.

'They saw her body in January. They refuse to make the discovery and so more time passes. The Church authorities say, "What are we going to do now? Let's invent the story of a leaking roof." Some tiles were broken because they had to say, "Some tiles are broken and water is coming in." The company [called to do the repairs] does three surveys, and an extremely senior priest goes up there twice. A priest of that sort doesn't get involved in inspections for works!' Gildo says scornfully. 'The company cleans up the water on the terrace but they're called back. "It's further on."' Gildo points his finger, imitating with sarcasm the action of the priest who was doing everything he could to lead the workers to the cadaver. '"You've got to look under the *sottotetto*."'

But despite all his scorn for the authorities, both legal and ecclesiastical, Gildo is warm in his descriptions of his fellow citizens. 'The people of Potenza', he says, 'have been very, very solidly behind us. They've been close to us and are following everything in an incredible way. All of Italy is asking for truth and justice for Elisa. People arrive from all over, bringing flowers, placing them outside the church.'

Gildo knows that although the story of Elisa is his family's story, it's also one that has touched and moved millions of people across the peninsula. It's possible that some people in his position might be almost protective of it, not wanting other people to claim ownership of, or participate in, his family's anger and sorrow. But the reason Gildo is so admired in the city, and across the country, is that he sees the story of Elisa as something that might shake the country out of its current state. It's a story that so clearly illustrates injustice and incompetence, misinformation and corruption, that it's an opportunity for Italians to recognise the state of the nation and do something about it. 'There is', he explains, 'so much anger. People have lost all their references. It's so evident what has happened. This little provincial city feels under shock. When I go out, people say, "Keep going," and "Don't give up."'

*

Inevitably, perhaps, there were to be other slaps in the face for the Claps family. Various items from the garret had been entrusted to Professor Vincenzo Pascali, a geneticist from the Università Cattolica del Sacro Cuore (the Catholic University of the Sacred Heart) in Rome. Pascali seems to have conducted a very hasty analysis, writing what should have been a complex report in, by his own admission, a single evening. In it he announced that the DNA of Danilo Restivo wasn't present in any of the materials he had been given. The news was leaked to Ansa, the Italian news agency, and within minutes Mario Marinelli, Restivo's long-serving lawyer, was proclaiming once again that his client was clearly innocent.

The Claps family had already been wary of Pascali. An email had been sent to their lawyer, Giuliana Scarpetta, only a few weeks previously, in which an engineer had outlined his doubts regarding his professionalism. There were other instances, too, in which his work appeared to have been, to say the least, slapdash. Then there was the niggling suspicion that a man who worked for an overtly Catholic institution might have been leant on, might have been asked to turn a blind eye to certain findings. Either way, it seemed incredible that Pascali had conducted examinations on only a few of the items handed to him; there were more than twenty items on which he hadn't worked at all, saying that the quantities of biological material were too negligible to take into consideration. The material from the garret was as close as investigators would ever get to a smoking gun, but Pascali was effectively saying that it wasn't worth looking at. The bombastic explanation – 'reasons of analytic economy' – seemed like shorthand for 'can't be bothered'. In such an important case one of the leading experts involved seemed to be shrugging his shoulders. He had used old-fashioned kit and outdated methods. Little wonder, other experts felt, that he hadn't found any traces of Restivo's DNA.

The magistrate now in charge of the investigation, Rosa Volpe, realised that Pascali's work was inadequate and commissioned an entirely new study. She entrusted the work to the RIS, the Reparto Investigazioni Scientifiche, the department of scientific investigations. It all meant further agony for the Claps family. They not only had to put up with Marinelli crowing about Restivo's innocence, they also knew that it would now be many, many more months before they would, finally, be able to bury Elisa. They wanted to be able to give her a tomb, a place where they could visit her and mourn in peace. Instead, further investigations would drag on well into the autumn of 2010 and beyond.

*

The family and their supporters continued to make appeals. 'If there's someone, and surely there is someone, who knows the truth,' Filomena said publicly, 'they know where to find me. I'm prepared to meet anyone face to face, how they want, where they want. I have no fear of meeting *mafiosi* or delinquents. I'm ready for anything to know the truth.'

'Potenza isn't a *città omertosa* [a city of silence],' said Don Marcello, 'but in this city there have been too many silences. Other than the body,' he asked, 'what was there to hide that so many people became complicit in this lie?'

It was a sentiment echoed by the founder of Libera, the anti-Mafia organisation. Don Luigi Ciotti said of the Elisa Claps case: 'You could feel in the air that there were too many lies and that there were too many superficialities in the investigation.' Potenza, he said, 'is a place where there's been too much suffering'.

*

Fortunately the RIS were as thorough and painstaking as Pascali had been sloppy. The man in charge of the new investigation was Lieutenant Colonel Gianpietro Lago, a tall, thin man with glasses and salt-and-pepper hair. He concentrated on the jumper that had been worn by Elisa. It was, by now, extremely fragile, falling apart in his hands each time it was touched. Dark brown and looking more tangled than knitted, the jumper appeared rather like seaweed on the beach. He divided the jumper into four parts and, after initial testing, then concentrated on one of those parts, dividing it into nine sections rather like a noughts-and-crosses board: there was A1, A2 and A3; B1, B2 and B3; and C1, C2 and C3. In each of those sections his team conducted four tests, looking for evidence of blood, semen, saliva and DNA. Blood, semen and saliva are known to be DNA-rich sources, unlike skin, sweat or urine, which are less so. All the sections were negative for semen. Many were positive for blood and some were positive for saliva.

Lago concentrated his attention on the one tiny area of the

jumper that had given a positive result for blood but a negative one for saliva: B3. B3 also had the highest total of male DNA. The quantity mattered because it was mixed with female DNA, and the close parity between the quantity of male and female DNA suggested that they had come from the same source: not something innocent like saliva, but from blood. Lago, however, was a methodical scientist. He knew that there was a danger of contamination, that there was the liquid of putrefaction and so on. He couldn't be certain that his tests hadn't missed something or, possibly, picked up something erroneously. But the fact that after seventeen years he had still been able to isolate and identify so much DNA suggested that originally there had been a great quantity of bodily fluid on that B3 sample; and, since the tests there for semen and saliva were negative, that left only blood as the possible source. Even more vitally, when that profile of male DNA was compared with that of Danilo Restivo, it was seen to be an exact match. At last it seemed as if investigators had found the *prova regina*, the indisputable evidence that, after all the doubts and gossip and guesses, could finally nail Elisa's assassin. Here was a proof that couldn't be contradicted or *insabbiata*, 'sanded up': Restivo's blood was on the back of her jumper. The fact that he had almost 'signed' the crime scene by leaving hair in Elisa's hands merely confirmed what was, by now, obvious to everyone: Danilo Restivo had killed Elisa Claps on the day of her disappearance.

Before he was tried for that murder, however, he was due to appear on the other side of Europe, at Winchester Crown Court. He was finally going to be tried for the murder of Heather Barnett.

Eight

'Time is the old justice that examines all such offenders, and let Time try.'
Shakespeare

7 November 2010: Gildo and Filomena arrive at Bristol airport. Gildo's face is badly bruised after a fall from his motorbike and he seems tired by the long journey. As soon as we're out of the airport, a camera crew from *Chi l'ha visto?* does an interview with Filomena. I watch from behind the cameraman as she puts on the determined, gritty face she always has when talking about Elisa. 'I hope he's condemned here,' she says, pointing at the ground. It's her first time in England, but she's convinced that our justice system offers more hope than the Italian one. 'And I want him to serve his sentence here,' she says. 'In Italy,' she says to me later in the car, 'Restivo will always find an *escamotage*.' She uses the French word, implying that Restivo could trick his way out of prison.

We drive the short distance to my house. As always, I'm surprised by how much my wife and I laugh in their company. On television they seem understandably steely, but in person they're relaxed and warm. They've brought hats, scarves and jumpers for our children, and Filomena, despite the long journey, sits down and plays with them. She knows exactly how to entertain – and gently chide – them. She insists they speak Italian to her and, even though for years they've pretended they can't, she won't put up with any nonsense. Within minutes she's got them chattering away in her language. 'My grandchildren', she says, 'gave me my life back. Until they came along there was less to live for.' We don't talk about what's going to happen tomorrow – the pre-trial hearing in Winchester.

My wife Francesca has dug up some of our Jerusalem artichokes and made a risotto. A long debate begins with Gildo about what such a vegetable is called in Italian. He roars with laughter as I try and tell him that it's called, from the French, *topinambour* in Italian.

'*Topinambour*? I've never heard of it,' he laughs loudly. 'You're making it up.'

Filomena, who grows and cooks plenty of plants, tries to guess at what the strange vegetable is called in the south. I tell them something I had heard: that since the plant is related to the sunflower, it was originally called *girasole*, the Italian for 'sunflower', but because the English couldn't pronounce the word, it became 'Jerusalem' instead.

'You're just making it up.' Gildo is still guffawing, looking at the rice on his fork.

'Actually,' I say, getting into my stride, 'it's called *topinambour* in Italian because the vegetable was first cultivated by a native South American tribe called the tupinambas.'

By now Gildo's sure I'm pulling his leg and is roaring with laughter. 'Tupinambas,' he says, shaking his head and holding his palm in my direction to show the table I'm clearly nuts. 'That's good.' He and Fra laugh about some line from *Non ci resta che piangere*, the Roberto Benigni and Massimo Troisi film. It's a fun evening.

The next morning is very different. We get up at the crack of dawn and it's a horrible day: bitterly cold, windy and wet. It's still dark as we set out for Winchester Crown Court, and all the humour of last night has gone. Filomena is talking about Restivo, describing exactly what she would like to do if she got hold of him. 'The one I really blame is the father,' she says. 'Danilo should have been helped. There were all sorts of warning signs from his youth, right from his earliest schooldays.'

'I'm worried,' says Gildo. 'I'm worried that they [the Dorset police] don't have conclusive proof, that they only brought him in after Elisa was found in order to get to him before the Italian authorities. What they have might only prove to be circumstantial.' I ask Gildo when he last saw Restivo. 'I haven't seen him since I went to Bournemouth back in 2004. But he knew I would never, ever give up, that I would always keep breathing down his neck.'

'He thought he had got off scot-free,' Filomena says. 'Not this time. There's no one to protect him here.'

We drive on in the rain, barely able to see anything other than oncoming headlights as we cross Salisbury Plain. When we get to the court, it's clear that the hearing is a big news event in Italy. There are half a dozen camera crews and about a dozen journalists. Filomena has come all this way with the sole intention of staring at Restivo, of letting him know that she is still here, still fighting. She's devastated to realise that the public gallery is above the glass cage of the accused. Restivo won't see her, and vice versa. We try to slalom past the court officials to sit in the press box, but Gildo and his mother are too well known. We go upstairs and meet Heather Barnett's sister, Denise, and her husband, Roger.

Being simply a pre-trial hearing, it's over very quickly. Restivo pleads not guilty, and the trial is set for the beginning of May next year. I sit in the public gallery translating everything for Filomena and Gildo. They're amazed by the precision of the court, by the ability to set a trial date so far ahead and to say that it will last between six and eight weeks. In Italy a court case can last for many months, even years, as hearings happen only intermittently and get repeatedly postponed and interrupted. Filomena sighs gratefully when it's announced that Restivo will remain in prison until the trial. But, overall, she's bitterly disappointed to have made the long journey and not be seen by Restivo. That was her main reason for coming, and she feels thwarted. Perhaps worse is the thought that the trial won't start for another six months, and so his trial in Italy won't start for, at the earliest, another year. It means yet more waiting for justice.

On the way back we stop at Stonehenge and eat sandwiches in the car. It's a bleak autumnal day, and we sit there looking out of the windscreen at the windswept plain. I think how strange it must be for Filomena to be here, looking at those ancient stones through the rain; how bizarre that destiny has brought her here, of all places, in her search for justice for her daughter. And, even now, all she thinks of is other people. She's glad, she says, that Gildo has fallen asleep in the car. 'He's so tired.'

*

Easter 2011. A few weeks before the trial begins in Winchester, I go and spend Easter with Gildo and his family. Gildo greets me on crutches: six months on from the last crash, he's had another accident on his motorbike. He's clearly in a lot of pain and needs help getting his plastered leg on and off footrests.

Filomena tells me that her husband, Antonio, is joining us for lunch. I've never met him; I've only heard about his silent suffering. 'Later we'll talk about Elisa,' she says to me before he comes in. 'Don't mention her when he's here.'

Luciano, Gildo's brother, arrives with his wife Caterina and their daughter Sara. As always, I'm amazed how many laughs there are in the household. Luciano tries to get his daughter and niece to nick Gildo's crutches and run off with them. Even Antonio has a glint in his eye and a cheeky smile. Fairly short and barrel-chested, he jokes that if I need a hotel in the area I should stay right here, in Gildo's house. Only at the end of the meal, as we're finishing the bottle of wine, does his bitterness emerge. He says how rotten the modern world is, how it's all gone wrong, that all people care about nowadays is money. Caterina catches my eye and suggests we move on, have a coffee and talk about something else.

After lunch, Luciano drives me up into the densely forested mountains outside Potenza. It's a beautiful spring day, and the view from a clearing on the summit is spectacular. His daughter runs through the trees picking flowers as we look out across the peaks. 'This is where I come to feel at peace with the world,' he says. We drive on to another sanctuary in the mountains, to another statue of Christ with his arms spread wide. We don't talk about Elisa, but we both know the trial is about to start and that, hopefully, this is the beginning of the end.

*

May 2011. Winchester is one of those old towns that seems soaked in history. It was called Venta Belgarum by the Romans and was made the capital of Wessex by King Alfred the Great. Ever since it has remained central to English history. It was here that the Domesday Book was compiled and kept; it's where the apocryphal Round Table of King Arthur hangs. The Great Hall, with the huge Round Table, was where justice was administered right up until the 1970s, and it was here that Sir Walter Raleigh was sentenced to death. The Royal Mint operated in Winchester until 1279. The oldest school in England, Winchester College, was founded here by Bishop William of Wykeham in 1387. Even the names of the streets – like Parchment Street – seem somehow old-fashioned.

The courtroom is large and modern. At the back, in the middle, is a long box of thick glass where the defendant sits. The public gallery, four or five metres above that, is accessed from the next floor up. The police sit to the left of the glass box with, nearest the exit, the press. Opposite them is the jury. In the centre are the two teams of lawyers and, on the bench at the front, Mr Justice Burnett in his large red leather chair. There are pencil microphones and vertical Bose speakers on the wall, and two large screens either side of the judge. A few weeks ago, a hearing in London signalled the first major victory for the prosecution: the judge allowed all the details of the Elisa Claps murder to be heard because of the 'striking similarity' to the Heather Barnett killing. It means that the members of the jury will have to believe in a number of extraordinary coincidences if they are going to acquit Restivo. But it also means that the trial will be very long by British standards, probably close to two months. Many prospective jurors have other commitments and, of the sixty potential jurors called in, only twenty-seven can commit for that length of time. Eventually, the jury of five women and seven men is chosen, and the case can begin. Most of them look young, in their twenties.

Filomena is here for the first day of the trial. I try and take her into the press box, from where she'll be able to see Restivo, but court officials are adamant that she must go up to the public gallery. One of the journalists from *Chi l'ha visto?* goes and talks to Gennaro, a shaven-headed court security guard who happens to be from Italy. Up in the press gallery, diminutive Filomena is moving to the left and right, leaning dangerously over the edge in the hope of getting a glimpse of where Restivo will sit. I tell her that she can't possibly see him from up here, but she won't take no for an answer. 'He has to see me,' she says, staring with determination, her teeth showing. 'He has to know I'm here.' After much lobbying, she's allowed downstairs. Gennaro, the Italian connection, appears to have worked some magic, and the judge has allowed Filomena to sit in the courtroom. The other Italian journalists and I exchange smiles as we watch her tiny figure sitting a few feet in front of the defendant's glass box.

When Restivo is ushered in, she spins round and stares at him, her face hardening. Her eyes flash with fury and her lips are pulled tightly over her teeth. '*Io sto qui*,' she hisses – 'I'm here.' She's pointing at the ground. '*Io sto qui*,' she says again. He doesn't acknowledge her; he only stares straight ahead, but he must have seen her.

It's the first time I've seen Restivo in the flesh. He looks so different to the fresh-faced boy filmed at the trials in the 1990s. He looks thickset now, his shirt bulging over his paunch. His hair is thinning and he has sideburns. His large eyes bulge behind his glasses. He's wearing a tie, but it only comes halfway down his stomach. His nose and forehead slope at exactly the same angle, and his mouth is narrow, even though his lips are thick. He looks a bit shabby and rather odd.

Michael Bowes QC is prosecuting counsel. A shortish man with glasses, his opening speech is slow and methodical. He outlines everything the jury will hear during the trial, mentioning the 'striking similarities' between the two cases and calling the placing of the hair in the victims' hands as 'akin to a hallmark'. He talks for the entirety of the first day and for much of the second. During breaks, Filomena and I share sandwiches, and she repeatedly expresses astonishment that the state pays for Restivo's defence team. 'He should have to pay for it himself.'

The first piece of evidence the court hears is the testimony of Terry Marsh, recorded on video the day after his mother Heather's murder almost nine years ago. The chilling part is when the policewoman interviewing him asks why his mother had recently replaced the locks, and Terry tells her that the Italian living opposite had accidentally taken the spare key. I look over at Restivo, sitting only a few metres away in his glass box, but he's completely impassive. It still seems remarkable, in retrospect, that police missed that clue; that they were told an Italian living opposite had taken Heather Barnett's key and that he wasn't thoroughly investigated.

Other witnesses are called. Sergeant Paul Vacher describes going to 211 Capstone Road on the day of the murder and finding Terry 'absolutely distraught'. 'All he could say was "bathroom" and "mother".' The officer 'gingerly opened the door' to the bathroom and then concentrated on crime-scene preservation. Two other policemen who took part in the investigation go into the witness box. One, Detective Constable Anthony Merrifield, had walked from various bus stops to see how long it might have taken Restivo to return to Capstone Road had he got on the bus but jumped off after just one stop. The prosecution alleges that Restivo had only bought a bus ticket on the number 30 at Richmond Park Road to shore up his alibi. He had kept the ticket, which clearly showed the time at which he had purchased it – 08.44. The prosecution believes that he got on the bus, got off at the next stop and walked back to Capstone Road. If Restivo had travelled one stop, to the Alma Road stop, it would only have taken him eight minutes to return to Heather Barnett's home. If he had walked a long way round to avoid being seen, it would only have taken eleven minutes. He could have been at the flat by 09.00 that morning.

The court was then shown CCTV footage taken from a camera mounted on the wall of the Richmond Arms pub. From the screens either side of the judge, the court saw the last sighting of Heather Barnett alive, as she turned her white Fiat Punto left into her street. Roughly half an hour later, at 09.23, a man was seen walking away from her road, apparently pulling a hood over his head. The footage was jerky and the image blurry. Identification was almost impossible.

The next witness to give evidence was Dr Allen Anscombe, a forensic pathologist. The post-mortem that Dr Anscombe conducted the day after the murder made for gruesome listening. For over an hour he listed Heather Barnett's injuries in precise detail and recreated what might have happened during the attack. As the court adjourned for lunch, people filed out with glazed looks on their faces. No one had much of an appetite. In the press gallery, journalists were debating how much of the pathologist's evidence their readers or viewers could stomach. I looked over at Restivo and the young female interpreter sat next to him. I wondered what it must have been like for her, translating all those harrowing injuries into the ear of the man who was accused of making them. She had, I couldn't help noticing, long dark hair that was falling over her shoulder and down her back.

After lunch the prosecution called Claire George, the woman who had identified the man in the CCTV footage as Danilo Restivo after she had seen it broadcast on *Crimewatch* in 2006. George had short white hair, glasses, a slim necklace and small earrings. She looked nervous, occasionally chewing her lower lip and speaking softly. Defence barrister David Jeremy QC asked her about her knowledge of the case, about the fact that she had printed off material about Restivo from the Internet, and she became increasingly defensive and strangely adamant. He asked whether 'all that background knowledge influenced the way in which you looked at that clip?' 'I don't think so,' she said. 'No.'

Another policeman went into the witness box. Inspector Peter Browning was wearing a dark suit and had short, greying, gingerish hair. It was he who had visited Restivo on 17 November 2002, five days after the murder, to gather DNA for the purposes of eliminating people from police inquiries. He asked Restivo to show him the footwear that he had been wearing on the twelfth. 'He showed me', Inspector Browning said, 'to the bathroom, where he indicated two trainers that were in the bath. They were wet and a smell of bleach [was] prominent. He said they were being washed because they were dirty.' His curiosity aroused by this behaviour, Inspector Browning took possession of the trainers.

*

Geoffrey Robinson was the forensic scientist who had examined the crime scene at Heather Barnett's flat. As had happened with the pathologist a few days earlier, it was strange hearing a professional, dispassionate analysis of something so messy and violent as murder. 'It perplexed me', he said, 'why there wasn't more chaos in there. The indications were that very, very quickly Miss Barnett was subdued.' That said, he did believe that 'the perpetrator would almost certainly have been significantly bloodstained'. He described his analysis of the bloodstaining in the flat, and his hypothesis that Barnett had been dragged to the bathroom. He found fibres on the door handle of the bathroom that appeared to be the same as those that had created 'line marks' on the inside of Barnett's knickers.

It was a confident, compelling performance. In great detail, he had methodically reconstructed the likely chain of events, at each turn backing up his hypotheses with the available evidence. But as frequently happened during the trial, the defence QC rose to question him, and within a matter of minutes that cool, clear presentation was being knocked and doubted and I could see jurors frowning in confusion. David Jeremy began asking about false positives and false negatives in tests for blood, eventually arriving at a question that even the judge had to reiterate for the witness: 'If you use Luminol [an agent for blood detection] and you get a positive result, that may be a false positive. There may not in fact be blood there. Now, if you try to compensate for that deficiency in that capacity of Luminol by then applying one of these presumptive tests, and one of those presumptive tests turned out to be negative, you cannot assume there's no blood because it's capable of giving false negatives?' After a quarter of an hour of confusion, the clarity of the prosecution's case seemed a distant memory. Male

DNA had been found on Heather Barnett's knickers, but that, said the defence, 'did not match the profile of Danilo Restivo'.

'That's right,' said Robinson.

*

Claire Stangoe was another forensic consultant, an expert in DNA analysis. Ash blonde, in a black suit, she had a soft Scottish accent and a slight lisp. She would use her hands a lot as she spoke to the jury about her findings. It was Stangoe who had conducted tests on the green towel which Restivo claims to have given Heather Barnett in order to get a colour match for the curtains he wanted to commission. Stangoe had repeatedly taken tapings from areas of interest on the towel.

'We obtained', she says, looking at the jury, 'a mixed DNA profile with DNA from at least two individuals. Heather Barnett had contributed the majority of the DNA. We then looked at the remaining minor components . . . and these matched the profile of Danilo Restivo. The DNA could have come from him. We then go on to statistically evaluate that result.' Stangoe estimated that the possibility that that DNA had come from someone other than Restivo was as low as one in fifty-seven thousand. The prosecution alleges Restivo never gave Barnett a towel, and that he actually used it to wipe blood from his face. He only made up the story of giving it to her as a colour match, the prosecution suggests, once he had been informed that his DNA had been found on the bloodstained towel. It was Stangoe who had discovered minute traces of blood on the inside of Restivo's trainers.

In an attempt to build up a picture of Restivo as a hair fetishist, the prosecution calls Detective Constable Michael Davies. He had searched Restivo's house on 21 November 2006, over four years after the murder, and had found evidence of Restivo's obsession with hair. He reads from his notebook: 'Seized a lock of brown hair, tied with green cotton.' It had been in 'a Tesco carrier bag full of photographs and photograph envelopes . . . this bag was found on the floor at the bottom of the chest of drawers'. The lock of hair is produced for court in a sealed evidence bag. It's passed to the judge and the jurors. The court doesn't see the photos in the Tesco carrier bag, but is told that they're mainly photographs of Fiamma Marsango's family.

Mr Jeremy, the defence barrister, rises to his feet and asks if the photos contained pictures of very young children.

'I don't recall,' says DC Davies.

'I'm going to suggest they included photos of young children,' says Mr Jeremy. The implication is obvious: the lock of hair is nothing more sinister than a memory of childhood, a keepsake from another era.

The next witness is Paul Barnett, the crime-scene investigator who recovered hair from both of Heather Barnett's hands. Each piece of evidence from the crime scene is given the initials of the person who finds them, so the hair found by Barnett under the right hand was given the initials PJB6. PJB25 was the code given to the hairs from the victim's left hand. 'There was a clump', says Barnett, 'or a number of hairs that were only really visible once the left hand had been moved slightly. Initially I didn't realise any hairs were present. I was preparing the body to be transported to the mortuary, and that involved bagging the deceased's hands for any evidence. I lifted the wrist of the left hand and there was a further clump.'

Carole Evans was the forensic scientist tasked with testing those hairs. The result, she said, was that PJB6, the hairs in the right hand of Heather Barnett, matched none of the samples taken from the Claps and Barnett families. PJB25, the hairs in the left hand, however, provided a match with Heather Barnett. MJD2, the hairs found tied with a green ribbon in the Tesco plastic bag, also matched none of the samples. As usual, the evidence given to the court hardly seems to build a cast-iron case against Restivo. Witnesses are called to give evidence, but the evidence is often that a DNA match wasn't found. And the presence of that witness merely gives the defence barrister a chance to muddy the waters. Mr Jeremy asks Evans about DNA testing on Heather Barnett's knickers.

'Did it match the profile of Mr Restivo?' asks Mr Jeremy.

'No, it didn't.'

In fact, that DNA sample matched the profile of Terry Marsh. The chances were that, as they shared the same house, Terry's DNA had simply got onto his mother's clothing. But, once again, the evidence seemed to point as much away from as it did towards the defendant. And after an opening week of seemingly endless forensic details, the jury are looking baffled. The evidence is often so complicated that it's hard to understand, let alone comprehend the criminal implications. Moreover, it can sometimes take an hour or two of clarification and contextualisation before the killer question is asked. And, even then, the answer isn't always clear-cut.

*

Craig Wilson was the forensic computer expert who had first ana-lysed the hard drive of the computer at Nacro. He's a bulky man with short grey hair, a striped shirt and red tie. Danilo Restivo's alibi for the morning of 12 November was that he was working on that computer. The following day, the computer was seized, and years later, in August 2010, Wilson was asked to perform an 'evidential capture' of the hard drive to prove whether there was any activity on the computer when Restivo claims to have been using it.

Wilson drew up a computer-activity timeline drawing on all the available applications. He discovered that there was no human activity on the computer between 09.08 and 10.10 on the morning of the murder. He found that the computer had also subsequently been used to search for details of the police investigation.

David Jeremy, for the defence, pointed out that Wilson had corrected the prosecuting QC, who had said there was no computer activity: 'You corrected him, you said there's no *evidence* of computer activity. You would not agree with the proposition that you can be sure there was no user activity. The most you can say is there's no evidence of user activity?'

'That's correct, My Lord.'

'You can only speak of the evidence you find?'

'That's correct, My Lord.'

'Does it not follow from that answer that you very properly have given that you cannot say that you are sure that you have recovered all of the data relating to 12 November 2002?'

'All I can say is that [the evidence] suggests the computer was idle.'

Once again I'm left in awe of the ability of lawyers to make eloquent experts qualify their conclusions and start hedging their bets. Every time you think that a witness has well and truly proved their case, the cross-examination plants a seed of doubt.

*

I'm beginning to worry that the case is becoming an obsession. I can't wash it out of my head at night any more. I see Heather Barnett's bathroom or Elisa in the loft. Each time I see a stray hair somewhere it gives me the creeps, it brings me back to that sad man and his lonely obsession. I'm beginning to long for it all to be over.

I go for a walk through the meadows outside Winchester to clear my head. It's a warm summer's day and there are men in whites playing cricket. They're far away, and the sound of the ball reaches me long after it's been hit. I sit on a bench and watch the game for a while. This, I've read, is where Keats wrote 'Ode to Autumn'. I bought a copy in Waterstone's on the way here and pull it out now to read. 'Seasons of mists and mellow fruitfulness,' it starts. But even this apparently bucolic poem drags me back to the case with the image of 'hair soft-lifted by the winnowing wind'. It should be the most gentle image, but 'hair' for me no longer has innocent associations. I'm not sure I'll ever look at it the same way again. I close the book and just watch the cricket.

I walk further on to the Hospital of St Cross. It's a beautiful setting, the so-called 'hospital' contained within an old wall that backs onto a meadow full of butterflies and wild flowers. It provides sheltered living for elderly men and was founded by Bishop Henry de Blois in 1136. It was stipulated that the hospital should feed one hundred poor people a day, although the 'wayfarers' dole' of bread and ale is, today, a symbolic crumb and a sip, nothing more. The Brothers of St Cross traditionally wear black gowns adorned with the Jerusalem cross, while the Brothers of the Almshouse of Noble Poverty, founded by Cardinal Beaufort in 1445, wear red with a cardinal's badge.

There's a lot of history here. This is where, in the early nineteenth century, Francis North allegedly embezzled a large sum of money, an act which prompted Trollope to write his fourth novel, *The Warden*. But this ancient Norman church is also where crusaders gathered before departing for the Holy Land. It is, at least, a remote connection with Metaponto, with those Paladin Tables I saw so long ago where crusaders also met. I'm glad to have found some connection, other than Restivo, between this part of Britain and Basilicata. I go and sit on a pew. The only noise is the birdsong outside. The evening sun is slanting through the high windows, and I put my forehead on my forearms and fall fast asleep.

*

Philip Webster was the forensic scientist who had analysed the bloodied footprints at Heather Barnett's house. He described his findings: that the body had been dragged to the bathroom, and that bloodied footprints then went from there to the sewing room, at which point they disappeared.

'If the attacker', asks Mr Bowes, the prosecuting QC, 'went back down towards the patio door, moved round changing footwear, would that be compatible with a lack of blood?'

'Yes.'

'And if the offender had picked up contaminant blood on a sock, that could be transferred to a trainer?'

'That's correct, yes.'

What seemed like a convincing reconstruction of events was, as usual, strained when examined by the defence barrister. Mr Jeremy pointed out to Webster that there were, inexplicably, four missing footprints that were unaccounted for, as if the blood had suddenly vanished from the offender's shoes or as if he had started, rather improbably, hopping instead of walking. 'This is not a science', said Mr Jeremy, 'where there's a beautiful, consistent diminution of blood apparent. You can have a footprint, then not a footprint.' It was conceded that this wasn't a neat crime scene where there was a puddle of blood followed by diminishing imprints of blood, but a complex one where blood could have been picked up by shoes from any number of sources. Webster conceded that this was 'a complicated area'. As had happened the day before, Mr Jeremy pointed out that the witness had corrected the prosecution lawyer: when Mr Bowes had referred to the hallway having 'no blood',

Webster had corrected him by saying 'no detectable blood'.

At lunch I see the defence team in a huddle. They're laughing and seem somehow jubilant. They appear happy with the way they're slowly planting seeds of doubt in the minds of the weary jurors. The prosecution team, by contrast, seem sombre. The impression so far is that the prosecution case relies on the jury to join a lot of dots: there's endless forensic evidence – traces of blood and DNA and so on – but it's always relentlessly queried by the defence, and the evidence is delivered in such a slow, detailed, scientific fashion that the jury appear to glaze over. Nothing is as clear-cut as it seemed after the prosecutor's opening statement, and slowly I'm beginning to wonder whether, incredibly, Restivo might walk free. I express my concerns to one of the team of prosecutors in the corridor outside the court. He smiles confidently and jokes that I have said the unspeakable: 'Wash your mouth out,' he smiles.

*

Various people who had had their hair cut by Restivo went into the witness box: Holly Marie Stroud, Katie McGoldrick and Sonia Taylor all described how they had only realised, in retrospect, that they had lost clumps of hair. Mark Goddard, the man who had seen Restivo cutting the hair of an unidentified woman on a bus, also gave evidence. More than once the suggestion emerged that Restivo was masturbating while having his hands, and the girls' hair, under his jacket.

*

Detective Sergeant Robert Lee was one of the officers responsible for the covert surveillance of Danilo Restivo in April and May

2004. The court was shown the video footage of Restivo. Watching the footage in silence is strange: there's obviously no commentary, and the court is completely quiet as we all watch his bizarre rituals. For once we're not being prompted or persuaded; we've simply got this compelling, disconcerting footage of Restivo taking off and putting on identical clothes. He looks, quite simply, extremely dodgy. It's not hard to come to a conclusion about what he was up to. The next day was, significantly, the twelfth of the month – the same day that Elisa, Heather and Oki, the South Korean student, had all been murdered. The surveillance team were so alarmed by his behaviour that they sent in uniformed officers.

*

Day nine of the trial is a site visit to Bournemouth. The day feels a bit like a school field trip, when the formality and distance of teachers is replaced by something approaching camaraderie. The judge and the lawyers are neither robed nor wigged, and they appear unexpectedly normal in their suits. The jury, having sat across the court from the press for the last couple of weeks, are now trudging along the pavements with us. None of us reporters say a word to them, and they, rightly, ignore us. An Italian colleague expresses incredulity that none of us have approached a juror to get an exclusive or an inside opinion on the trial. 'That would have happened in Italy the minute they got off the bus,' he jokes.

We gather outside Heather Barnett's old flat, and it's striking how small it is. You suddenly realise how little time would be needed to commit the murder and mutilation. In court it's taken hours and hours to describe what happened, but here you can understand that it might have occurred in a matter of minutes. The other striking thing is that directly opposite is 93 Chatsworth Road. The two roads converge exactly at this point, and Danilo Restivo's residence would have looked directly into Heather Barnett's bedroom and bathroom. For a voyeur it would be a perfect vantage point.

From there, the jury are taken to the various locations of CCTV cameras and bus stops that they've heard about in court. Then we all go to Nacro, the educational centre on the Poole–Bournemouth boundary, where Restivo claims to have been on the morning of the murder. It's a red-brick, art-deco building with a crouching lion on a plinth. 'Lion Works,' it says in big letters. There's a small pond in the middle of the drive. Nacro's mission, it says in the hallway, is 'to reduce crime by changing lives'. This, obviously, isn't the kind of publicity they want: their most famous student didn't change a life but, allegedly, ended one. We're shown to the small computer room where Restivo says he was working on the morning of 12 November. I ask one of the people present what he was like. 'He didn't seem able to connect,' they say. 'It was like he was closed, not there almost.' I've heard of him having to be told by one of the tutors to stop staring so insistently at female students.

After lunch the jury are taken to the park where yesterday's footage of Restivo acting strangely had been filmed. It's obvious, from here, just how secluded a spot it is: with various trees and long grass, it's exactly the kind of place someone could hide, or stalk, or kill. We're visiting at about the same time of year as when the surveillance footage of Restivo was taken. Today, many people are wearing neither jumpers nor jackets, and the idea that someone had to wear gloves or a balaclava is blatantly weird. Occasionally, the group pauses as the detective inspector in charge of the visit describes the various locations of the surveillance footage we saw yesterday. The jury are taking it all in, and for the first time I feel optimistic that they've understood just who Restivo is.

*

It's the start of the evidence from Italy, and the video link to a courtroom in Potenza works surprisingly well. The only trouble, predictably, is that the verbose Italian judge doesn't pause for breath as he begins intoning the formalities, and the interpreter in the Winchester courtroom has no time to translate. The English judge intervenes to ask his Italian counterpart to pause occasionally, but to no avail. The Italian gives the address of the court, says it's in a basement, lists all the people present, records the time of day. It's a surprise he doesn't mention the weather and what he had for breakfast.

The first witness is a blonde woman, Angela Campochiaro. She describes going to a cinema with her then boyfriend, now husband, 'seventeen or eighteen years ago'. Her hair was dark and long, down to the small of her back. She felt a pull on her hair and 'at first I thought he [Restivo] had his knee in the back of the chair and was catching the hair'. She turned round to look at him 'two or three times'. Her husband also turned round, and saw that Restivo had his hands under his jacket, which was placed on his lap, and that the jacket was moving up and down. When Restivo eventually moved, he went to sit behind 'three young girls'. Campochiaro only realised the next day that her hair had been cut.

Nicola Marino, her husband, was the next witness. He had been sitting next to her in the cinema all those years ago. 'When I pushed him [Restivo] away, I could see what he was doing with his hands. It was very visible what he was doing . . . I saw the gesture of masturbation.' The defence barrister pursued the point, wanting to see the exact actions Marino had seen. Marino demonstrated a jacket moving up and down on his lap, but because the camera in the Italian courtroom would only zoom in on who was talking, the screen reverted to a wide angle unless he made some noise, so we were all treated to the embarrassing spectacle of a poor man in Potenza having to simulate masturbation at the same time as making enough noise for the camera to zoom in on him. Things got even worse because, for the defence, it wasn't enough that Marino had seen the movements. Mr Jeremy wanted to know what Restivo had had in his hands. By now Marino, impatient with and embarrassed by the ponderous, precise questioning from far away, has lost his cool. 'I saw that he had his penis in his hands. When you're masturbating, it's not as if you have anything else in your hands. Come on!' Everyone in the court – including the judge and jury – laughs quietly at the robust riposte.

The next witness to be heard is Giovanni Motta, the ex-boyfriend of Danilo Restivo's sister, Anna. He has a sort of flat face, with floppy hair, a beige jacket and glasses. He describes that Sunday eighteen years ago when Elisa had gone missing. Anna and he had got back to the Restivo household for lunch at around 13.00 to see Danilo walking towards them. 'He was very sweaty and had a very quick step. He was quite agitated and asked me to accompany him immediately to hospital.' Restivo's clothes, Motta says later, were 'soaked'.

Motta describes the tiny cut on Restivo's hand between the index finger and thumb. 'It was a small cut, a centimetre, more or less. It was bleeding a little, but not in such a way as to have to go to hospital. I asked him how he came by the injury, and he replied that he had gone to the escalators out of curiosity.' Restivo insisted they go to hospital, so Motta and Restivo's sister had accompanied him there. A doctor had put a single stitch in the wound.

Just as the judge is thanking Motta for his testimony, he surprises the court by launching into a new, unsolicited revelation. 'I would like to add that I received threats by telephone . . .' he begins, before being abruptly interrupted by the judge, who reiterates that his evidence has concluded.

Paola Santarsiere is next up. She's slim with short black hair, and she looks slightly timid. She was the woman Restivo had been keen on early that autumn. They had met a few times, and Restivo had mentioned Santarsiere as having accompanied him to the escalators, not on the Sunday but a few days before.

'Did you ever go to the escalators construction site with Danilo Restivo?' Mr Bowes asks.

'No.'

She goes on to confirm that Restivo had told her that he knew all the secrets of the churches; that he had keys to one of them and knew all its hidden corners. 'He once told me that he was good, but if someone made him angry he was capable of brutal actions.'

Angelica Abbruzzese is the next witness. When she comes on screen, I'm surprised by her age. One of Elisa's best friends, she was just a teenager when Elisa disappeared, and that's how I always imagined her: an innocent girl caught up in a terrible tragedy. But here she is on screen and she's obviously approaching middle age. It's a reminder of how long this story has been going on. And as she recounts the events of that Sunday morning, you realise how those few hours completely changed her life. One minute she, Eliana, Elisa and all the others were normal kids, walking up and down the main street, bumping into each other, making new friends. They would stand outside ice-cream parlours, chatting and joking and gossiping. And then one morning their innocence, as well as Elisa's life, was suddenly snatched away. Ever since, Angelica had spent her life telling and retelling the same account of that fateful morning. She had gone to Mass at the Chiesa della Trinità and, on leaving, saw Eliana De Cillis, the girl who was supposed to be going to the countryside with Elisa.

'Did you ask Eliana, "Where is Elisa?"?' Bowes asks her.

'Yes, of course.'

'What did she say?'

'She told me that she [Elisa] was due to meet Danilo Restivo at the Trinità because he was going to give her a present.'

[253]

Restivo has always denied that he said he was going to give Elisa a present. The meeting took place, he says, in order that he could seek advice from Elisa about a girl. But many other women have come forward in recent years saying that Restivo used the strategy of a *regalino* – a little present – in order to tempt young women into secluded, isolated spots.

Abbruzzese says that, later, she had spoken to Restivo. 'I asked him how Elisa had seemed, if she had seemed worried when he had seen her. In the first place he said she was tranquil. Then, though, he said that Elisa was a bit nervous because there was someone who had been annoying her.'

'Did he say anything more about this person?'

'No. Personally, I didn't believe him.'

*

After lunch, it's Gildo's turn to testify in person in the Winchester courtroom. He hobbles in on crutches, looking rather pained. He's wearing an open-necked shirt and a suit. He takes the oath sitting down.

'In 1993, did you know Danilo Restivo?' Bowes asks him.

'Yes. I knew him because in Via Pretoria, the street where you walk, he made himself known as a character.'

'In the summer of 1993, did Elisa speak to you about Danilo Restivo?'

'More than talked. A month before her disappearance Elisa and I spent a few days of holiday at the seaside, at a village called Montegiordano, on the Ionian coast. We were walking along, and at a certain point I felt her squeeze my arm and she exclaimed, "My god, Danilo Restivo again. Not only do I have to meet him in Potenza but I have to meet him here." I asked her for an explanation. "Are there problems, is he annoying you?" She told me that on more than one occasion in Potenza he had been insistent with her. In a few minutes' time he approached us. And, of course, he turned to Elisa straight away, inviting her to take a walk. At that point my sister squeezed my arm very tightly as if to say, "Don't leave me." I was very abrupt with him. "She doesn't have any wish to walk with you. Please go away." He tried to insist, but then confronted by my firmness he went away. I knew exactly who Danilo Restivo was on the day that Elisa Claps disappeared. I tried to get more explanations from Elisa because I didn't like his insistence and the way he looked at her. My sister said it doesn't matter, he's a boy who is always on his own, and to let it go, not to put myself in the middle of the thing. I would have wanted to intervene with more determination.'

'That evening [prior to her disappearance], were you aware of a telephone call to her from Danilo Restivo?'

'I remember it perfectly. That afternoon there had been a big storm, so I was at home, and at about 5 p.m. he phoned, and Elisa went and answered. I didn't use to listen to the phone calls of my sister, but I distinctly heard the name Danilo. Obviously, I didn't pay much attention to the rest of the conversation. When she hung up she came to me, and I saw her looking very annoyed. I asked who was on the phone, and she said, "That Danilo again." "Is he annoying you?" "No. Don't worry, nothing important, it's OK." I didn't ask anything else.'

'Did she mention anything to you about a meeting with him the next day?'

'No, not that afternoon.'

The next day, Elisa was, he says, 'completely fine, happy because we were going to the countryside and Eliana her friend was coming as a guest'.

'The plan was that she was coming to your house for lunch?'

'Yes. They were due to go out together, go to Mass, and around

[255]

12.30 or 12.45 the plan was to come back to Via Mazzini because I had the car and we were going to go together. My parents and my brother had already left early in the morning.'

'Did you see Elisa leave the house with Eliana?'

'Yes. That was the last time I saw my sister.'

Gildo describes what happened in the following hours: the confusion, the rising sense of fear, the frantic searching and the little lies that Eliana had told. 'I had a funny feeling,' he says. 'I knew Elisa too well. What Eliana had recounted to me didn't convince me properly. I began to organise a search. In the meantime, I thought of going back to Eliana, who was at my home. Then I challenged her with much more decisiveness. At that point she told me the truth, that they had never gone to Mass.'

Significantly, Gildo says that, from what he remembers, Eliana had said Elisa was due to meet Danilo 'behind the church', by the back door, not the main entrance. From there, there was a staircase up to the Newman Centre and beyond. 'At that point, when I hear the name of Danilo Restivo, my anxiety increases even further.' Shortly afterwards, he says, 'My parents and my brother arrived, as they'd hurried home. My mother had a feeling that perhaps something serious had happened.

'Then I discovered that the priest of the church had just left for a thermal place near Rome, so the church was shut. Strange. I asked to talk to someone who had the keys, and they opened it for me and I went behind the altar, because I still had in mind what Restivo had said, but I didn't find anything. The door that gave access to the Newman Centre was closed. They said that they didn't have the keys, only the priest had the keys . . . I stayed a bit longer in the church, but I didn't find anything useful. That afternoon was a succession of events, and we were beginning to have the sensation that something serious had happened . . .'

At the end of his testimony, when told he can leave the stand, he pushes himself up on his crutches and stares at Restivo. He fixes on him for four or five seconds, just glaring as if he were taking aim. During his testimony I could see a couple of jurors weeping quietly, and when we meet for dinner later Gildo tells me that the interpreter had hugged him in the waiting room afterwards.

As usual, when Gildo emerges from the courtroom, there are a dozen Italian journalists wanting to interview him. He looks exhausted, but he feels it his duty to talk to reporters and he patiently speaks to everyone. 'I hope that the hour of justice has arrived. And we're waiting for him in Italy because we're hoping, as we have for eighteen years, that he'll be tried and sentenced for Elisa's murder.'

That evening we go for dinner with a couple of other journalists and Gildo's wife, Irene. As always, Gildo is good-humoured, making everyone laugh and guffawing when someone amuses him. But he looks shattered. Partly because he's on crutches and his leg is very painful, he moves slowly, wincing every few metres. 'Today', he says to me as we're standing outside the restaurant, 'really took it out of me.'

*

It's beginning to feel a bit like Groundhog Day: every morning the same faces in the same places; the same rituals at the same times. 'Court rise,' the usher barks, and we all stand and bow to the judge. The huge red leather chair is pushed in behind him as he sits. 'Yes, Mr Bowes,' he says to the prosecuting QC, who is on his feet. There are discussions about procedure and admissions before the jury is brought in. We hear evidence at great length. Most days I wonder whether the jury will be able to follow this torrent of facts. Sometimes I see them yawning and their heads hanging low, chin on chest, as if being dragged towards sleep. Sometimes I feel pulled that way myself. The court usher plays patience on her computer. The High Sheriff of Hampshire visits for the day and yawns repeatedly on the dais by the judge.

By now I know the court staff so well that they barely check my bag when going through security. One day I realise, with embarrassment, that I've tried to wander into court with various air-rifle pellets in my pocket. They were in my jacket from last weekend's attempt to kill some grey squirrels that were damaging some young trees. The metal detector went off and I had to explain to the Italian security guard, Gennaro, just why I was taking something similar to bullets into the courtroom. Days become weeks, and you get used to the rhythm of the courtroom. Michael Bowes QC, counsel for the prosecution, buys coffees and Kit-Kats for his staff. Jeremy, Restivo's barrister, has to put up with notes from Restivo being passed to him through the slits in the dock. 'Listen to me very carefully,' he says, exasperated, on one occasion. 'Stop telling me to ask silly questions, as it's not going to help your defence.' One of the barristers working alongside Bowes asks me to let him know if I, with my 'encyclopaedic knowledge' of the case, think they've missed anything that might be useful. I'm more amused than flattered by the idea that I might be roped in to help the prosecution.

There are constant pauses and delays: witnesses are on holiday, or are available but have to be heard in conjunction with someone else who is testifying at another trial somewhere else in the country. The case plods on, but it's barely being reported in the British media. Apart from the first day, when the prosecution's opening statement was reported, the case has been almost completely ignored by the nationals. Only the *Daily Echo* from Bournemouth and local ITV and BBC reporters are still in court. It's hard to know why a story which I find so extraordinary, so compelling and sad, has been so thoroughly ignored. It might be because it's running almost parallel with the Milly Dowler murder trial, or because the case is so complicated that it can't be encapsulated in a few paragraphs. But most of us journalists who are still here reckon, sadly, that the case has been overlooked for the daft reason that the victim wasn't an attractive blonde in her teens.

More witnesses are heard via video link: the doctor who had put a stitch in Restivo's hand after the alleged fall down the escalators on 12 September 1993; the policeman who accompanied Restivo to those escalators the following day; another who had interviewed him. I get increasingly frustrated with the woeful translator in the Winchester court, who repeatedly gets things completely wrong: she's unable to translate *lamiera* ('sheet' or 'plate'), *pozzanghera* ('puddle') or *cerotto* ('plaster'); she mistranslates *parroco* for *parrocchia*, so that the question 'To which parish did you belong?' becomes 'To which priest did you belong?', which the witness finds understandably weird. She assumes *galleria* means 'gallery' (it's actually a tunnel) and, perhaps because of prudishness, doesn't translate the words 'masturbation' or 'penis' at all. An Italian journalist and I are squirming in our seats most of the time, wondering what she'll get wrong next. Eventually, even the monoglots realise there's a problem, and a new translator is brought in.

*

Professor Francesco Introna arrives from Bari to give evidence. A professor of legal medicine, he was the first forensic pathologist to examine the body of Elisa Claps on 17 March 2010. The jury is shown a photograph of the mummified body. It's the first time I've seen the image, and suddenly the whole horror of the case rears up. I'm so used to seeing that familiar, smiling shot of Elisa but this is brutal and black: there are dark stains against the wall where her pelvis and chest would have been, though now they've shrunk and disappeared and all that's left is a black memory on the wall. There are two shoes at odd angles with barely any legs left; a jumper that looks more like a string vest; a head with some teeth, but it's disconnected from the spinal cord. Elisa has been reduced to black dust. There are tiles on top of the body, and there, by her feet and half covered with dust and debris, are her perfectly folded glasses. It's a terrible, moving image, a reminder that a sixteen-year-old girl with her life before her was just left here to rot, to sink into dust all alone.

I listen to Professor Introna's evidence in a sort of trance. He describes his hypothesis that, because of the position of Elisa's hair, the body had been dragged. He thinks she had reached the garret alive because the staircase leading there was so steep and the door so small. The two semicircular stains on the wall corresponding to the pelvis and shoulders 'both indicate that the body touched the wall and all the decomposition and skeletonisation happened in that place'. He describes details that are noticeably similar to the Heather Barnett murder: the lowering of the trousers and the cutting of the bra. He then describes the lesions to the bones that enabled him to reconstruct the stab wounds. There's a ripple of laughter as he asks the new interpreter, a veiled woman from Sardinia, to stand up and turn around so that he can demonstrate the assailant's stabs on her back. It's strange what we laugh at.

Haemorrhages in intimate parts of the body lead him to suspect that there was a sexual element to the attack. He describes how his team had realised that the only way to get such a perfectly straight cut along a clump of hair was for it to be cut when glued together by dried blood. Introna confirms that 'exactly above the body a piece of wood from the roof had been removed to increase the ventilation of the place'.

Another forensics expert, Professor Cristina Cattaneo, in a red velvet trouser suit, gives her evidence in fluent English. It was she

who had analysed Elisa's hands and identified 'pelliferous formations' that appeared to be hanks of hair in both of her palms. Later
the same day, Dr Eva Sacchi describes the state of Elisa's clothing:
various cuts had been made with scissors to the jeans, jumper and
bra. She talks about the stones found in the tread of Elisa's shoes.

'Did you', Bowes asks, 'conduct matching exercises between
stones in her shoe and stones in the loft where her body was found?'

'Yes.'

'Without going into detail, did you find similarities between
stones in her shoe and stones in the loft?'

'Yes.'

'Does the finding of the stones help you to say whether Elisa
Claps walked, a little bit at least, in the loft?'

'Yes.'

'And your opinion?'

'I think that Elisa Claps arrived alive.'

*

Various transcripts of interviews with Restivo and recorded
conversations from covert surveillance were read into the court
record. For hours a lawyer reads page after page of material, sometimes doing a double-act with a policeman who plays the part
of Restivo's wife. Certain sentences make you sit up, offering as
they do a tiny insight into the strange man on trial. 'My dream
was to be admitted to the faculty of dentistry,' Restivo had said in
court proceedings in Italy in February 1995. '[It's something] I had
promised my grandmother on her deathbed.' Explaining why he
had gone to the escalators by himself, he said: 'It may seem odd
that I was alone, but for me it was normal. It gives me time to
think . . .' He describes the effect blood has on him: 'Normally the
sight of blood upsets me . . . Many times it has happened, I faint

at the sight of blood.' Interestingly, there's evidence, from email exchanges, that he actually got an almost sexual excitement from seeing blood. There are also examples of his bizarre logic. Asked whether he had met the Albanian, Eris Gega, before Elisa's disappearance, he responds: 'Without a doubt I know many people. I may have said it [that Gega should deny knowing him], but that doesn't mean I [did] know him.'

Covert recording from June 2004 hears Restivo musing about 'my wonderful innocence', and two years later he talks about what happens when he gets hold of someone's hair: '[When I] touch the hair, hold it in the hand . . . then everything is visible, everything.' It sounds to me as if he's not just explaining to his wife that he does everything openly, but that it transports him to a place of almost visionary ecstasy: 'everything is visible'.

*

One of the last witnesses to take the stand before Danilo Restivo himself is Eliana De Cillis. The court in Winchester has no power to compel the citizens of other states to testify, and given the fact that she has always avoided further comment on the case, I never expected her to show up. But she comes up on the large screens. The last time I had seen her face was on TV during her trial in the 1990s, when she looked like a rather lost young girl: she had a thin, slightly spotty face and frizzy gingerish hair. Now, though, she's in her thirties. She's wearing a skin-tight purple top and still has long frizzy hair. It looks blonder. Her voice is hoarse and, although she now lives in the north, in Reggio Emilia, she still has a thick southern accent. There is something rather sad about her, and it's moving to think that as a timid teenager Eliana had been caught in the glare of a national story and that her dissimulations have haunted her ever since.

'The night before [her disappearance],' Mr Bowes reminded her, 'Elisa had said, "I'll tell you more about the meeting with Danilo Restivo when I see you." When you saw her at about eleven that morning, did she tell you more?'

'I remember that she had to see him because of a present for passing her retakes.' Eliana goes on to describe seeing Elisa go off for the meeting 'out of the corner of my eye'.

'Was that the last time you ever saw Elisa?'

'Yes.'

'Did you go to the phone boxes?'

'Yes.'

'Did you wait there for Elisa Claps?'

'Yes.'

'You had arranged to meet her at about 11.45?'

'Yes.'

'When she did not appear, what did you do?'

'I waited at the phone boxes.'

'For how long?'

'For five or ten minutes, then I moved, but I was always thereabouts. I was waiting.'

Inevitably, the cross-examination was tough on her. Restivo's defence team obviously knew that De Cillis had been tried for perjury, and they attacked her from the start.

'Have you always told the truth about the day on which Elisa disappeared?' asked Jeremy.

'Yes, I always said the truth.'

'Did you tell the truth to Elisa's brother, Gildo?'

'Yes.'

'The first time that you spoke to him that day, after Elisa had failed to meet you at the phone booths, was when you went to his house to speak to him on the intercom?'

She nods. 'I went to intercom him.'

'And he was worried as to why Elisa was not with you?'

'Yes.'

'And did you give him a truthful account of where you had last seen Elisa?'

'I told him that we had been to Mass because Elisa didn't want it to be known that she had met Danilo Restivo. That's what I had understood.'

'You didn't tell Gildo the truth, did you?'

'No. In that moment, no.'

Jeremy quoted a long passage from De Cillis's earlier evidence to an Italian court in which she said that she had considered telling a lie regarding her whereabouts to her own parents. 'Do you remember giving that evidence to the court in 1995?'

'I always told the truth.'

'My question was, do you remember giving that evidence to the court that day in 1995?'

'I always told the truth. I don't remember what was asked in 1995.' Her arms are crossed and she's looking defensive now. The Italian judge interrupts the interrogation to say that the witness doesn't remember what she said in 1995, but that she remembers telling the truth at the time.

'I always told the truth,' she says again.

*

Lieutenant Colonel Gianpietro Lago comes in person to the court. He was one of the forensic scientists who examined Elisa's clothing. He called her jumper exhibit 44. He had divided it into four sections. The only one showing male DNA was called section 44.1, which was then divided into ten areas for further sampling. 44.1.10 alone produced a mix of male and female DNA. That area was then divided into a nine-section grid, and

DNA matching the profile of Danilo Restivo was found on section B3.

'What was the source of that DNA?' the prosecution asks.

'In our opinion and our experience,' Lago says in accented English, 'this is compatible with three kinds of body fluids in a forensic field. Typically these are blood, semen and saliva.' A deposit of saliva would require 'direct and long contact with the mouth', and all tests for saliva were negative. All tests for semen were also negative.

'What opinion, then, do you have on this body fluid?'

'With regard to the information and data, my opinion is that the body fluid from which the DNA came is blood.'

He is asked to give the probability that it was, indeed, blood. 'My conclusion is that, with a high probability, the DNA we found in B3 comes from blood. The expression of my level of confidence is that there's an extremely strong probability that the cells and DNA come from blood. For the second hypothesis [that it was from saliva], the probability is very, very low.'

That expression of probability is hotly contested by the defence. To many of us sat in the court, the provenance of the DNA hardly seemed to matter much. It would, presumably, have been more damning if it were, indeed, from blood, especially since Restivo obviously had a cut to his hand; but even saliva would have been telling and, given that DNA in that quantity from saliva could only have been deposited by sucking or repeated spitting on the jumper, it didn't seem likely that an innocent, everyday encounter was the cause. But more experts are called, and all offer their expertise on the minutiae of DNA testing and the likelihood that the source of Restivo's DNA was blood. There is debate, detail and, for the layman, a lot of confusion. And all this despite the fact that Restivo isn't even on trial for the murder of Elisa Claps. Not for the first time during the trial, it becomes very difficult to see the wood for the trees. The simple fact is that Restivo's DNA was on the jumper.

*

17 June 2011. There's a buzz in the courtroom this morning as Danilo Restivo is due to go into the witness box. The press box and public gallery are full, and there's a tangible sense of anticipation and excitement. The first sign something is wrong comes when, before the jury has entered, Restivo calls his counsel over and they have a long, whispered exchange. The defendant, it emerges, has a headache and doesn't feel up to taking the stand. His QC is visibly frustrated, and debate ensues about what should be done. The judge expresses himself 'concerned and disappointed' at another hiccup, but is reluctant to force an allegedly ill man to defend himself, and – after an hour's deliberation – the hearing is delayed until after the weekend. Journalists flood out, calling their editors to say that Restivo has, effectively, pulled a sickie.

The following Monday, however, on 20 June, Restivo does testify. He's wearing a blue shirt, a blue-and-white diagonally striped tie and a pinstripe suit. His thinning hair has been swept back and, from here, it's possible to see that his sideburns are greying. He confirms that he's thirty-nine, that he was born on 3 April 1972 in Erice, Sicily. He lived in Sardinia for ten years, in Cagliari, before moving to mainland Italy because of his father's work.

Jeremy's tactic throughout the questioning appears to be to take the wind out of the prosecution's sails and ask every awkward question he can of his client.

'When was the first time that you cut the hair of a woman or young girl?' he asks.

'When I was fifteen or sixteen years old, at the scientific school.'

Restivo's voice is still slightly high-pitched and childlike. He replies in Italian, and his translator renders it in English. 'It started as a bet between schoolmates and classmates. [I did it] to try and get accepted into a group of friends.' That would become a constant throughout the following days: Restivo desperately trying to be accepted and repeatedly finding himself rejected.

'That was the first time?'

'Yes.'

'Did you continue to do it?'

'Yes, I kept doing it.'

'Still because of a bet?'

'The first three times because of a bet. After I started liking it and I did not mean any harm to anybody. I didn't do it because I had a dislike of a particular girl. The problem is that I like touching hair and smelling hair, but I couldn't smell any odour, that was the problem, because I had a problem with my nose.' He starts agitating his fingers under his nose, acting out the frustration that he can't smell the hair. Many people have suggested that Restivo might be impotent and that his inability to smell hair might be some spooky kind of metaphor for that.

'What was it about what you did that you liked?'

'I liked touching hair and smelling hair, but I couldn't smell the hair. And then I would throw the hair on the street.'

'We have heard from a young couple describing a cinema where you cut hair, and they had the impression you were masturbating. Were you?'

'No, I have never masturbated in public places because of the education that I received from my family. It's a very serious offence to masturbate in public in Italy . . . and I guess it's the same in other countries.'

It's a reply that would constantly be repeated over the following days, explaining bizarre behaviour, or denying it, through reference to the good behaviour his uncles or parents or employers had taught him.

'Is it not an offence to assault women by cutting hair?'

'I never knew that it was an offence, and if it is I apologise.'

Throughout the questioning, Jeremy is almost impatient and gives Restivo very short shrift. It's as if he himself were the prosecuting lawyer. Restivo talks about how women, or their parents, used to get angry or scared when he sent them flowers. He couldn't understand why they didn't want to receive flowers from him. He cuts an almost pitiful figure, that of a man longing to be accepted but whose every gesture was either scary or laughable. Restivo presents himself as a thoughtful, caring man who's just a bit unlucky, what they would call in Italian *sfigato*, jinxed. And watching him he is, indeed, a sorry figure: the interpreter has to help him find things on the map; he knocks a folder off the edge of the witness box; he knocks over the microphone.

But over the course of the ensuing hours another side of him emerges. When describing his solitary confinement while awaiting trail in 1994, he becomes very self-pitying and angry. 'I was in isolation for thirty-seven days,' he says, showing his teeth and, it seems, almost on the edge of tears. He's almost shaking with rage. 'I was physically and psychologically abused.'

Very soon it becomes clear that Restivo is an extraordinary hypochondriac. Jeremy asks him questions about his health, and Restivo is unstoppable, talking and talking about the problems he's suffered. 'Medical records', he says bombastically, 'show that I was operated on in 2001 for a thyroidectomy. My vocal cords were paralysed and my voice was affected until treated with injections.'

'In what way was your voice affected?' Jeremy asks.

Rather than describing a hoarse voice, Restivo then growls, making some of the jurors either jump or laugh. He describes then his photophobia, which he says is a consequence of a dosage of thyroxine.

'What effect did that have on your appearance?'

'My eyes look bulging,' he says, taking off his glasses and thrusting his face forwards to show his proptosis, the eyeballs almost jumping out of his head like a cartoon. Again, the jury and members of the public laugh at this strange display, and Restivo immediately looks offended and rejected again.

'In 2006, I was suffering from sleep apnoea.' The consequence, he says, is that he forgets things.

'Is that a complete summary of your medical conditions?' Jeremy asks wearily.

Restivo describes a hernia operation. Then he had another hernia problem 'as a consequence of me dragging a flower pot of three and a half kilos'.

'Does that complete the summary?' Jeremy asks again.

Restivo then describes an operation on his nose, since his nostrils were too small, which was why he couldn't smell.

'Does that complete the summary of your medical condition?'

'In 1994, I dislocated both my shoulders and I've suffered from tendonitis since 1985. And between 2002 and 2004 I had to undergo treatment for that problem.'

The list of ailments goes on and on, and each time Restivo gives minute details and explanations. It seems as if he's somehow so terrified about his own well-being that, perhaps, he disregards everybody else's. Eventually, Jeremy simply barks 'pause' at his client and leads the questioning elsewhere. Even then, however, Restivo's poor health re-emerges in explanations. It took him thirty-four minutes to walk the hundred metres from his house to the bus stop on the morning Heather Barnett was murdered because he was, he says, hyperventilating due to the paralysis of his left vocal nerve and a loss of feeling on the left side of his neck. At one point during a rambling reply, Jeremy appears so impatient with his client that he asks bluntly: 'Does "cut to the chase" translate into Italian?'

After years of reading and researching Restivo, imagining him to be some kind of monster, I'm surprised to find myself feeling almost sorry for him. He is truly pathetic, and the description of the house he shared with Fiamma sounds desolate. He wanted to buy her curtains, he says, 'because Fiamma's bedroom was in a pitiful state when I met her. Rain came through the roof, there was mould, the curtains were ruined, the bed was damaged . . .' None of his family are here. He occasionally looks up at the public gallery, and once even asks why his wife isn't present. It's as if everyone has abandoned him. When I express my sense of unexpected sympathy for Restivo, a more hard-bitten Italian journalist shakes his head, explaining that this is the tactic Restivo has always used to encourage people to care for him, to take pity on him. It's an act, he says, one calculated to make women, in particular, feel called to mother him.

Soon afterwards, an instance of Restivo's so-called caring is described, and suddenly I remember what this man has done.

'According to the witness statement,' Jeremy says, talking about Terry and Caitlin minutes after they had seen their murdered mother, 'you hugged those children?'

'Yes.'

'You understand that the prosecution case is that that morning you had murdered their mother?'

'I've never killed anybody.'

'You were playing out a repulsive charade, you understand that is the prosecution case?'

'No, it was sincere.'

Sometimes his excuses and reasoning provoke titters in the public gallery. When asked why he had a balaclava in his coat pocket on a warm spring day in the park in Bournemouth, he once again launches into his medical history. 'Earlier you asked about my medical condition. I told you there was something I hadn't remembered. And among these medical conditions there is the chronic sinus condition, an inflammation of the nerves. The balaclava was suggested to me by my GP for when it was too cold, and given that in my car the heating didn't work, when I turned the engine on for ten minutes to heat the car I would use the balaclava to protect myself from the cold. I've never driven with my balaclava on.' The image of him sat there in the car for ten minutes wearing a balaclava because that's what his doctor had told him to do for his sinuses was too much even for the jury, and one or two visibly giggled at the absurdity of the explanation.

'You had a balaclava to keep your sinuses warm inside the car?'

'Yes.'

There are many more surreal moments. When asked why he had a bag with only tissues and a filleting knife, Restivo explains that he had animals at home – a bearded dragon, a lizard and five geckos – and that he used to feed insects to those animals. So he had the knife and tissues to capture insects and put them in the bag. When asked why he kept acrylic hair in a drawer, he explains that he had used it for a moustache at a fancy-dress party where he got dressed up as a Mexican.

If his own defence counsel had been scathing towards Restivo, Michael Bowes, QC for the prosecution, demolishes what little is left of his credibility over the following two and a half days. Bowes is like a weary headmaster: methodical, patient and seemingly kind. He often bounces his palms slowly up and down, as if honking an invisible horn, as he explains his questions. But he can also be lethal, spotting any tiny inconsistency and asking questions that drip with incredulity and sarcasm. He also frequently manages to needle Restivo sufficiently that he becomes infuriated and reveals a very nasty, aggressive side.

Bowes's opening gambit is to underline the extraordinary similarities in the murders.

'Both victims had their hair cut after death, didn't they?' he asks.

'Based on what the documents say, yes.' Restivo stares at him with his head to one side.

'Do you agree that is a similar feature?'

'I haven't cut hair . . .'

'I didn't ask that. I asked: "Do you agree that it is a similar feature?"'

'I don't know, I don't know.'

'Do you agree that both victims having their bra cut is a similar feature?'

'I don't know.'

'That both having their trousers and pants pulled down is a similar feature?'

'I don't know, I don't know.'

'Do you agree that in each case it looks as though the killer liked cutting hair?'

'I don't know this, I haven't killed either Elisa Claps or Heather Barnett. You are suggesting that the killer is me, and I'm telling you that it's not me.'

'At the moment,' Bowes says in a soft, almost soothing voice, 'we're just talking about the killer generally. From everything you've seen and heard, does it look like the killer of both women liked cutting hair?'

'I don't know.'

'Two murders, nine years apart, yes? And in different countries, yes? And you had a connection with both victims, didn't you?'

Restivo doesn't answer.

'Yesterday,' says Bowes, his voice still soft, 'you talked about touching hair, but of course you cut it as well, didn't you? That means you must have had scissors with you, doesn't it? Did you take them with you every day?'

'The scissors had a rounded edge so as not to harm anybody.'

'That wasn't the question.'

'Yes, perhaps.'

'So you would go on the bus and look for girls with long hair?'

'Yes.'

'I'm going to suggest to you that a certain amount of stalking and planning went into your hair-cutting episodes.'

'No, it wasn't planned and I wasn't stalking them . . . in my opinion stalking is when you stare and follow this person everywhere and you exasperate this person. This is not what happened in my case, it was something that just happened.'

'When Holly [Stroud] got to school, she found a sticky something in her hair. What did you put in her hair?'

'I didn't put anything in it. Because my nose was blocked, I had in my pocket a substance, an oily substance. It's possible that the pot got broken, and perhaps if I touched her hair somehow this oil got transferred.'

Bowes repeats the testimony of one witness who saw Restivo take off his anorak and touch a girl's hair.

'I used to do it, I admit that, but it was one of my techniques . . .'

'Explain a little more about your techniques.'

'I used my jacket to cover my hands and then I would pull the hair and cut the hair from underneath the jacket.'

'With the hair, you liked the touch, and so you cut the hair, yes? And then you'd got your trophy, hadn't you?'

'Yes.'

'Didn't you want to keep your trophy?'

'As I said, I tried to smell it, but I couldn't, so I threw it away. I would feel the touch of the hair and then throw it on the streets.'

'If you're telling the truth, you couldn't smell anyway.'

'Perhaps this was one of the reasons why I cut hair, because I couldn't smell the scent of a woman.'

'And so what you wanted to do was touch the hair, yes? If you're just going to throw it away, what's the point in cutting it?'

'Because I wanted to feel the touch.'

'But you've already touched it.'

'But I kept touching it afterwards.'

'When would you throw it away?'

'When I got off the bus, just enough time to smell the hair. I kept touching the hair and would then throw it away.'

Repeatedly, when Bowes points out blatant contradictions in Restivo's replies to police from his first arrest in 2004 or from interviews after his arrest in 2010, Restivo's tactic is to say that he lied because he didn't trust the police and because they were leaking material to the Italian press. As Restivo gets more and more irate, he starts pointing the finger at various police officers and journalists sitting in court. As Bowes slowly points out the inconsistencies in the various versions Restivo has given – mainly regarding the green towel and computer activity at Nacro – Restivo is backed into a corner and resorts to absurd lies, often changing his version in front of the whole court. Occasionally Bowes interrupts him and asks the obvious, and damning, question: 'Mr Restivo,' he says, shaking his head, 'you're just making this up, aren't you?'

Restivo's defensive tactics vary: he often invokes his ill health and says that sleep apnoea causes loss of memory.

'The prosecution doesn't accept that,' Bowes says sharply. 'It accepts you have sleep apnoea, but not that it affects your memory.'

'You don't accept anything, that's the problem,' Restivo says.

At other times Restivo claims that it's other people who have a memory problem. Pressed as to why his wife said that he was daft to put his trainers in bleach because he should have smelt it first, Restivo says: 'My wife has the problem that she had forgotten that until 2003 I had no sense of smell. As I said earlier, my nose was operated on in August 2004. From August 2004, I could only smell lightly. I had a light perception. And I also remember that the 17 March 2010, I had the same problem with my nose, and I went to the Poole hospital . . .' On and on it goes, talking about the woe with his nostrils.

At other times he pompously announces that he has a startling revelation to make. On one occasion the judge steps in to clarify that Restivo is, indeed, challenging the testimony of the computer expert who had testified that there was no human activity on the computer at Nacro. 'Yes, I can demonstrate it. It will be my defence barrister who will demonstrate it because I have given him a note to that effect.' We break for lunch and afterwards Restivo merely says: 'I apologise. It was an automatic update [on the computer]. I'm sorry about that.'

Most frequently, however, he just repeats the same line again and again: '*Io, il dodici novembre duemiladue, ero al Nacro*' – 'I, on 12 November 2002, was at Nacro.' He repeats it ad nauseam, his eyelids lowered and his head to one side. Sometimes he says it softly, sometimes angrily, sometimes like he's almost bored of saying it, but the words never change.

Bowes starts asking him about his habit of going to Pig Shoot Lane outside Bournemouth with a change of clothing and shoes. 'You're seen [on police surveillance videos] removing your clothing, taking off over-trousers and changing trainers. Why?'

Restivo comes up with more zany explanations: 'The shoes that I was wearing had a sole full of mud. If I had driven with shoes full of mud, the shoes on the accelerator or the brakes would have slipped and I could have caused an accident. This was taught to me both by the garden centre where I used to work . . . and the person who taught me how to drive in Italy.'

'Were you scared the shirt would get muddy as well?' Bowes asks sarcastically.

'The problem that I have with the thyroid', Restivo says, launching into another dubious explanation, 'is the regulation of my body temperature. I give you this information so that we understand each other. In 1997, I developed a condition [Graves' disease] which affected the thyroid. I had a hyper-production of thyroxine in the blood . . . One of the side effects is warm and cold hands, warm body and cold body . . . when they removed my thyroid in 2001, my body had to absorb thyroxine from outside. The correct dosage wasn't accepted by my body and I had, since 2001 until 2006 and 2007, the problem of the correct dosage of thyroxine in my blood. In this period of time, my dosage went from 125 mg to 250 mg to 125 mg to 150 mg to 175 mg. This different dosage was due to the fact that my body wouldn't accept the right dosage, and the temperature of my body changes. Sometimes I'm cold, sometimes I sweat. Now with 175 mg, even though the dosage is slightly high, I manage to maintain the same body temperature.'

'Finished?' Bowes says aggressively.

Restivo stares at him angrily, surprised that not everyone is fascinated by his medical meanderings. So why, Bowes wonders, would he bend down in the long grass when women walked past?

'Can I point something out?' Restivo asks. 'I've said in previous days that I used to collect insects in order to feed my geckos. When I bent over I had just caught some insect. I point out that I bent down and I must have collected the insect, and in the meantime just by chance the woman must have gone past. I went to that park just because I like nature. I like to observe birds, jays, kingfishers, swans, the ducks. I like nature, I like dogs. I must have stopped many people, which you can't see from the video, who had dogs. Before coming here I had a dog. I had a Dobermann who took part in beauty contests . . .'

The idea of Restivo having a Dobermann that was dressed up in ribbons for dog pageants is too much for me. There's something so absurd and ridiculous about this sinister man parading a dog that I get the giggles and struggle to stifle them. It's terrible to be laughing in a murder trial, but the more I try to stop, the harder it is. Many of the jurors, too, are openly chuckling as the explanations for his behaviour become more and more unbelievable.

Restivo starts suggesting that he had picked up the filleting knife in order to protect children who were playing near by, but Bowes points out that it was a school day.

'Mr Restivo, you're just making up a story about the little children and the knife. It's just a fantasy, isn't it?'

Restivo shakes his head.

'Lying there gleaming, was it?' Bowes is back at his most sarcastic.

'I don't remember, honestly. You're asking me questions from 2004. How it gleamed, I don't know.'

'It was your knife you took to Throop, but once police had taken it, you had to buy a new box set. What you were doing at Throop with a bag and knife and balaclava was stalking women.'

'No, no, no, I was simply relaxing and enjoying nature, and was there to collect insects. Never, ever have I stalked women. OK?'

'Except on buses?'

Restivo is by now getting angry. Bowes seems to needle him deliberately just minutes before we're due to break for lunch or for the end of the day. It's as if it's a tactic to wind up Restivo into one of his frothing, furious states so that the jurors have that picture of him in their minds during the pause: that snarling, crepuscular face going red, his teeth literally bared, his dead eyes fixed on Bowes as he spits his anger at him. It's fascinating watching Restivo, seeing how quickly he can go from being peeved and childish to pompous and legalistic; how quickly he moves from the wounded, humiliated hypochondriac to the threatening, rather frightening figure he is now. There seem to be multiple personalities in there and, before the whole court, he slips from one to the other in a matter of minutes.

The next day, Bowes takes Restivo through the day of Elisa Claps's murder. Just like when he was accused of Barnett's murder, Restivo now resorts to one line that he repeats again and again. 'I saw Elisa Claps leave the church at 11.50,' he says in reply to every question about the loft, about him having the keys to the church, about him enticing Elisa up there on the pretext of him having a present for her.

'In the course of the struggle she cut her own hand deeply, didn't she, by grasping the knife you were using?'

'I saw Elisa Claps leaving the church at 11.50 . . .'

'And in the course of knifing her and struggling, your knife slipped a bit and you caught yourself on the right hand?'

'I saw Elisa Claps leaving the church at 11.50. I got injured on the escalator.'

'You were injured by your own knife, weren't you?'

'I saw Elisa Claps leaving the church at 11.50, OK?'

When Bowes asks Restivo about the escalators where he claims to have been cut, the prosecuting QC is again at his most sarcastic. Why on earth, he wonders, would someone rushing back for lunch on their mother's saint's day want to stop and look at some escalators? What was so fascinating about them? Bowes takes him through the police photographs of the escalators one by one, asking Restivo what it was that he found interesting in these dull, concrete tunnels. Restivo mutters a brief, unconvincing explanation, saying that there wasn't much to do in Potenza back in those days. But you had only been there a few days before, Bowes says, so why did you need to go back?

'I hadn't seen all of them [the staircases].'

Restivo claims to have been there just a few days before with Paola, the woman he fancied. Bowes again ridicules the idea that a construction site was an appropriate place for a date.

Bowes looks at the defendant with raised eyebrows. 'What did you say to this girl? "Paola, let's go to a building site"?'

'I might have said, "Paola, I'm curious to see [it]. If you're curious as well, we could go."'

'To a building site, for an evening out?'

Bowes then reads out Restivo's description of his fall on those escalators, which is taken from his statement in 1993: '"I tripped . . . I must point out that I did not fall straight away, I lost my balance but did not fall. [There were] two or three steps with my right foot, two or three with my left foot, two or three with my right foot . . ."' He then rolled down the entire flight of steps, holding, bizarrely, a hand over his teeth to protect them. The whole reconstruction has a ring of absurdity about it. It sounds more as if he were dancing, moving from foot to foot and then somersaulting all the way down the stairs.

Bowes concludes his cross-examination by putting to the defendant the central accusation: 'On 12 November 2002, you went into Heather Barnett's house. You went . . .'

'On 12 November 2002,' Restivo says, interrupting, 'I was at Nacro.'

'In almost exactly the same way, on 12 September 1993 . . .'

'I didn't kill Elisa Claps,' Restivo says. 'I saw her leave the church at 11.50, and I was at Nacro on 12 November at 9 a.m. OK?'

'Elisa Claps's body was found last year in the loft where you left her.'

'I never knew of and I never saw the loft. I saw Elisa Claps leaving the church at 11.50. I followed her with my gaze . . .'

'And just like Heather Barnett, her hair was cut after death, her bra had been cut, her knickers and trousers lowered . . .'

'I've never killed anybody. I wasn't at Heather Barnett's house on 12 November. I was at Nacro.'

'You had murdered both of them.'

'I haven't killed anybody. I saw Elisa Claps leave the church at 11.50 through the curtains, and 12 November 2002 I was at Nacro.'

'No further questions, My Lord,' Bowes says, drawing to a close two and a half extraordinary days of cross-examination.

By then, Restivo was finished. He didn't have a shred of credibility left. Sometimes he could remember things too clearly: when he was lying he would make up absurdly detailed reconstructions, mentioning things from eighteen years ago that no one could possibly have remembered. At those moments he would put both index fingers vertically in the air and rotate them like cogs that were connected and making each other move. And other times he would have forgotten everything and, due to some medical ailment, would claim that he couldn't remember why he had done or said something. He had been both surly and obsequious, sometimes turning to the judge and saying 'My Lord' in heavily accented English. Sometimes you almost thought he had glimpsed one of his other personalities when he said that Elisa complained to him of being harassed by a man on that fateful morning in September 1993. It was, clearly, Restivo that had harassed her. Quite often, though, you watched him and wondered how he had got away with both murders for so very long. He appeared astonishingly stupid in the box. Every story he told rang false. He was slippery and deceitful. 'That's always been his strategy,' another Italian journalist said to me. 'He appears like the village idiot, and people underestimate him. He's actually very clever, very wily.' In the end my final impression of him was similar to that damning line Norman Douglas once used to describe Italian bureaucrats: the 'only intelligible expression is one of malice striving to break through a crust of congenital cretinism'.

In his final speech for the Crown, Michael Bowes was, as he had been throughout the trial, slow and precise. He put his head forward for emphasis on certain words or put his palm towards the jury, pushing it down as if it were on a pedal.

'You know what the prosecution case is,' he said. 'The one thing you don't leave outside the court is your common sense, and we submit that common sense does play a very substantial role in this case. It might seem quite complicated, but in the end it's actually straightforward: Restivo is indeed the man who murdered Heather Barnett . . . Let's remind ourselves of the basic similarities [between the two murders]: when Heather Barnett was found, the killer had placed a lock of someone else's hair in her right hand and her own hair in her left; her bra was cut, possibly torn, at the front, after death; and the position of her trousers and underwear were lowered just enough to reveal the pubic region. What had happened nine years earlier? Elisa Claps was murdered, her hair was cut after death, her bra was cut at the front, and the position of the trousers and the pants was the same. Two murders nine years apart in two different countries. Where does the defendant come in? He had links to both of them, he was very close by when both died. Elisa Claps never came out into the Potenza sunlight that Sunday morning. She had been lured to that loft by the promise of a present . . . his DNA was on her pullover . . . if her pullover has such rich traces of DNA, that's not his saliva, that's his blood.

'Throughout you may think he [Restivo] was evasive in the extreme. From time to time he had what we submit was selective amnesia; the fog of convenience came down. But when it helped him, his memory was razor sharp.'

With regard to hair-cutting, Bowes said that 'in each case there must have been stalking and planning. He murdered Heather

Barnett having stalked and planned. Every time he cut hair he took scissors with him. He stalked and selected and preyed. He was used to being tooled up. He agreed it must have been frightening and intrusive. All he cared about was himself and gratifying what he wanted to do. He's not harmless, he's very harmful indeed.'

Bowes went over all the evidence once more, outlining all the occasions on which Restivo's story 'just got more and more ridiculous'. Elisa, he said, had been a young girl who 'had been pestered quite a lot. What's the chance you would want to go with him into the church? Common sense is you want to stay out in the open. You might go to a cafe. It matters for his account. They didn't meet in the church. No one saw them at all. He said, "Let's go to the Newman Centre, let's just go a bit further, I've got a present for you." Realistically, his account of her going out into the sunshine is just nonsense. Eliana and Angelica were looking for her within minutes. They didn't see him either. Why? Because he wasn't there, he was up in the loft, murdering Elisa Claps.' Bowes pauses, looking down at his notes before talking rather more softly. 'Very awfully, it seems she didn't die immediately but might have lived for another fifteen minutes and effectively died in her own blood.

'Shortly after having butchered Elisa Claps, he's back outside, but he has a problem: he has that cut. He comes up with a story and is then stuck with it, the absolutely absurd one that he trips head-over-heels down a whole flight of stairs. There's no injury, but the one thing that did happen is that a tiny piece of metal sprung up and embedded itself in him. He has to try and give more detail. It was one to two centimetres long, triangular in shape and very thin, "absolutely tiny". It was a stupid lie but on and on it went. He had a sudden fascination with the architecture of concrete steps . . . The explanation is nonsense from beginning to end.'

As Bowes is talking, and appealing repeatedly to common sense, all I can think about is the Italian investigation in 1993. It's absurd that anyone ever believed Restivo's story. The more you hear it, the more ridiculous it sounds.

The lack of blood at Heather Barnett's house, and on Restivo, said Bowes, 'is a bit like Sherlock Holmes with the dog that didn't bark. What isn't there that should be there? The answer: more blood. Couldn't all the blood have been used up? No, definitely not, you'd certainly get blood. What has happened is, of course, quite obvious. Danilo Restivo changed his outer clothing and his trainers, transferring blood into the inside of his trainers, and that is what has caught him out.' He changed his trainers because he was, said Bowes, 'forensically aware'. The bins were collected that morning, as Restivo knew they would be. He must have simply dumped his bloodied clothes there, knowing they would be taken away.

With his usual sarcasm, Bowes described Restivo's habit of lying and, with regard to the use of the computer at Nacro, Restivo offered 'a particularly special treat – no fewer than three explanations. Version one: when interviewed in June 2004, he says he went straight to the computer room and got on with work. But police put it to him that there was no activity until much later. "Ah," he thinks – version two coming up, you'll like this one – "I didn't use it then, I had to wait for my turn to get onto it." But that didn't work either. Craig Wilson's report tells him there was no activity until 10.10. Oops, that's blown it. "I know, brilliant, [the tutor] Jim Todd has died, I can say I had the password. But I've got one problem left: I was asked in 2004 if I had the password, and I said I never knew it, only the tutor had the password. Ah, that's blown it. I know, I'll have to try one of my specials – a ridiculous explanation. I'll say that in 2004 I quite deliberately lied [because of distrust of the police and journalists]." It's absolutely absurd and his lies have found him out.

'And so', says Bowes, 'I now come to the end. Both murders were clearly committed by the same person. He says, "I can't explain my DNA on Elisa Claps's jumper . . . I can't explain the blood on my trainers." The reason he can't explain is because it's him. The identity of the killer becomes crystal clear, doesn't it? The reason every piece of evidence points to him is because it was him.'

The final speech of Restivo's defence barrister, David Jeremy, was rather admirable. Jeremy had, throughout the trial, chipped away at the prosecution case, looking for any inconsistencies or contradictions. He didn't find many, but his questions were always probing. He knew that, in being asked to defend Restivo, he hadn't just been dealt a bad hand, he barely had a hand at all. And yet for almost two months Jeremy had fought his corner, often even making the people in court smile with his wit and impish grin.

'I have asked myself the question "What am I going to tell the jury?" repeatedly in recent days,' he started. 'By the time Danilo Restivo had left the witness box, I was asking that question with expletives deleted. I doubt you'll ever see another case in which the defending barrister has so many bad things to say about his client. When you think of Restivo, good words do not fly from the pen. He is not a "my word is my bond" kind of a guy. You don't think for an instant that he traps insects with his bare hands and puts them in a holdall.

'I'm going to approach this [final speech] with the idea that Danilo Restivo told you many ridiculous lies. He is not, you may think, just a liar. He has a highly developed persecution complex . . . not trusting the police or the media. He has undoubtedly had health issues, and hypochondria should have been inserted in the list of health problems. He is wholly unable to answer a simple question with a simple answer. He has a hair fetish, causing obviously fear and anxiety. He is never-endingly garrulous and self-pitying. He presents a deeply unattractive oddity. Restivo is a gift to any prosecution, a gift.'

And yet, despite admitting that, Jeremy warned the jury about the dangers of the case: of the fact that the police were convinced he was their man, and that, 'however well-intended, the investigation ceases to be a search for evidence that will identify the murderer and becomes a search for evidence that will nail the suspect, evidence that will shore up a theory of guilt.

'In a case of this horror, it's a revealing fact that you laughed. It was completely understandable that you should do so: even in the context of this case some of what he had to say was laughable. Mr Bowes watched while Danilo Restivo self-destructed, no idea of the spectacle he had made of himself. He has had months if not years to invent a story. It was almost as if he were setting out to make things worse for himself. There was a childlike quality to Danilo Restivo in the witness box, and I hope I'm not being unfair to children. The changing lie, the failure to see how ridiculous a lie is, the constant resort to illness as an excuse . . . Danilo Restivo almost became a fairground attraction.'

Jeremy conceded that Restivo was 'odd, unusual, deeply unsympathetic', but said that there's 'an element of the beauty competition to a murder trial, and in a beauty competition Danilo Restivo would come last'. Don't judge him, Jeremy was effectively saying, on his oddities. Why, he asked, had it taken so long to bring this prosecution? Because there were weaknesses in their case, weaknesses that Jeremy listed one by one. There was no trial until now, he suggested, because of a 'lack of confidence' in the evidence.

It was telling that in inviting the jury to make up their own minds, he said that 'the dignity with which the Claps family have behaved will inspire you'.

Mr Justice Burnett, in his summing up, reiterated what had been obvious to everyone: that Restivo gave 'long, discursive, irrelevant answers and returned to his central themes regardless of what he was asked. Many aspects were contradictory and he often lied. He often gave what Mr Jeremy called "preposterous" answers. The central lie advanced by the defendant concerns his whereabouts at the time Heather Barnett was murdered.' It was the jury's job, he said, to 'consider whether there might be an innocent explanation for the lie'.

'Surreptitious cutting', he said, 'is bizarre and reprehensible and suggests a fetish of some sort. The fact that somebody has a fetish does not make him more likely to commit murder or serious crime. But an inevitable inference to be drawn is that the killer had a fetish for hair . . .' He then went through the facts of the case one by one, reiterating everything the jury had heard with succinct clarity.

*

It was late morning by the time the jury was sent out to consider its verdict. It was a surreal period, sitting in the chairs outside the courtroom just waiting. There wasn't anything to do but just hang around. The corridors slowly filled up with more reporters coming in for the final show.

I sat next to Phil James, the policeman who had led the original inquiry into the Heather Barnett murder until his retirement. I asked him what his impression of Danilo Restivo was. 'I think', he said, 'that he's a man who thinks he's cleverer than everyone else but isn't. He's slightly delusional, but he's not a stupid man. He looks it – he comes across as a bumbling idiot – but this is a man who clearly learned from the murder of Elisa Claps and, as a result of learning from that, he was able to think and plan much better. He needed an alibi because he didn't have an alibi for Elisa Claps; he put himself there with her. He needed to make sure he didn't have blood and other material on him. I think he was able to adapt, he was forensically aware. He's not stupid.'

We were just beginning to assume that no verdict was going to come in that day when the PA called all those concerned with the trial of Danilo Restivo back to court. Suddenly, people put away books and laptops and dictaphones and rushed upstairs. Within minutes everyone was sitting silently in court. The jury filed in and the foreman was asked if they had reached a verdict. They had. He was asked how they found the defendant.

'Guilty.'

As the judge and jury file out, the police look jubilant. They turn round to shake each other's hands and slap backs. They've been sitting next to us in the press box for almost two months now, and some journalists go over and congratulate them. My overwhelming feeling is one of relief: relief that the young jury has found Restivo guilty; relief that he won't be a danger for a very long time; relief for the Claps family that his true character has been revealed in all its horror. They, of course, are still waiting for another verdict in another murder trial, but this will, at least, give them some meagre comfort. More selfishly, I'm also relieved that, within a few days, I'll finally be able to go home. It's strange listening to months of material about parents desperately missing and mourning a child, and children missing and mourning a mother, when you haven't been home for so long.

A dozen journalists have already run out of the courtroom by now. It's just gone four o'clock, and if they're to make this evening's news, or tomorrow's paper, they've got to rush. I call Gildo to tell him the verdict. He, of course, has already heard.

*

Sentencing was the following day. Mr Justice Burnett had, until then, appeared as a meticulous but also softly spoken and solicitous

man. He was often apologising to the jury for delays and inconve-
niences. But when it came to sentencing, he was as hard as nails.
'Danilo Restivo,' he said, 'you have been convicted of the murder
of Heather Barnett on 12 November 2002. The evidence of your
guilt was overwhelming. In the course of your trial the jury also
heard evidence about the murder of Elisa Claps in 1993. Without
doubt you were responsible for her murder too. It is important
background because I approach this sentence on the basis that you
killed before. It would be quite unrealistic to pretend that you had
not.'

The judge briefly described what had happened to Heather
Barnett and Elisa Claps. He mentioned the mutilations and the
locks of hair. 'At least in part your motivation was sexual. You had
a long-standing hair fetish which you indulged by cutting wom-
en's hair in buses and cinemas . . . your planning was careful and
involved a good deal of guile.'

Most damning of all, in the eyes of the judge, was the fact that
Restivo knew that the children would find their mother's body. 'You
knew they would return home. You knew that they would find their
mother butchered on the bathroom floor. That will haunt those who
have sat through this trial . . . and the stark reality of the destructive
forces you unleashed continue to reverberate and will continue to
do so down the years. "Inhuman depravity" is an apt description.'
He told Restivo he had killed to satisfy 'a sadistic sexual appetite'; he
was, he said, a 'cold, depraved, calculating killer'.

'The depravity of this killing, the planning and premeditation,
the sexual content and the previous killing drive me to the starting point that thirty years would not be appropriate . . . I can find
no mitigation in this case, and none has been advanced on your
behalf. Having considered all the factors, I come to the conclusion
that there is no minimum period that could be set. You will never
be released from prison. Take him down.'

We file out of the courtroom, all amazed at the severity of the sentence. Various police officers and lawyers are shaking hands. I wander off to the window halfway down the steps, overlooking the cathedral. I can't believe it's all over. I pull out my phone.

'Gildo?'

'*Ciao*, Tobias.'

'Have you heard?'

'No. What?'

'Sentencing's just finished. He'll never be released.'

He sighs audibly and then there's silence at the other end of the phone. 'Thank you. That's very good. He won't be able to hurt anyone else.'

'No, he won't.'

'When are you getting here?' Gildo asks.

'Tomorrow,' I say. 'Tomorrow morning.'

'OK, give me a bell when you arrive.'

'Will do. *Un abbraccio.*'

By a strange twist of fate, within forty-eight hours of Restivo being sentenced in Winchester, Elisa is finally being laid to rest in Potenza.

Postscript

'I tuoi occhi son come la giovinezza
grandi, perduti, lasciano il mondo.
Potrebbero dirti morta senza rumore
e incamminare su te il cielo
passo a passo, seguendo l'alba.
Tu sei l'amore da portare in braccio
di corsa sino al vento, sino al mare:
e dirti fredda da scaldare al fuoco,
e dirti triste coi capelli neri
da pettinare eternamente, è come
deporti nel silenzio, starti accanto
udendo l'acqua battere alle rive.'
Alfonso Gatto, 'Potrebbero Dirti Morta'

1 July 2011. I'm driving towards Potenza. The terrible end is in sight: tomorrow Gildo and his family will finally be able to lay Elisa to rest. It's what they've wanted to be able to do for almost sixteen months, ever since she was found in that garret. In those eighteen years between her disappearance and now, they've longed to have her back and to have a place where they could bring flowers.

Today, as I head towards Potenza from Naples, they're driving to Bari to collect her remains. I'm pleased for them that they might get closure, or at least the beginning of it; not least because the timing, so soon after Restivo was sentenced to life in prison, seems apt. Personally, I'm relieved that this journey is finally, after years of following the story, coming to an end. I'm even content to be heading back to Potenza, a city that is so spectacularly unattractive at first sight but which I nonetheless warm to every time I come. I know all the roads that lead you there: the long tunnels; the transparent, tubular footbridges with spray-painted slogans of love; the mountains and towns on the way. I've grown very fond of the people of Potenza. It's almost as if I'm coming home.

But the closer I get, the more melancholic I feel. I turn off the music in the car and drive on in silence. A hint of the finality of what's about to happen is creeping up on me. It's as if all the emotions I've experienced while researching and writing this book have suddenly been concentrated into this one, tragic trip, and I get a tiny insight into what Gildo and his family must have been going through over all these years: disbelief, astonishment, anger, hope, fury, impotence, sorrow. I'm still a hundred miles from Potenza but even now I know that the ritual is going to be gruelling.

When I get there, it's immediately obvious that the whole city is expressing solidarity with the Claps family. Almost all the shops have A4 printouts in their windows saying that tomorrow, the day of the funeral, they'll be shut until 11.00 in memory of Elisa. When I get to the hotel, the woman on the reception desk asks why I've come. I tell her, and she shakes my hand, saying: 'Thank you for coming here for Elisa. Thank you for coming to Potenza.' I flick on the TV in my room and, on the local channel, there's a static screen with a message for viewers. It's a strange, overtly religious announcement which somehow sounds odd in English:

Civic Mourning
For Elisa and the Claps Family
God is truth and life. Man can delay truth but never impede it.
After the turbid, the divine source of the truth returns to gush
more limpid than ever.
I am life. After days of torment the seized souls return to
hope in rebirth.
Who believes in God, the sum of justice, will live in eternity.

After lunch I walk down towards Elisa's old school, the Liceo Classico Quinto Orazio Flacco. I take the lift down from the central square and turn right at the bottom towards the stadium. As I get closer I can see men and women from the *protezione civile* in their green fluorescent trousers ushering the long queues of citizens in the right direction. All around I can see TV vans, their huge antennas facing the sky.

I join the queue that snakes around the building. This is the *camera ardente*, where people can pay their respects before the funeral. We slowly shuffle forwards into the main hall of the school, with its rust-coloured walls and long wooden benches. There, in front of us, is Elisa's white coffin. White is the colour always used to indicate a deceased's innocence. One by one, people move forwards to touch it. Some kneel or make a sign of the cross. It seems unbelievable that it's her, that her remains are, after so many years of mystery, actually here in front of us all. A large photograph of her is projected onto the wall behind the coffin. The juxtaposition of the smiling, teenage face and this, almost eighteen years later, is terrible. A small cushion saying *'sempre insieme'* – 'always together' – has been placed in front of the coffin.

About a hundred people are sat in silence. The quiet and the sense of reverence are incredible. I can see Gildo and his family off to one side, greeting mourners. The whole hall is completely still. Most people are either praying or staring at the projected photo of Elisa, looking at her and trying to work out what this was all about, how it happened and how it was allowed to happen. Every half hour or so someone walks up to the lectern and reads something. I listen to a woman reading Psalm 31, and its words seem amazingly appropriate. I look over at Filomena in the corner, talking to people, as I listen to the words: 'My eyes grow weak with sorrow, my soul and body with grief. My life is consumed by anguish and my years by groaning.' And then, as I stare in bewilderment at Elisa's coffin, I hear the woman saying: 'I am forgotten as though I were dead; I have become like broken pottery. They conspire against me and plot to take my life.' I hear the words in a daze because by now it's too much for me, and I put my head in my hands.

I sit there for another hour, watching people coming in and out as I think about Elisa. I never knew her but it feels like I've been looking at her and for her for so long that I've got to know her through her absence, through the hole she left behind. I've traced the contours of that hole through those who felt it most, her family. I've seen their courage and dignity and can, through them, begin to glimpse what Elisa must have been like: fun, kind, honest, simple in the deepest sense of the word.

I walk over to the roped-off area where the family are sitting and say hello to Filomena. As usual in these situations it's hard to know what to say. 'I'm sorry' sounds a bit weak, to say the least, and it's too late, but I say it anyway. Filomena, as always, is extraordinary. She hugs me tightly and asks after Francesca and the children. She apologises that she hasn't cleaned her country house because she wanted me to stay there in comfort instead of in a hotel. Even during the vigil prior to her daughter's funeral, she's thinking of everyone but herself. We hug each other again, and I try and tell her what I think about her and her family.

*

The following morning I'm up early and back in the school's main hall with the family. Marco Gallo, the private detective, offers to give me a lift, and we walk to his car. One by one the cars all form a line. Police outriders keep the rest of the traffic at bay as the funeral cortège moves off through the streets of Potenza. As we pass the block of flats where Elisa used to live we see large white bed sheets hanging out of the windows and balconies. They, too, are a symbol of lost innocence. About a mile further on we come to a large *piazza*, a modern concrete square where the open-air funeral will take place. Filomena was determined that Elisa would never go back inside a church.

It's only once we've walked through the barriers and into the central zone reserved for close family and friends that we realise the size of the crowd: there must be many thousands of people here. Some are standing either side of where we're now taking our seats, but behind us there's a river of people as far as the eye can see. Here, too, white sheets and tablecloths are hanging off people's balconies, and there's a large bank of photographers and cameramen off to the left. To the right are about two dozen local politicians and mayors from Potenza and surrounding towns, all wearing the oblique tricolour across their suits. At the front I can see Don Marcello, the priest from the Libera organisation, in a white cassock. He's flanked by thirteen other priests and the choir from the church in which Elisa used to sing.

The coffin is brought forward from the back of the *piazza* and is applauded as it moves through the crowd. When it is placed on trestles in front of Don Marcello, he simply says: 'Welcome back, Elisa.'

It's a long, moving service under the baking heat of the sun. There's no shade in the centre of the *piazza* and Boy Scouts and Girl Guides are giving out bottles of water to the mourners. Someone reads that passage from Ezekiel about the valley of dry bones: '. . . as I was prophesying, there was a noise, a rattling sound, and the bones came together, bone to bone. I looked, and tendons and flesh appeared on them and skin covered them . . .' One of Elisa's cousins gives a brief, moving tribute to her friend, remembering how back in 1993 they had made an appointment to see each other at the end of the summer holidays. 'I've waited eighteen years to touch a white coffin,' she lamented. There's a reading about Jesus's raising of Lazarus.

Don Marcello's sermon is fiery and heartfelt. For fifteen years he has sat with the family, listening to their fears, sharing their pain; he has written letters, organised events, put up posters. He, like Gildo and Filomena, has kept the case alive, and now here he is, trying to make sense of it as a man of God. He doesn't hold back, his amplified voice booming around the *piazza* as he poses question after angry question:

Lord, why wasn't Elisa allowed to live that explosion of spring that is adolescence? Why did a murderous hand stop her from dreaming about the season of love? Why were Mamma Filomena and Father Antonio denied the custody of their daughter as she was looking out on life? Why couldn't Elisa see Luciano and Gildo become men . . .? Lord, how was it possible? How was it possible that the life of a just-blossoming flower was cut off and then left to rot in a dark corner like some throwaway weed? How was it possible to cover up, deviate, deter . . . and how was it possible that all that happened in a church, in your church, Lord?

As he's posing the questions, the volume of his voice rises and applause builds around the *piazza*. Sometimes it is so long and loud that he has to start the next sentence two or three times, trying to find space amidst the noise. It's as if the indignation of a city that feels insulted and slurred is suddenly emerging, that the anger of an entire community is finally audible. Don Marcello continues to give voice to that indignation, wanting to confide in his God all the terrible things connected to this case:

We would like to tell you, for example, about who in this case was more concerned to look after their own social image rather than restore sacredness . . . We would like to confide in you the lonely pain of a family that too often saw the rights of a caste's honour put before the rights of their own pain. We would like to tell you about a state, with its institutions, that has been sometimes absent, and when it's been present it has been unworthily represented. We would like to talk to you, with so much suffering in our heart, about those who preferred to whisper rather than shout, to forget rather than keep attention alive . . . how many times, Lord, prudence and tactics of all kinds were preferred to truth, as if you had never said that truth, only truth can set us free.

He complains that in Basilicata 'the truth is often left under the roof, as with Elisa'. He then addresses himself directly to Danilo Restivo:

Cain, our brother, you who have barbarously broken Elisa's life, take away the boulder in front of that sepulchre of lies and falseness in which you have condemned yourself to live for ever. There is no other way in which you can restore your dignity and which will lead you to God's forgiveness. Take away that stone, you men and women without name . . . you that have covered up for and hidden the fugitive Cain: let the roar of remorse wake you up. Take away that boulder that kept Elisa hidden for eighteen years and let out all the truth. Because a half-truth means condemning a family and an entire community to stay for ever in that sepulchre. Take away the stone, then, let's roll away those huge boulders that in our region hide so many more secrets that cannot be confessed . . . too many clientelistic dependencies. Let's dissolve the bandages that force us into lives resigned to suffering what others decide for us, let's break the perverse ties that stop us living freely . . .

Once again, the applause rises from the back of the *piazza*, increasing in volume and intensity at it arrives at the front. Don Marcello hasn't pulled any punches and, in a city that is fed up with the disinformation and half-truths of this case, the people appreciate his bluntness. It's a very Italian kind of bluntness, full of long, florid, rhetorical sentences, but his message is unmistakable: he doesn't believe that Danilo Restivo acted alone, that he wasn't helped and protected.

At the end of the funeral we get back in our cars and the cortège moves on to the city's cemetery. It's not a burial as such, because the white coffin is put in a *loculo*, a niche in a wall of the cemetery. The walls are three or four metres high and each has dozens of bricked-up niches carrying the name of the deceased and, usually, a photograph. There's quite a crush as family and friends file past, touching Elisa's coffin for the last time. It feels strange, touching that shiny white coffin now, knowing that this really is the end. This is it. There's a man near by, ready with his trowel, water, mortar and bricks. She's going to be walled up, and it feels even worse than when the first fistful of mud hits the lid of a coffin in a traditional burial. At least then you feel the horror of helping to bury someone you loved, whereas here you just watch a man build a tiny wall at the end of the niche. It feels cold and clinical, and all you can do is look on as Elisa disappears for the last time.

I move away from the crush and wander to the next-door wall of *loculi*. I read the names and ages and look at all the photographs of the faces. I look up at the top row and can't believe who's there. Almost exactly opposite Elisa, way up high on the next wall, is the *loculo* of Monsignor Domenico Sabia, the man everyone knew as Don Mimì, the priest of the Chiesa della Santissima Trinità. It's a bizarre coincidence, one of those eerie twists of fate that make this story so unbelievable. It's almost as if they're confronting each other in death, the patrician priest staring down on the innocent teenager. On his plaque it gives his dates, '1923–2008', and there's a glowing tribute: 'The bequest of his example will burn, like a flame, perennially in our hearts.' There's someone standing beside me now, following my gaze and reading the same line.

'Huh,' says the other mourner with derision, 'some bequest.'

We slowly start moving away, walking back down the central path that leads through the grand, private burial temples and back to the car park. I see Gildo and wander over to him. He's dressed very casually, ever the nonconformist: a black polo shirt with an orange bag over his shoulder. He's still limping heavily because of the accident, and I offer him my arm. We walk like that for a while, me thinking about the promise he made Elisa all those years ago: that he would fight to find her and that he would fight for justice.

'You kept your promise,' I say.

He sighs heavily and nods. He looks at our intertwined arms and at the suit and tie I'm wearing and guffaws loudly. 'Dressed like that, it looks like you're walking me up the aisle.'

He keeps laughing, and the friends and family that are walking with us join in, looking at him with admiration as he limps towards the glinting metal of the cars.

*

On 8 and 10 November 2011, Danilo Restivo was tried for the murder of Elisa Claps in a court in Salerno. He had chosen to be tried in a 'shortened rite', a quick trial in which the evidence wasn't disputed and he wasn't himself present. It meant, frustratingly for the Claps family, that it wasn't possible to cross-examine him. The choice of a 'shortened rite' and the fact that certain associated crimes had fallen under the statute of limitations (meaning that so much time had elapsed that he couldn't be prosecuted for them) meant that a life sentence was impossible. However, on 11 November 2011, Danilo Restivo was sentenced to thirty years for the murder of Elisa Claps.

It was a very moving moment. Gildo and Filomena both wept.

'Dear sister,' Gildo said, 'we've done it.' Afterwards, he said to various journalists who had covered the case for years: 'The day of her disappearance I promised Elisa that I wouldn't find peace until I had found her assassin, and today justice has been done.'

'I'm Christian, but I will never forgive,' Filomena said. 'If he [Restivo] had let me find the body, if he had let me touch it, maybe things would have been different, but I can never forgive him for the way he's behaved.' She appealed directly to Restivo to 'take paper and pen and write the truth, tell me finally the truth'. She also appealed to others, to those unknown accomplices who had helped Restivo: 'To who knows,' she said, 'and to who has to clean their conscience.' Her main anger was reserved, however, for the Church. With incredible tactlessness, the Diocese of Potenza had applied to be a plaintiff in the case against Danilo Restivo, implying that it had been hurt by the affair. The presiding judge in the case, Elisabetta Boccassini, rejected the application, saying that the Church 'had not been diligent in the control and management of the space'. 'The Church', Filomena said after the verdict, 'shouldn't have done what it did, not to me and not to Elisa. And it's the truth about the Church that I want. The truth about the Church must come out at all cost. Don Mimì Sabia can't have been the only priest who was in a position to know, he can't have done everything by himself . . .'

After the verdict I chat to Gildo. I wonder what it will be like for him and his mother now that a battle they had waged for almost two decades is finally over.

'What scares me', he says, 'is re-entering normal life. I struggle even to imagine what a normal life is. All my adulthood I've been completely absorbed by this struggle. I'll have to find a new objective, a new aim.' He wants, he says, to take advantage of his notoriety to help all those relatives of other missing persons and 'invisibles' who haven't been able to interest the media in their stories. And yet it's clear that he's not ready to leave the battlefield. 'It's obvious that one chapter is closed,' he says, 'but others remain open. I want to know clearly, at the very least, what happened as regards the discovery of the body. Because I don't accept that only Danilo Restivo should pay. All these years we've spent looking for Elisa are only in part due to him. The Church is also responsible. That's why it's a very Italian story,' he says, 'because it involves the Church. No other state has a Church that is so strong, that has so much influence, and in which criticising it is such a taboo. And we're in a very small provincial city in which the relationships between people are very close. There's a lack of civic spirit and an involuntary complicity.'

I wonder how he remembers Elisa when he thinks of her now. 'I'm glad that Elisa has spoken so much,' he says metaphorically, 'that she allowed us to know what happened. She wanted justice, and without her body we would still have an unpunished killer and there would have been other victims. I don't think, after every-thing we've been through, that we'll ever be at peace. But she can be. She can finally repose in peace.'

Despite the speed of the trial, new evidence did emerge. There was the testimony of a woman who had, a year before Elisa's mur-der, risked a similar fate. It was revealed that Antonia Camardese had been enticed by Restivo to go to the terrace of the Chiesa della Santissima Trinità. He had approached her during Mass on the pretext that, as with Elisa, he had a present to give her. She had accompanied him all the way to the terrace but, on seeing the tiny garret, had told him she wasn't interested in any present and returned downstairs. It was a chilling insight into the tactics he must have used on Elisa.

The conclusion of Restivo's trial wasn't, however, the end of the investigations regarding the case. There are still two inquir-ies under way: one into the initial forensic analysis of Vincenzo

Pascali; and another into the circumstances of the discovery of the body. The judge conducting the preliminary investigation into the latter has called the testimony of one of the cleaning ladies 'absolutely inexplicable and at times also irrational'. The circumstances of the discovery of Elisa's body were so confused that the telephones of the bishop and various priests had been put under surveillance in an attempt to understand just who knew what and when.

It also emerged that the telephone of Maurizio Restivo had been monitored. A conversation between him and his daughter, Anna, was released in which even after the discovery of her body he spoke of Elisa in the most vulgar, derogatory terms. Even his daughter refused to continue the conversation, calling him an 'accursed pig'. Another bugged phone call between Maurizio Restivo and his lawyer shortly after Danilo's first interrogation, way back in 1993, revealed the fact that both men were pleased with Felicia Genovese, the investigating magistrate; both were satisfied that she had gone easy on Danilo. Indeed, years later, when Danilo's parents' house was searched, a Post-It note was found with Genovese's personal number on it. There was, it appeared, an inexplicable proximity between the accused's family and the investigator.

The most extraordinary revelation that month, however, came from an intelligence officer from Sisde, the former domestic arm of the Italian intelligence agency. He had conducted an inquiry into Elisa Claps's disappearance back in 1997 and had, in November 2011, been tracked down by a journalist. 'The essence of the briefing', he said to the reporter, 'was that the disappearance of the girl was due to the fact that Claps had been killed in Potenza. And that the presumed author was the person always considered as such [i.e. Danilo Restivo]. The briefing said that Elisa had been killed the same day as her disappearance, 12 September 1993. We were involved because we had an informer and in order to give an input to the investigators.' The report, he said, had been passed to his superiors but had, evidently, been buried. The most explosive part of the interview, however, came when he was asked about the hypothesis that other people knew about the murder. 'Yes, there was a priest,' he said.

Everyone assumed that priest was Don Mimì, but in the days after the trial it emerged that magistrates had had the phone of another priest under surveillance: Don Pierluigi Vignola. He was the man who stood in for Don Mimì after Elisa's disappearance. A bald, rotund man with a chubby face, thin lips and thick glasses, Don Pierluigi had had links to masons in the past and, bizarrely, denied that he had ever heard of Elisa. He was now the chaplain to the police in Potenza. When his name emerged in the press, he went to ground, preferring to avoid rather than face the mounting questions. 'It's deplorable,' was Filomena's characteristically blunt assessment. 'There's a priest who has a conscience more black than the cassock he wears.'

In fact, although Elisa's burial and the conviction of Restivo appear to bring the case to a close, there are still unanswered questions. Many wonder whether Restivo was responsible for the murder of Oki, the South Korean girl in Bournemouth. Omar Benguit remains in prison for her murder, adamant that he's the victim of a miscarriage of justice. The authorities in the Valle d'Aosta, in the far north of Italy, have also opened an inquiry into whether Restivo was connected to the disappearance of another South Korean girl, Erika Ansermin. Adopted by an Italian family, she disappeared on 20 April 2003, and a photograph of her was found on Restivo's computer in Bournemouth. He has also, inevitably and sometimes rather fancifully, been linked to other murders and disappearances across Europe.

Perhaps the greatest mystery that remains is how Restivo became the way he is: a pitiful, deceitful, scared, aggressive hypochondriac, as well as a fetishistic killer. Because of his Sicilian origins, some people have suggested that he was inspired in his sadism by the story of the Sicilian Christian martyr, Saint Agatha, whose breasts were cut off. Others believe that his father's intellectual interests reveal a home life that was far from normal. Whether the twelfth – the day of the month on which Elisa, Heather Barnett and, incidentally, Oki were all killed – was coincidental or somehow meaningful to Restivo will also, presumably, remain a mystery.

*

Years ago, I read Ann Cornelisen's extraordinary book about Lucania, *Torregreca*. It was an account of her struggle to set up a nursery in the suspicious, claustrophobic mountain town of 'Torregreca' (real name Tricarico). Her descriptions of the society were not unlike Carlo Levi's a few years before: she painted a picture of incredible deprivation and superstition, of resentments and jealousies and feuds. But she also discovered unrivalled generosity and idealism. She described the locals' habit of gossiping and 'fantasticating', and wrote about the fact that 'nothing was so suspicious as the obvious. Only a fool accepted it. The simplest event, to be understood, must be analyzed and reconstructed until it was a lacework of deception and evil intentions.'

That is what happened in the Elisa Claps case. What should have been obvious was ignored because it was too straightforward and simple. It was a dull and boring possibility compared to the fabulous, fantastic theories and hunches that a nation's fertile imagination could invent. It should have been blatantly clear, as it was to the Claps family, that Danilo Restivo was responsible for Elisa's disappearance and that, in all probability, she was to be found within a very short distance of where the two had met. But fantasy yearns not for simplicity, for things that are close to hand, but for gothic, improbable, far-fetched scenarios; it longs for exoticism, for contorted, incredible surprises. So much so that it begins to invent ideas and notions that are so extraordinary that even the fantasist can be surprised by their own invention. They are taken in by the bluff, and become convinced that their version is closer to the truth than the dull and terrible reality that the more sober, sorrowful family had always dreaded.

That frenetic fantasising is called *dietrologia*, 'behindery', or conspiracy-theorising. It's a game in which you can display your vertiginous intelligence, perception and imagination, one that helps demonstrate that you alone are not credulous. The trouble is that overactive, suspicious minds don't always tend towards clarity. It means that the most obvious, blatant explanation is obscured and derided as simplistic. For seventeen years the Claps family, desperate for any information, had to put up with the fantasists and, on many occasions, go along with their delusions. Every avenue had to be explored, just in case. And every time it was a dead end. Sometimes the false leads were innocent, introduced into the case by people who genuinely wanted to help; but very often they were deliberate, either part of the crackpot game of some maniac who enjoyed being the centre of attention for a fleeting moment or, worse, a determined effort to skew the investigation and deflect suspicion away from the one man who really knew what had happened. It was a surprisingly successful strategy. With hindsight, it seems astonishing that Danilo Restivo was allowed to wander round Italy, continuing to cut hair, to go to Britain and to murder again. But until recently he was just another character, albeit a leading one, in the crazy cast of this perverse drama.

Just as reality finally replaced fantasy in the Elisa Claps case, so too did hard facts eventually dispatch the baloney of Silvio Berlusconi. In the same week that Danilo Restivo was sentenced, Italy was convulsed by an economic crisis. As the yield on the country's ten-year bonds surpassed the critical 7 per cent mark, the point at which Ireland, Portugal and Greece had all had to request a bail-out, there were increasing concerns about the size of Italy's debt and its ability to pay back its loans. Berlusconi, the media mogul who had entered politics in the autumn that Elisa went missing, was forced from power by defections within his own ranks. The man who, it was thought, would lead Italy towards another economic miracle had merely led the country to the very brink of bankruptcy. Rather than a King Midas, he was, it appeared, just another robber baron, a man who was in power not in the national interest but merely because of the immunity it afforded him.

In a strange way, it seemed fitting that Berlusconi's rise and fall mirrored so precisely the timeline of the Elisa Claps case. In talking to Gildo about his sister over the years, he would often suggest that Elisa's disappearance wasn't just an isolated, irrelevant story but one which was emblematic of what was happening in the country at large; it was a story, he said, that could give you an insight into Italy's politicians and priests and provinces. It wasn't, usually, a flattering picture, and he would repeatedly talk about Italians' *smarrimento* – their bewilderment or dismay – at the state of their nation. But there was always, too, a tentative optimism that civic society might one day be reborn and that Italians would finally get the meritocratic, efficient institutions and the honest, statesman-like politicians they longed for. The political eclipse of Silvio Berlusconi and the conviction of Danilo Restivo seemed to suggest that there were, at least, some grounds for that optimism.

Acknowledgements

During the research for this book, I've been privileged to be encouraged by the Claps family. I am very grateful for their hospitality, humour and co-operation. They are an extraordinary family.

Stephen Page and Walter Donohue at Faber courageously commissioned the book long before there was any judicial conclusion to the case. I admire their bravery in doing so, and I'm very grateful to everyone at Faber for their support and enthusiasm. My agent, Georgina Capel, and all her colleagues have always been exemplary. I'm very thankful for the many long chats I enjoyed with Selina Walker at the outset of my research. I'm also grateful to Luca Formenton, Matteo Battarra and Luca Fontana.

I'm indebted to Euan Wallace for libationary encouragement; to Laurie Rousham, Tui Dunleavy, Debra Salmon, Ruby Elliot, Dennis Massey, Lucy Ollis, Daniela Calebich and my parents, Bob and Jane Jones, for holding the fort, and looking after livestock and children, in my absence. James McConnachie and Alice Hunt frequently gave me a bed and a lot of laughs. I'm grateful, too, to Nic Bowes, Dickon Edwards and Simon Stanley for their expert advice.

Not for the first time I've been amazed by the generosity of Italian journalists. I happily acknowledge the help offered to me over the years by Federica Sciarelli, Paolo Fattori, Matteo Berdini, Domenico Sammartino, Fabio Amendolara, Massimo Brancati, Pierangelo Maurizio and Mattia Bagnoli. Gildo's memoir of the case, *Per Elisa*, was published shortly before this book went to press. Co-authored with Federica Sciarelli, it has been invaluable in allowing me to check facts and quotations, and I'm indebted to it.

I'm grateful, too, to many British journalists: to Harry Crawford, Martin Dowse, Andy Martin, Daniel Flynn, Paula Roberts, Ben Moore, Tony Serpini, Nick Squires and Emily Nash. I thank especially various editors who have commissioned work during the course of this book, enabling me to find the funds to make repeated trips to Potenza: Tim Lewis, Emma John, Libby Brooks, Malik Meer, Clare Margetson, Anne Spackman, David Wastell, Marco Mathieu, Giovanni De Mauro, Jacopo Zanchini and Miles Warde.

I am, as usual, thankful to many friends in Parma for their advice and support over the years: to il Gallo, la Deni, il Davo, la Vale, lo Zivo, la Manu, l'Albe, la Betta, il Cris, Diego Saglia, Livio, la Gloria, Giovanni Granatiero, Lucia Sbravati and all the rest. Many kind *consiglieri* in Britain have put up with my obsession with this case: I'm very lucky to have had the chance to talk everything through with Julian Baggini, Antonia Macaro, Christopher Wakling and Gita Gyorffy, Steve Wharton, James and Paula Wilson, Ed and Claire Davis, Dan and Waf Green, Tim and Sue Snowdon, Jonathan and Suzi Herbert, Richard Beecham, Guy Walters, Annabel Venning and many more. Kate Banks, Emily Pitts, Katherine Grey, Kirsteen Heselton and Andrew and Valerie Hart have all offered incredible support over the last year.

I thank my children – Benedetta, Emma and Leonardo – for putting up with my absorption in a case which I was reluctant to share with them. And I owe a special debt of gratitude, as always, to my wife Francesca.

Any errors, of fact or interpretation, are obviously entirely my responsibility.

I am grateful for permission to reproduce extracts from the following:

Murder in the Cathedral, by T. S. Eliot (Faber and Faber, London, 1976)
Assalto al PM, by Luigi de Magistris (Chiaralettere, Milan, 2010).

Every effort has been made to trace or contact all copyright holders. The publishers would be pleased to rectify any omissions or errors brought to their notice at the earliest opportunity.